Inspired to Serve

INSPIRED

to SERVE

Today's Faith Activists

Mark H. Massé

INDIANA UNIVERSITY PRESS   BLOOMINGTON & INDIANAPOLIS

This book is a publication of

Indiana University Press
601 North Morton Street
Bloomington, IN 47404-3797 USA

http://iupress.indiana.edu

Telephone orders   800-842-6796
Fax orders   812-855-7931
Orders by e-mail   iuporder@indiana.edu

The paper used in this publication meets the minimum
requirements of American National Standard for Information Sciences — Permanence of Paper for Printed Library
Materials, ANSI Z39.48-1984.

Manufactured in the United States of America

Library of Congress Cataloging-in-Publication Data
Massé, Mark H., date
Inspired to serve : today's faith activists / Mark H. Massé.
p. cm.
Includes bibliographical references (p.   ) and index.
ISBN 0-253-34455-7 (cloth : alk. paper) — ISBN 0-253-21714-8 (pbk. : alk. paper)
1. Church and social problems — United States.
2. Religion and social problems — United States.
3. Social action — United States.
I. Title.
HN65.M37 2004
201'.7'092273 — DC22
2004004469

1 2 3 4 5 09 08 07 06 05 04

"Now faith is the substance of things hoped for, the evidence of things not seen."

—Hebrews 11:1

CONTENTS

INTRODUCTION: "LEAP OF FAITH"   1

FATHER GARY SMITH [1] "STREET ANGEL"   7

THE REVEREND DR. ISRAEL SUAREZ [2] "FIGHTING THE GOOD FIGHT"   12

SISTER ANN KENDRICK [3] "LA MONJITA OF THE FIELDS"   22

THE REVEREND DR. RICHARD L. TOLLIVER [4] "YOU CAN DO IT, RICHARD"   36

DOUG AND JUDY HALL [5] "BOSTON'S SERVANT LEADERS"   61

FATHER ROY BOURGEOIS [6] "THE COURAGE OF CONVICTIONS"   77

MARION MALCOLM [7] "JUSTICE FOR ALL SEASONS"   102

MARY NELSON [8] "REBUILDING WITH HOPE"   117

REVEREND SKIP LONG [9] "WHATEVER IT TAKES"   136

RABBI STEVE FOSTER [10] "NEVER IN DOUBT"   155

DR. M. BASHEER AHMED [11] "MESSENGER OF GOOD NEWS"   174

MARK GONNERMAN [12] "DHARMA ACTIVIST"   192

EPILOGUE: "LESSONS LEARNED"   208

ACKNOWLEDGMENTS   210

NOTES   212

BIBLIOGRAPHY   223

INDEX   225

Inspired to Serve

INTRODUCTION: "LEAP OF FAITH"

> In spite of our religious, cultural, racial, and ethnic differences, we all
> have an innate desire to serve humanity.
>
> —M. BASHEER AHMED, Arlington, Texas, psychiatrist and social activist

In this all too often skeptical age, I found hope and conviction in the stories of people trying to make the world a better place. These are tales of human transcendence, of "ordinary" individuals doing extraordinary work in the service of others. This is a collection of profiles, narratives of people of faith engaged in social activism (i.e., faith activists), with lessons for those willing to be informed and enlightened.

I have written these stories to reveal the lives of activists beyond the headlines of causes, movements, and protests, and beneath the surface descriptions of good works and good intentions. By immersing myself in their lives and missions, I have learned of their motivations, struggles, and aspirations. In the process I have tried to personalize contemporary societal issues, to illuminate the subject of social activism, and to contribute to an enhanced understanding of its impact on the human condition.

The initial profile in this book, "Father Gary Smith: Street Angel," was first written in 1997 and published in *Catholic Digest* magazine in June 1998. But my journey began years earlier when I met Gary, a Jesuit priest engaged in urban (street) ministry in Portland, Oregon. His story led me to other accounts of faith-driven activism and to a deeper examination of the subject.

As a former sociology major turned writer and journalism teacher, I had long been interested in social problems and in those who work to transform society. As a practicing Catholic (with patrilineal Jewish ancestry) who came of age in the 1960s, I was familiar with certain dynamics of religion, faith, and spirituality in driving historic activist causes, such as liberation theology and the social gospel, Catholic Worker, and civil rights movements. I knew the names of Mahatma Gandhi, Dr. Martin Luther King Jr., Dorothy Day, Cesar Chavez, and the Berrigan brothers (Philip and Daniel). I had also heard the litany of labels applied to these leaders and to countless others of the rank and file of society who were striving to

1

improve the quality of life for the less fortunate and mistreated. They were called do-gooders, rabble-rousers, protesters, radicals, reformers, liberals, progressives, pioneers, and social activists.

Years later, some would proclaim the passing of activism.

"I think there might be political reasons for this. The protest culture of the '60s was, by the late '70s, almost totally exhausted. Among a lot of people who had committed time to various causes, there was a feeling of utter weariness and defeat. Irony was absorbed into the culture as a defensive reflex and remained after the activism died," wrote essayist Roger Gathman in the January–February 1999 issue of *Poets & Writers* magazine.

That perspective seemed too bleak. It also challenged conventional wisdom that in troubled times throughout history people had stepped forward to make a difference. However, there was evidence from the religious front that formerly progressive Christian and Jewish congregations during the 1970s and 1980s had changed their priorities, often urging their clergy to be more involved with spiritual and pastoral rather than social concerns. But the more research I conducted, the more I was convinced that the activist spirit never died among a vigorous cadre of people driven by their faith and a commitment to social action. They remained dedicated to changing the status quo by empowering the poor and disenfranchised and by speaking out against poverty, injustice, and abuses of power. What had shifted was the emphasis from large-scale protests to a community-based focus on more mainstream social welfare programs.

By the late 1990s the term "faith-based" had entered public dialogue as a result of emerging political and religious developments. This had been sparked by a host of factors, including the Charitable Choice provisions in the 1996 welfare reform law that facilitated financial and working relationships between government and religious groups, while meeting the constitutional mandate for separation of church and state; innovative (biblical-based) social programs to address crime prevention, prison reform, and drug rehabilitation; and collaborative antipoverty efforts such as the evangelical Christian-led Call to Renewal program. At the dawn of a new millennium, the media were asking if the nation's religious communities and their legions of faithful might be equipped to address America's social ills, particularly where government programs had failed.

For decades religious charities and social service organizations had been receiving government funding to provide food, shelter, job training, and other basic services to needy Americans, as long as there was no proselytizing or denial of services on religious grounds. These and other precedents would support the launching of twenty-first-century federal governmental actions, including creation of a White House Office of

2

Faith-Based and Community Initiatives in 2001, issuance of a presidential executive order in 2002 to streamline religious organizations' competition for social service grants and contracts, and passage of the CARE (Charitable Aid, Recovery and Empowerment) Act in 2003, which encouraged donations to both religious and secular charities.

But despite religious groups' apparent gains in having greater access to financial contributions and social service contracts, political rhetoric had far exceeded reality, according to social activists such as Jim Wallis, editor-in-chief of *Sojourners* magazine and founder of Call to Renewal. In the July–August 2003 issue of *Sojourners,* Wallis described the impact of drastic budget cuts on faith-based service providers: "The administration's priorities are a disaster for the poor and a windfall for the wealthiest, and thus directly conflict with biblical priorities."

Another aspect of the faith-based discussion was the impact of religious beliefs on social responsibility. "From the beginning to the present, Americans from every religious tradition have expressed their faith through service to those in need," noted *Finding Common Ground,* produced by the thirty-three-member Working Group on Human Needs and Faith-Based and Community Initiatives, which included religious activists and civil libertarians.

The group's mission was to explore ways "for both nonreligious and religious Americans to work side by side to alleviate poverty and promote human betterment." Among its 2003 recommendations were increased philanthropic contributions to community-based and faith-based groups, tax incentives to promote charitable giving, technical assistance for grassroots organizations, and expansion of VISTA (Volunteers in Service to America) and AmeriCorps programs.

Winifred Gallagher had discussed similar themes when she wrote in her 1999 book, *Working on God:* "Research shows that America's religious institutions are the major source of community volunteers, and that their members are far likelier than others to donate to charities. When all is said and done, they're arguably society's greatest influence for good behavior."

Inspired to Serve: Today's Faith Activists is guided by the premise that those who are drawn to community service and social activism are more likely to be people of faith and conscience. In most instances, their early religious and spiritual experiences, training, and traditions have shaped their outlook, softened their hearts, and strengthened their resolve to improve the world around them.

By people of faith, I also refer to faith's secular definition: unquestioning belief, complete trust, confidence, reliance, allegiance, and loyalty. In writing these accounts, I have been even more concerned with a person's resolve and dedication to enact social change than with his or her theological orientation. Most of the activists I profiled are devout; others describe themselves as being more spiritual than religious. But what they have in common is an unbending belief in the power, potential, and rewards of service to others.

As Jim Wallis writes in his autobiography, *Faith Works:* "And hope is the single most important ingredient for changing the world. It has continued to provide the energy and sustenance I've needed, not just to keep going but to be continually renewed." The activists I chronicled would echo Wallis's words.

In researching and writing these accounts, I learned how activists are created by their response to events. Rabbi Steve Foster of Denver calls these "God moments." Other people may be affected by these same kinds of situations, but they react differently. They may choose the routes of passivity, retreat, apathy, or despair. Or they may decide to support a cause with financial donations or periodic volunteer efforts.

What sets faith activists apart is the depth and breadth of their service, vision, and sacrifice. There's more at stake for them. They may risk their reputations and careers, their health, even their lives in pursuit of social change. These activists are people who make a leap of faith and are transformed in the process.

White evangelical Christians Doug and Judy Hall in Boston and Mary Nelson in Chicago are caught in the wrath of inner-city riots in the 1960s. But they decide to stay and fight back with compassion and commitment. Through the decades they build nationally recognized organizations, providing education, jobs, housing, and support services for thousands of people. African American ministers Richard Tolliver and Skip Long triumph over prejudice, becoming leaders of successful community revitalization and economic development programs. They resolve to serve God while confronting social problems.

Rabbi Steve Foster encounters both hatred and heroism as a college student when he joins Dr. Martin Luther King Jr. and other activists during the Selma–Montgomery, Alabama, civil rights march in 1965. He dedicates his life to human rights advocacy. Marion Malcolm, daughter and granddaughter of Christian missionaries, is also reinvented during her college years, resulting in a lifetime of activism spanning five decades and featuring causes such as social justice, antiwar protest, and migrant worker rights.

Hispanic minister Israel Suarez overcomes childhood poverty and answers the call of indigent residents in southwest Florida, creating a diversified social service organization. Growing up in a comfortable upstate New York setting, Ann Kendrick didn't envision herself becoming a nun, much less working most of her adult life with migrant farmworkers in the rural South. But witnessing dire poverty and death in Central America as a high school and college student dramatically alters her worldview. Father Roy Bourgeois is also forever changed by loss; his epiphany is forged during his tour of duty in the Vietnam War. Afterward he becomes a Maryknoll priest, committed to a life of service and antimilitarism. Basheer Ahmed, a successful psychiatrist in North Texas, is struck by the influx of Muslim refugees from war-torn Bosnia, Somalia, and Iraq. He works to establish a community and medical center to serve low-income Muslims and others in need. Mark Gonnerman, raised Lutheran, now a practicing Buddhist, survives a near-fatal accident and pursues a path of enlightening others through community education. Father Gary Smith, a wayward youth and child of a nonreligious, troubled family, becomes a convert, Jesuit priest, and activist. His decades-long spiritual quest takes him to streets of the Northwest, where he serves in an outreach ministry.

The profiled activists (eleven individuals and one couple) include clergy, lay workers, and others, representing a mix of faiths, social issues, and geographic regions. They are Buddhist, Catholic, Jewish, Muslim, and evangelical, mainline, and Pentecostal Protestants. Nine of the activists are men; four are women. Four of the thirteen are men of color (African American, Hispanic, Asian Indian). Though I have strived to be thorough in my coverage, I don't claim complete demographic representation. I regret that several women activists of color were unable to participate due to schedule conflicts or other commitments.

I am first and foremost a nonfiction storyteller, not a scholar of religious studies. But in my accounts I have tried to honor the legacy of leaders such as Moses, Buddha, Jesus, and Muhammad and their followers, who for thousands of years have preached a message of responsibility for one's neighbors, especially the weak, afflicted, and downtrodden. I have also studied operations of religious organizations in this country to better understand their respective roles in the practice of social activism.

As a journalist, I was interested in how these activists try to balance their secular and spiritual lives in the face of daily challenges. I spent several days on-site with each of my subjects, joining them in meetings and meals as well as on protest marches, shadowing them for hours at a time on city streets, back roads, and open fields. I was granted generous access to their day-to-day worlds. I visited their offices, homes, and places of worship. I rode in their cars over countless bumpy roads, through major league traffic jams, and in occasional frantic forays into city and country.

This process was a leap of faith for me and for the people I was writing about. They didn't know exactly what to expect, and neither did I. That is the risk and reward of this type of immersion journalism. At times I wondered, was I wearing them down, or were they wearing me down? In retrospect, I would say it was probably a draw.

To supplement my ethnographic observations, I interviewed friends, colleagues, family members, and experts on religion, social activism, economic development, and social services. That reporting was buttressed by in-depth research, including dozens of books, periodicals, and newspaper stories, subscriptions to religious organization list servers, library databases, and online media archives. Although I tape recorded more than twenty-five hours of interviews, speeches, and presentations, my primary tools for reportage were pen and paper. I took about one thousand pages of notes during my research into the lives of reformers profiled in this book.

Some final reflections. The activists I've written about are interesting, impressive people of faith, but they are not saints. Nor would any of them claim to be—though several certainly have very healthy egos. But I found no universal character type for a social activist. The brash ones were balanced by self-effacing, almost reticent folks. Their personalities differed, but they were all leaders in their own style, able to motivate others and to achieve results. Each of these individuals demonstrated a remarkable work ethic. This was true from the youngest forty-something to the oldest sixty-something.

What helps sustain them, beyond their faith, is a buoyant sense of humor. For those who are married, I saw evidence of a deep commitment to their families. Others have chosen to remain single, either because they took religious vows or because the demands of their vocations seemed to dictate their lifestyle. Despite the sacrifices these social activists have made in their lives, they remain positive, forward-thinking people.

That is perhaps the best lesson they have to offer anyone who wants to "take arms against a sea of troubles" in their community. Your attitude will largely determine how successful you are at leaving the world a better place. If the experiences of these social activists are your guide, you will need a resilient spirit for the long and winding road ahead.

* * *

Author's Note: This book is written as an anthology of narratives, covering a span of six years (1997 to 2003). The order of the twelve chapters of activist profiles follows the chronology of my research, reporting, and writing. Four were written prior to 2000. Two were researched in 2002. Material on the remaining six stories was gathered during 2003. Brief updates will be provided in chapter introductions.

[1]

FATHER GARY SMITH "STREET ANGEL"

My first meeting with Father Gary Smith was prompted by an article published in The Catholic Sentinel newspaper (September 16, 1994). I saw a photo of a tall priest with longish gray hair and moustache, dressed in jeans and sneakers, carrying a backpack. I thought, "This man has a story to tell." We began talking over coffee in early 1995. I would make the two-hour drive from Eugene to Portland, Oregon, where Smith was working the streets of the Burnside neighborhood. His profile, which I wrote in 1997, was published in the June 1998 issue of Catholic Digest. In September 2000, Smith sent me an e-mail saying he was leaving Oregon for eastern Africa en route to Uganda, where he would work with the Jesuit Refugee Service. Three years later I again heard from him. He had come to the United States for a brief visit, but was soon returning to northern Uganda to serve Sudanese refugees in a place called Rhino Camp. Smith had good news to report. His memoir Radical Compassion, documenting his years living and working among the poor of Portland, Oregon, had been issued in 2002 by Chicago-based publisher Jesuit Way. He said this was the "latest effort to say where I am in the universe." It would fill me in on much of the "Smithonian saga since our talks in Portland."

> Redeem: to deliver from sin and its penalties, as by a sacrifice made for
> the sinner; to fulfill a promise or pledge; to make amends or atone for;
> to restore (oneself) to favor by making amends; to make worthwhile.
>
> —*Webster's New World Dictionary*, Second College Edition

On a mild, slate-gray spring day in Portland, Oregon, a scruffy but solidly built man in his thirties wanders into the St. Vincent de Paul chapel from the streets of Old Town in search of a tube of toothpaste. His face sports a week's worth of stubble, and his jeans are in need of a wash. Though his eyes dart about, his words are polite as he waits in the lobby for a volunteer from the Macdonald Center, a social service program located in the basement. As the man steps across a freshly mopped spot on the floor, he excuses himself.

In response, a crusty custodian with a patch over his right eye, wearing a paint-spattered blue work shirt, just grunts. The toothpaste seeker returns to his seat and waits.

"They treat you nice here," he says, glancing quickly to the right and then back at the small space in front of him.

According to the chapel receptionist, Father Gary Smith, S.J. hasn't arrived yet. "But knowing him," she says with a wisp of a smile, "he'll come bounding through that door any minute."

When Smith finally arrives, he doesn't bound as promised, but he does seem to glide with the brisk, fluid steps of a well-coordinated athlete. Watching the six-foot, three-inch Smith move, one can easily imagine how he might have looked running a fast break as a college basketball star in California in the late 1950s.

These days he looks and acts like someone defying the imminent arrival of his sixtieth year. He is agile, energetic, with a shock of frosty hair, a rakish silver moustache, and riveting blue eyes. His jogging shoes, Levi's, and casual blue-and-white-striped T-shirt complete the youthful image. His positive attitude only partially explains why he lives with such conviction.

"My passion," Smith says, "comes from my love affair with Christ and with my calling to serve Him."

Later, as he begins his daily walking tour of the area, he passes the Sisters of the Road Café, where handwritten window signs boast of hot meals for $1.50. The café has become a refuge for area poor seeking to eat amid an atmosphere of courtesy and respect—rare commodities, it seems, for society's discarded, shunned, and forgotten.

A café volunteer in a green apron stands outside, push broom in hand. The man is gangly, with a full Afro and a toothless grin; his eyes brighten when Father Smith stops to shake his hand. But several men loitering nearby give Smith the once-over as he passes.

"Who's the dude?"

"That's Father Gary, man," says the café volunteer.

"A priest? Get out. That dude's really a priest? For real?"

* * *

Father Gary Smith is for real. He is one of several angels of the street who serve the poor and needy as members of Outreach Ministry (OM) in what's known as the Burnside area of downtown Portland. In doing so, Father Smith says, he is striving to reaffirm the mission of the gospel while continuing on his own path to spiritual fulfillment. In a column for a ministry newsletter called *Outreach Update,* Smith writes: "We are called to be bearers of God's love and truth, and, as bearers, we take that love and truth into our culture where there exists the bruises and flickering flames caused by homelessness, loneliness, excessive wealth, racism, injustice."

According to Smith, Outreach Ministry helps meet the basic needs of more than fifty people. Through the ministry, individuals can get help in finding an inexpensive room in one of Old Town's hotels, in obtaining medical care, or in budgeting welfare or disability checks to afford food, clothing, and other essentials. Sometimes, though, what matters most is simple, compassionate human contact.

Father Smith is quick to credit Sister Maria Francis Waugh, O.S.F., who founded Outreach Ministry in the 1980s, as well as staff members and countless volunteers who fuel the program with love and hard work. Smith says that by helping other needy human beings, a person can grow closer to God. A sign in the street-front OM offices best sums up their mission: "We are continuing what He began."

* * *

Smith settles his angular frame into a sturdy coffee-shop chair, stretching his long legs out onto the black-and-white-checked linoleum floor. He slowly sips a mug of black decaf. He speaks softly, measuring his words and carefully weaving his stories, with anecdotes tumbling out as if fresh from a vivid dream. His blue eyes reflect the road to redemption—one moment liquid and tear-filled, the next beaming with joy.

He talks of discovering the social dimension of the gospel in the mid-1960s when he was teaching at a Jesuit prep school in Phoenix. During those turbulent years, Smith protested the Vietnam War and the injustice of racism and poverty. The more he participated in activism, the greater his desire to work on social problems. He left teaching in 1968 and traveled to Toronto, where he served as a prison chaplain during his theological studies. In 1971 he was ordained a Jesuit priest.

"I knew I had to translate my theology to poor people," he says, describing his prison counseling and later his eight years working with a team of Jesuit community organizers and neighborhood activists in Oakland, California. From 1984 until 1992, he served as director of Nativity House, a street drop-in center in Tacoma, Washington's skid row. He chronicled his experiences at the center in a 1994 autobiographical account, *Street Journal: Finding God in the Homeless,* two years after he came to Portland, Oregon.

Smith acknowledges that his activist ideals from the 1960s have evolved into his street ministry in the Northwest. But he says his true motivation is more Bible- than politics-based. He says he is following Christ's teachings to serve those rejected by mainstream society and to tell them of God's love. "I believe the conscience of the Church lies with serving the poor and less fortunate of the world," he adds. "And it is our duty to remind everyone that we truly are our brother's keeper."

At Outreach Ministry, those are not just words. Smith and his organization serve the poorest of the poor—the desperate, troubled, addicted, feeble, and self-destructive. On an "average" day, Father Gary Smith counsels Jesse,* an ex-offender who had killed a fellow transient in an alcohol-fueled rage and is trying to rebuild his life. He prays with Robert,* a frequent visitor to the Macdonald Center. Diagnosed as a paranoid schizophrenic, Robert has lost everything over the years: a good job, a home, and a family. Now he is dependent on social service providers. Out on the street, Smith helps Tommy* find his way back to his Old Town hotel. Tommy, an Outreach Ministry "regular," suffers from frequent blackouts and memory lapses, brought on by years of drinking and brawling.

Smith can relate to these troubled souls. He knows what it's like to lose your way. He understands the meaning of emptiness, pain, and despair because he has lived it. One of four children of working-class alcoholic parents, the Modesto, California, native had grown up exploiting people in order to survive. As a self-indulgent college student in the late 1950s, Smith quickly hit rock bottom—no religion, no faith, no sense of spirituality. Yet, all the while, Gary Smith was searching desperately for meaning in life.

"By the time I was a sophomore at San Jose State University," Smith says, "my personal life was a mess." Desperate for answers, he started reading voraciously: literature, philosophy, political science. One evening a Catholic roommate loaned him a Bible. "I was listening to jazz on a San Francisco station, and I started reading the Gospel of Mark," Smith recalls. "I was so struck by the straightforward, honest, and good relationship Jesus had with people. I liked the structure and order of the writing. I sat there and said, 'That's it.'"

Soon, Smith was reading the works of Trappist monk Thomas Merton, engaging in all-night discussions on religion, and attending Mass.

---

*A pseudonym.

"I was like a sponge," he says.

Within a year, Smith had converted to Catholicism and transferred to Santa Clara University. By his senior year, he had decided to become a priest—a Jesuit. As his spiritual journey continued, Smith soon discovered how St. Ignatius Loyola, sixteenth-century founder of the Jesuit order, had also been redeemed by the power of the Bible.

"It's a mystery how God enters someone's life," says Smith, finishing another cup of coffee. "I would call it grace and the love of God. It's been almost forty years since I was transformed, but I can still remember what it was like to live in darkness."

Reflecting on his decades-long evolution, Smith returns to the central theme of his life as a religious social activist. "The Church's credibility lies with its solidarity with the poor," he adds. "The poor Christ always comes back to haunt and—in the end—empower us."

Smith, who has a bachelor's degree in political science and graduate degrees in counseling and theology, says as a young man he thought he would enjoy getting a Ph.D. and teaching at a Jesuit university. But a lifetime of serving others changed his perspective. "What makes me genuinely happy is establishing meaningful relationships with people on the street."

As dusk falls on Portland, Father Gary Smith once again glides out the door. He moves swiftly down the sidewalks of Burnside. He hurries back to the chapel where he will say evening Mass, open his heart, and share the good news of God's grace and compassion.

[2]

THE REVEREND DR. ISRAEL
SUAREZ "FIGHTING THE GOOD FIGHT"

Photo by Thomas A. Price

Reverend Israel Suarez sounded just as enthusiastic in the summer of 2003 as he had when I profiled him five years earlier. He told me about the new headquarters building for Nations Association Charities, Inc. (NAC), about four miles from its previous facility. Suarez eagerly described the walk-in medical clinic, where area poor could receive screenings and prescription assistance, a legal aid clinic for immigration-related concerns, a computer training facility, and a job placement service. He said the organization had added "Charities" to its name in 2002 to reinforce its nonprofit identity. But in its twenty-fifth year, its mission still focused on providing Lee County residents with basic services, including food, clothing, furniture, appliances, job readiness services, financial assistance, youth programs, and a variety of other programs, including disaster relief. The organization had started with an informal group of volunteers helping troubled youth. Today NAC has almost 150 volunteers who supplement staff operations in serving the needs of low-income and minority residents. Much has changed since its founding in 1978, but the organization's driving force remains the Reverend Dr. Israel Suarez.

> In Spanish, I think Suarez means relentless.
>
> —ANDREW STEELE, Fort Myers, Florida, business owner

You would swear that the Reverend Israel Suarez was running for office. The short, stocky dynamo with the ready smile and piercing eyes knows how to work this room full of flush suburbanites. The Kiwanis Club is holding its weekly 7 A.M. breakfast meeting in the air-conditioned multipurpose room adjacent to the Cypress Lake Presbyterian Church. The beautiful white church is on sun-splashed Cypress Lake Drive not far from Thomas Edison's onetime summer home in Fort Myers, Florida.

Half a century after Edison journeyed here from the Northeast, Reverend Suarez arrived in 1976. He had come from Brooklyn, New York, his adopted home. He had come to Florida's Gulf Coast to enjoy the climate, embark on a new career, and raise his family in more comfortable surroundings. He had come to build a better life for his wife, Ruth, and three daughters, Susan, Dianne, and Catherine.

He hadn't come to preach or serve. He thought he was leaving his Pentecostal pastoral days behind in the Assembly of God church back in Brooklyn. But the good Lord had other ideas for Israel. His name gives one pause: a biblical name for a man, a nation, and a people. "Israel" is a popular appellation in Puerto Rico, Suarez's birthplace. The name seems well suited for a man of faith dedicated to serving God.

Two decades after his quiet arrival in this Gulf Coast community, Suarez has arguably become the area's best-known Good Samaritan. His reputation stretches from the poor Hispanic and African American neighborhoods to the affluent sections of town such as tree-lined McGregor Boulevard. Suarez has made many powerful friends during the last two decades. Former mayor Wilbur "Billy" Smith readily congratulates Suarez and his organization. State's attorney (for Lee County) Joe D'Allesandro openly endorses Suarez. Such political support is vital to the Nations Association's continued operations.

The Nations Association, the social service organization that Suarez has directed since 1978, publishes an annual report that boasts such sponsors as Merrill Lynch, NationsBank, Re/Max Realty, and major retailers and professional service firms. In 1997 the association's private donors accounted for slightly more than half of its approximate $350,000 annual revenues. City and county grants combined provided another 15 percent, slightly more than thrift store sales. Private foundation grants (7.1 percent) were more than double the $11,000, or 3.1 percent, received in Federal Emergency Management Agency (FEMA) grant funding.

The association's revenue streams are diverse, but Suarez knows that most of his funding depends on the good intentions of individuals and organizations such as the Kiwanis. Here at the Cypress Lake Presbyterian Church, well-heeled, longtime residents like banker Dilman Thomas praise fifty-five-year-old Israel Suarez's devotion to social causes. "He never gives up," says Thomas, dressed in shirt and tie, as are more than twenty of his fellow Kiwanians. "He's successful because he works within the system."

These nice upper-crust chaps smile sheepishly as the Puerto Rican–born minister presses the flesh. Suarez is grinning, but he appears nervous, distracted. He makes polite chatter, but his dark eyes roam the room behind tinted gold-rimmed glasses. His mind is clicking off the tasks he has before him today. He keeps it all up in his head—all of his appointments, schedules, and activities.

After he eats this bland breakfast of scrambled eggs, sweet roll, and lukewarm orange juice, he will drive his large white delivery truck to Sanibel Island to load two rooms of donated furniture. He will do most of the loading himself, as the burly spiritual stevedore usually does. Then, as the humidity drapes the streets and the temperature climbs into the mid-nineties, Suarez will distribute the dressers, beds, chairs, and couches to needy families around town.

Later, he will take an elderly couple to the Housing Authority to find out why they can't get their air-conditioning repaired. Suarez was formerly a board member, and he still has friends there, friends who know that Suarez will keep coming back until he gets some answers, some resolution.

Here, there, and everywhere. Suarez seems to be always coming or going, usually in a hurry. This needs to be done; that needs to be done. Keep moving; keep busy. Don't rest, can't rest. He knows how he got out of poverty: He worked his way out of it. He out-hustled it. He out-hustled poverty and the devil himself. So keep moving, Reverend Suarez. Keep moving.

He will return to the Nations Association offices on Dr. Martin Luther King Jr. Boulevard several times during the day to check in with his wife and program coordinator, Ruth, and his office manager, José ("Joe") Cardona. Suarez will pick up his messages, make sure the soup kitchen has enough food for the midday meal, and see how many customers are browsing and buying in the thrift store. Then he'll be on the road again— to make deliveries, distribute press releases, transport clients, and even haul away garbage from the men's transitional shelter that his private, nonprofit organization operates.

But first the highly motivated, hyperkinetic minister has to put in face time here at the Kiwanis breakfast in fashionable Cypress Lake. He's been doing this since 1988, and he'll keep showing up so people like Dilman Thomas don't forget about him and his mission: to provide a helping hand and a word of hope to those in need.

"You can't wait for people to start caring," Suarez says. "You have to go after them and keep after them."

He leads by example. It has been that way for Suarez here since 1976, when he started as a volunteer counselor for at-risk teens. Now he directs

14

well over one hundred volunteers who regularly serve the needs of the Nations Association. "I'm a creator," he says matter-of-factly. "I get things done, and that's why people support me." People like the Kiwanians of Fort Myers.

This morning Suarez is dressed in a floral print shirt, black slacks, and tassel loafers. His bronze skin and calloused hands make him stand out among these lighter-hued, white-collar citizens. These men seem to stroll to their seats, while Suarez strides like a thick-legged middleweight boxer moving about the ring.

"Won't you lead us in the morning prayer, Reverend?" an older fellow asks, and the assembled bow their heads.

"Dear Father in heaven," Suarez begins his prayer. Now he's at peace, in power. These men are listening to his words, his invocation. He is leading them in prayer. Suarez is soaring now like an eagle above the crowd. He is leading them in prayer. Later he will bid them goodbye. But they know he'll be back. He just never gives up, does he?

* * *

What's the story with these Good Samaritans like Israel Suarez? How do they manage to give so much of themselves to those less fortunate? Is this altruism, or are these modern-day disciples hedging their bets for the Second Coming? What do they expect for their life's work?

"We don't do good works to be saved. We do good works because we're saved," says Suarez as he drives his white delivery truck through the steamy streets of Fort Myers.

Florida seems even hotter and more humid in the month of the fires: June 1998. The skies are heavy and gray with a lingering acrid stench as upwards of half a million acres burn across the state. Fire seems an apt symbol for a story on a religious social activist: Pentecost and images of fiery tongues atop the heads of the disciples. The Holy Spirit descends and transforms ordinary, fearful men into extraordinary preachers and martyrs. Was it the fire of the Holy Spirit that forever changed Suarez, and thus eased the burden of thousands of Florida's poor?

It certainly didn't start out that way.

* * *

"I didn't come here to be a pastor or to run any social service programs," Suarez says, wiping beads of sweat from his balding palate. "But everything changed when I saw so many needy people."

15

Waiting to be helped. Waiting to be saved by the Holy Spirit. One can almost finish the sentence with the words Suarez has spoken to his congregations since being ordained an Assembly of God minister in New York in the mid-1960s. Though Suarez says he wasn't expecting the fiery tongue to descend upon him as he journeyed south to Florida.

But wasn't that just like God? Wasn't that how it usually was with matters of faith? Man plans. God laughs. And so does Suarez's wife, Ruth, as she relates her husband's failed attempts at finding work other than preaching or social service. "He made a lousy carpenter," says Ruth with a delightful chuckle. She describes how Israel showed up on a construction site that first day years ago wearing a shirt and tie and carrying a Bible in his briefcase. After a few weeks, Suarez went searching for another line of work.

He became a job counselor for residents of low-income housing projects. He also started working part-time as an announcer for a Spanish radio station. In 1977 he began volunteering as a counselor at a local detention center. He learned how many of the teens' problems (drug addiction, delinquency, pregnancy) could be traced to family crises such as unemployment, lack of shelter, poor nutrition, and a loss of hope.

In the process of dealing with troubled teens, Suarez rediscovered his calling. He had found his path and a new mission in Fort Myers, Florida. Once again, he became a pastor (the First Spanish Assembly of God Church). In 1978 he and other concerned citizens started the Nations Association. The term "Nations" was inspired by a host of biblical references (e.g., Psalms 86:9—"All nations whom thou hast made shall come and worship before thee, O Lord; and shall glorify thy name."). Suarez decided to dedicate himself full-time to the fledgling organization.

With a modest CETA (Comprehensive Employment Training Act) grant, Suarez began working in a donated small mobile home parked behind his church on Catalina Street. He helped poor people find jobs, shelter, and health care services. He was a tireless advocate and friend, especially for the area's Spanish-speaking residents. But all the good being done couldn't protect the Nations Association from ill will and violence.

In early 1980 someone broke into the trailer and destroyed records, office equipment, and furniture. A year later, on Good Friday 1981, someone again broke in. This time the mobile home was doused with gasoline and burned to the ground. Suarez moved the operations of the Nations Association into a couple of Sunday school rooms in his church.

By 1982 Suarez had received small governmental grants to help fund operations. Additional staff was hired, and the association moved to a former skid row boarding house, which would one day become the men's transitional shelter. In this location, the association's services were expanded to include a walk-in medical clinic for low-income people, including new émigrés from Cuba and Haiti.

In 1983 Suarez rented a warehouse to store donated furniture, clothes, and household items. Four years later, the Nations Association bought the warehouse and opened a thrift store and a permanent soup kitchen on the premises. By 1990, the association's offices and service space were located in their present location: a one-story multipurpose building on Dr. Martin Luther King Jr. Boulevard.

For more than twenty years, Suarez has tried to better people's lives by raising the consciousness of the community's affluent and politically powerful. This burly evangelist with the Popeye forearms and contagious smile has a simple formula: "Never give up." It's as if he wants to carry the needs and concerns of the people on his broad shoulders. "A job had to be done, and He chose me," Suarez says simply over a plate of shrimp and rice at his favorite Shoney's restaurant, before he heads back to the Nations Association office.

Suarez doesn't have time for extended introspection. There's furniture to be picked up and delivered, food drives to organize, bureaucrats to lobby, and donors to nudge. "Hey, my friend, call me, or you know I'll call you," Suarez says to a man on his way out of the restaurant, repeating one of his trademark lines.

* * *

"I know what it's like to be poor," Reverend Suarez says. He isn't smiling now, and his dark eyes are those of a boy who learned early how to hustle to survive on the streets. When you're one of ten children raised in poverty in Guyanabo, Puerto Rico, you can't wait for a handout. By age seven Suarez was shining shoes to help his mother put food on the table. But it was never enough. Suarez remembers all too well what it was like to eat his meals from the same plate as one of his brothers.

He tells others how he prayed to God to help him escape his poverty. Help me, and I will help somebody else, he vowed.

When Suarez was eleven, his mother moved him and his siblings to the hard-edged Bedford-Stuyvesant section of Brooklyn, New York. Though he had escaped the poverty of his native Puerto Rico, Suarez was faced with a challenge far greater than hunger: losing his soul to temptations of the street.

Then he found God. He and his brothers and sisters were baptized in an Assembly of God church in New York City. One of those watching Suarez's

17

family join the church was a pretty neighborhood girl from Delancey Street named Ruthie Rodriquez. She watched as Israel grew into a handsome, proud teenager. Suarez worked as a model for a men's store, and he would strut down the streets, advertising the latest fashions.

"The girls in the neighborhood were crazy about him," says Mrs. Ruth ("Ruthie") Suarez as she and her husband eat lemon cake and sip coffee at 10 P.M. in their tidy three-bedroom ranch house in Fort Myers Shores. After dessert, Israel Suarez will head for his worn recliner, where he'll watch the news and *Nightline,* often falling asleep with the remote control in his hand.

As Ruth watches Israel leave the room, she returns to her story of how she was courted by the good-looking, popular young man. In June 1963 they were married. She was twenty; he was nineteen. In June 1998 Ruth and Israel celebrated their thirty-fifth anniversary. Photographs of their three daughters and five grandchildren adorn the walls of the Suarez home, focal point for family gatherings and a source of comfort and renewal for Israel in his rare moments of relaxation.

Ruth says her hard-charging husband could have become a successful entrepreneur or political leader, but he stayed true to his mother's wishes and entered theology school. Soon he was in the pulpit preaching away. "Boy, could he roll," says Ruth, laughing contagiously as she imitates her husband's energetic sermons, sermons she used to help him type out the night before.

Though Israel Suarez respects the legacy of other charismatic activist ministers such as Dr. Martin Luther King Jr., he says he has no role models except Jesus Christ, who showed him the way. He cites Scripture: "Because he hath anointed me to preach the gospel to the poor; he hath sent me to heal the broken-hearted, to preach deliverance to the captives, and recovering of sight to the blind, to set at liberty them that are bruised" (Luke 4:18–19).

* * *

En route to his church, Israel Suarez complains about area clergy who aren't following the Savior's example. They aren't trying to serve the poor. He passes a nearby church and clenches the truck's steering wheel a little tighter as his voice rises. "That church is just bricks. The pastor doesn't do anything for his parishioners or for the community."

Suarez can't understand how a man of God can turn away from those in need. His words echo comments made in an October 23, 1983, Fort Myers *News-Press* article by Ann Rodgers: "If all the churches got together, they could work a miracle to help people. They have a responsibility to create programs to help needy people," he said. "If God has called us to a ministry, I don't think he has called us to deal with one kind of people. Maybe God has called me just to deal with the poor and other people just to deal with the rich."

His mood brightens as he pulls in the parking lot of his Buen Samartino ("Good Samaritan") church. It is a one-story building with a chapel that can seat about two hundred people. A wooden cross hangs above the altar area, which also includes two tall conga drums.

In his small church office to the rear of the building, Suarez licks his index finger and wipes away a smudge on his desktop.

"I keep my church nice, yes?"

Outside the chapel, but still inside the building, is a small glass case and counter displaying author Suarez's paperback books on religion—books of the prolific minister who is working on a doctorate in theology. The books are sold in Spain and Latin America, as well as the United States. But Suarez's words must be heard, not just read, if one is to feel the power of his conviction.

Adjacent to the counter is the entrance to a radio station (WWW6D 1620 AM). Suarez's radio station. Ever since he first worked in radio twenty-odd years ago, Suarez has embraced the airwaves as a means of reaching thousands of would-be church members. Each week he preaches at the radio station to his loyal listeners.

His show is not scheduled today, but he steps into the booth, puts his thick hands on the somewhat startled young Hispanic man's shoulders. The slender radio announcer relinquishes the microphone and stands awkwardly to the side as the burly Suarez slides into his chair. The afternoon's music is interrupted by the words of the Reverend Suarez.

"Mis amigos, es Israel Suarez. . . ."

His voice is smooth, resonant, seductive. He speaks rapidly, but enunciates his words. His hands splay as he moves his fingers through the air, as if parting imaginary curtains and peering into the homes of his listeners. While Suarez's melodic monologue continues, the slender young man smiles weakly. How long will this go on? Will he ever get the microphone back? What are the listeners thinking? Suarez keeps talking, lost in the sound of his own sonorous voice.

Later that night, his voice will rise in anger at his congregation. He stands at the front of his church like a father reprimanding his mischievous children. Suarez has found litter in the church parking lot. Litter shows disrespect, a lack of pride, and Suarez won't tolerate any disrespect toward his church, his *iglesia*. But after a flurry of fiery words, Suarez's face softens, and he smiles at his flock. Yes, he was mad, but no longer. He has a temper, he says. But it passes quickly like a thunderstorm racing down the coastline.

* * *

Suarez has been up since before 5 A.M. Twelve hours later, when most people are heading home to unwind after a day's work, Suarez is at the transitional shelter loading thirty-gallon black bags of rubbish into the back of his white delivery truck. He shouldn't have to be hauling this garbage away, but Scott,* the shelter director, hasn't taking care of the problem. So it is Suarez's problem.

A few minutes earlier, Suarez had toured the shelter, which provides temporary housing for about two dozen men. At the shelter they can get a meal, a shower, and a decent place to sleep.

Scott, who resembles a chubby Stephen Spielberg, was formerly homeless. He also has battled drug and other problems. Suarez gave him a chance, a new start a couple of years ago. He named Scott director of the shelter, and expected him to keep the place clean and orderly. Today the shelter is failing inspection, and Suarez is not pleased. He is tight-lipped as he tours the halls and public rooms, seeing clutter, grime, and disorganization. Suarez says later that he has been thinking of asking the Salvation Army in Fort Myers to run the shelter. It just isn't operating the way Suarez wants it to.

Eager to please, Scott shows Suarez around, trying to straighten up the shelter as he goes about on this surprise inspection. Scott is soft-spoken and amiable, but seems overwhelmed, like an absent-minded professor lost in an office full of paperwork and disarray. Before they reach the backyard, where countless black garbage bags have been tossed, Scott rambles on in a tribute to his boss, the Reverend Israel Suarez. "He's like Gandhi, man," Scott says. "Suarez is like from a different era. He's just amazing."

Minutes later, as the fetid rubbish is being loaded into the white delivery truck, Scott is subdued, a penitent handing bag after bag to Suarez, who will have to dispose of the rubbish before tonight's church service. Dressed in pressed black slacks, light sport shirt, and tassel loafers, Suarez keeps loading the garbage bags until the backyard is clear of refuse.

---

*A pseudonym.

When the last bag is loaded and the heavy truck door pulled shut, Suarez wipes his hands on his pants, takes off his gold-rimmed glasses for a few moments, and rubs his tired eyes.

As the truck pulls away, Scott waves, but Suarez doesn't return the gesture. The truck seems to groan as it pulls out on busy Dr. Martin Luther King Jr. Boulevard amidst the commuters seeking relief in their air-conditioned cars from another hot, sticky day in Fort Myers.

Two hours later, Suarez is dressed in a fresh white shirt, dark tie, and black slacks. He is smiling once again. More than sixty of his congregation are in the chapel listening to a young man singing while playing a guitar. It's a Bible reading tonight, but Suarez is not leading the service. Still people feel his presence and glance at him as he moves about the chapel. One of the readers asks him to say a few words, and he is happy to oblige. Again, one hears the beautiful melody of his words, words in his native Spanish that make the men, women, and children in this humble church nod and smile.

Once more, Suarez has given them something to cling to. Something to guide them. Something to encourage them.

When the service is over, Israel and Ruth Suarez stand outside the chapel, greeting people with strong handshakes, hugs, and resonant laughter. The minister sends his congregation on their way. They leave with words of faith, hope, and love to challenge their problems and counter their fears. They look at peace as they leave. They are smiling. Their minister, Reverend Israel Suarez, has the widest smile of them all.

[3]

SISTER ANN KENDRICK "LA MONJITA OF THE FIELDS"

Photo by Thomas A. Price

Sister Ann Kendrick is the kind of person who lifts your spirits with her infectious personality. She speaks with the same vitality whether reviewing achievements and recognition (she was profiled in the September 2003 Good Housekeeping magazine), discussing setbacks, or talking about new challenges. Kendrick notes that since many central Florida farms closed in the late 1990s, seasonal workers have had a difficult time being absorbed into the area's low-skilled work force. Also the Farmworker Association staff has been reduced due to funding cuts. But after more than thirty years, Kendrick and her three fellow sisters of the order of Notre Dame de Namur are still in Apopka, Florida, trying to better the lives of the poor. In November 2002, Amnesty International Orlando honored the four Roman Catholic nuns for their lifetime of service as "seekers of justice and peace." In accepting the award, Kendrick spoke of how she and her colleagues are recommitting to the path of human rights. She also said that in order to continue good works, activists must "take care of ourselves." That comment was particularly compelling in light of Kendrick's first public disclosure of her earlier struggles with alcoholism in a frank account in a December 6, 2001, feature story by Orlando Sentinel staff writer Kate Santich. In that article, Kendrick referred to the "gift of desperation" that drove her to seek treatment. She has now been sober for several years. "If my story helps other people deal with their problems, then I'm glad," she said in a recent phone call. Ann seemed in fine form during our conversation. When I hung up the phone, I felt better for having talked with her.

We have a great people among us, only we do not know it. They are the
poorest of the poor—the unwanted, the uncared for, the rejected, the
alcoholics, the crippled, the blind, the sick, the dying—people who have
nothing and have nobody. Their very life is prayer. They continually
intercede for us without knowing it.

—MOTHER TERESA

"Let's go," says Ann Kendrick, her pale blue eyes rimmed in red in the
wee hours of this late June morning as she marches into a sea of eight-foot-
high emerald cornstalks. The soil is powdery, fertile, dark silt from what
once was the bottom of Lake Apopka. For fifty years it has yielded some of
the richest harvests of corn, carrots, celery, and lettuce in the United
States. That will all end within days, and that's what brings Sister Ann
Kendrick to the farms this morning. The last harvest.

To restore the chronically polluted Lake Apopka, the St. John's Water
Management District has bought fourteen thousand acres of farmland
adjoining the lake. More than two thousand workers will lose their jobs
when the farms close in this sad summer of 1998. Kendrick says that people
are waiting for some kind of miracle, but no amount of prayer will stop this
land sale, this last harvest.

She plows into the rows of cornstalks armed with her Pentax camera.
After sixty or seventy yards, she reaches the "mule"—the giant green
harvesting machine that looks like something out of a silly monster movie.
It's about one hundred feet long and twenty feet high, and it groans,
growls, and wails as it devours row after row of crop. A score of Latino men
and women work the mule, most on the two-tiered machine, others on the
ground, following the "monster's" path. On this overcast morning, they
will finish the corn harvest and stack the wooden crates high on the mule.

"Sister Anna," the workers shout in unison as they see Kendrick's smiling
round, ruddy face. The voices are happy, celebratory. "La Monjita!" ("little
nun"—an endearment). ·

"Hola, Hola," Kendrick replies, still moving toward the mule. She's
taking pictures today to commemorate the last harvest. She hugs workers
in the field and laughs along with them. She has known some of these
people since they were infants. She has worked alongside them, alongside
their parents. She has fought for their rights to decent wages, housing,
health care, and schooling for the children.

She has served them for more than twenty-five years, and still she feels like
the lucky one. They've enriched her life while she's tried to empower theirs.

"Everybody who knows her, loves her," says Lidia Alameda, one of the AmeriCorps volunteers who works with the Office for Farmworker Ministry (OFM) that fifty-four-year-old Kendrick and the three other Sisters of Notre Dame de Namur operate in central Florida. Alameda came to these fields in poverty as a child from Mexico. Members of her family still work these fields. Alameda has known Sister Anna as long as she can remember. Her earliest memories are of the smiling nun in the fields.

Kendrick's white T-shirt and brown work shoes are coated with a thin layer of dust when she emerges from the cornstalks. She shakes her gray boyish-cut hair and adjusts her silver wire-rim glasses en route to the second mule in the fields of Lake Apopka this morning.

The Haitians act as if they know Sister Ann Kendrick, like they've seen her before. But these farmworkers don't have a long history with the nun from Apopka like the Hispanic workers do. Still, the Haitians know who she is. They have seen the small wooden crucifix around her neck. They have heard her friendly, booming voice trying to speak Creole. Most now avert their eyes when she arrives. A few shout to her.

"Money. *D'argent.* Money."

The Haitian mule is a rainbow tapestry of shirts, hats, and neckerchiefs: pink, green, blue, purple, red. These workers from Belle Glade, Florida, converse and laugh as they labor under the eyes of the stoic white supervisors who lean up against nearby pick-up trucks as a small dust storm of silt fills the air. On the mule, an assembly line of men and women separate cornhusks from fodder, load the wooden crates, and stack them.

One woman in a bright pink headscarf turns her face when Kendrick raises her camera. Superstitions are common among these Haitian workers, she says. Some believe that if you take their picture, you take their soul.

Why don't you take a hike, sister? Is this what these lanky white farm bosses are thinking as they watch this sturdy Catholic nun roam their fields talking with their workers? No words are spoken. These men in jeans, boots, and baseball caps look right through Kendrick as if she's a cornstalk, a weed, a prickly bush.

No words are spoken today, but plenty have been said in the past. Some have found their way into print. "She's trouble for us," said an anonymous Apopka fern grower in a February 28, 1993, story by Billy Bruce about the activist nun and union organizer that ran in the Daytona Beach *News-Journal.* "She's a thorn in our side, a troublemaker. She instigates labor problems."

The grower said that several employers in the area had stopped providing housing for their workers because of Sister Kendrick's efforts. "She's hurting the Hispanics, and her reputation is shot. She's hurt the industry, and she's hurt the workers. She has no idea what she's doing."

In that same article, former farmworker Carmen Rivera spoke fondly of Kendrick: "She's worked in the fields and lived as we live. She thinks she's a Mexican. She is one of us."

A cream-colored pickup truck roars past and kicks up mountains of dirt. Nobody seems to flinch. The mule moves farther away, but Kendrick doesn't follow. She brusquely thanks the field bosses for giving her access to the workers this morning. But Kendrick says later: "Wasn't that a bunch of crap? They're getting rich off these farm sales, while the workers are being left with nothing."

She drives away quickly from the fields, as if she doesn't want bad karma to follow. She has many stops to make. She has to check in on "her people," like Rosse, who just lost her husband. Rosse lives on an unpaved road in the black section of town, where once water and sewer lines didn't reach— until Ann Kendrick and her band of troublemaking nuns protested the miserable living conditions.

Today, Kendrick gives Rosse her African wooden earrings to wear to her husband's funeral. The woman, who bears a striking resemblance to poet Maya Angelou, hugs Sister Ann tightly as she says goodbye.

"I love you," Kendrick shouts heartily as she gets back in her teal Ford Escort with the worn shock absorbers, and she heads down the unpaved back road to visit more of the poor of Apopka, Florida.

* * *

The town of Apopka (population about twenty-seven thousand) is just north of Orlando, where a deity named Disney reigns. Here, Sister Ann Kendrick works to remind people that there's more to life than a megalomaniac mouse's corporate empire. Indigent families and those broken in body and spirit need to be cared for. These people deserve our attention, our support, our services, she says. Kendrick has been spreading the word among business and political leaders and everyday citizens since the early 1970s, when mentors such as Cesar Chavez were busy organizing a new generation of migrant farmworkers.

United with her fellow Sisters of Notre Dame (SND) Cathy Gorman, Gail Grimes, and Teresa McElwee, Kendrick has tried to ensure that proper educational, health care, housing, and other social services are provided to the needy in this central Florida community.

During the last three decades, these activist nuns have launched the Office for Farmworker Ministry, which provides tutoring, mentoring, family counseling, and immigration services for the mostly Hispanic and Haitian seasonal worker populations. They have helped create a community health clinic and a credit union for farmworkers. They have lobbied for worker rights. They have established counseling programs for pregnant teens and victims of domestic violence.

Perhaps their most innovative venture was the cofounding of the Farmworker Association of Florida (FAF), a sixty-five-hundred-member grassroots organization. It was established in 1983 to address economic, environmental, health, workplace, and other social justice issues. Today the association operates on a $750,000 annual budget at four sites in eleven counties in central and south Florida.

Tirso Moreno, a former fieldworker, is the general coordinator of FAF. When Kendrick met the Mexican-born Moreno, he was a powerfully built, soft-spoken family man and devout Catholic. Moreno and his wife, Blanca, befriended Kendrick in 1978 in an evening course for laypeople interested in the pastoral ministry. In that night class Kendrick introduced the Morenos to fundamentals of community organizing and social action. But it took years to convince Tirso and others that a grassroots farmworker association would be *their* organization.

"The founding vision of the Sisters of Notre Dame has been to serve the poor in the most abandoned places," says Kendrick. "But you can't just provide services; you must develop leaders in the community. Otherwise, you're pouring your work down a black hole." In time Kendrick's words of encouragement and vision were received, believed, and acted upon.

Tirso Moreno praises Kendrick and the other nuns of the OFM for earning the trust and respect of so many in the community. His wife, Blanca, is a teller at the Community Trust Federal Credit Union, the only farmworker-run credit union in the United States. With more than twenty-eight hundred clients and $4 million in deposits, this is a bona fide financial institution. An affiliated "Pennies for Power" Youth Credit Union has $27,000 in deposits and a priceless amount of "kiddy" pride and energy fueling its success.

Sister Ann Kendrick greets a room full of men, women, and children on payday at the storefront credit union, a few doors down from the OFM offices at 815 South Park Avenue. Nine-year-old Paulette, a Pennies for Power volunteer, sits typing depositor cards. Standing in the credit union as a steady stream of farmworkers and their families come and go, one thinks of the ordinary folks who patronized the Bailey Brothers Building and Loan in the movie *It's a Wonderful Life*. The way these hard-working folks shower Kendrick with love and affection, she might as well be a relative of "good old" George Bailey. "Her heart is right here," says Blanca Moreno. Right here in the community. Right here where help is needed.

How do Kendrick and her spirited cohorts stay dedicated year after year? That's what Farmworkers Association attorney Carl Webster asked five years earlier in a February 28, 1993, Daytona Beach *News-Journal* story: "I don't understand how they maintain that energy, although some say it comes from God. . . . Most people burn out and lose their level of idealism after that long. It's either their commitment to God, man, or both. I don't understand it."

Kendrick defines it as a mission. Following in the footsteps of legendary Catholic Worker cofounder Dorothy Day, Kendrick and her fellow sisters are human rights activists. They fight the status quo with a powerful combination of prayer and protest. Their goal is to awaken and enlighten people in the community, even those comfortably ensconced in the institutionalized Catholic Church.

"We take this Christian deal seriously. We're not talking a bunch of religious rhetoric and praying quietly. If you take this seriously, you just can't sit in your convent, or your home, or your classroom," Kendrick said in a December 23, 1989, story by *Orlando Sentinel* reporter Sharon McBreen. Today Kendrick, laughing heartily, adds, "We took vows of poverty, chastity, and obedience, but not silence."

* * *

Ann Kendrick grew up as an outspoken, upper-middle-class only child. A sister eighteen years her junior would come along when she was almost out of the house. ("Irish family planning," Kendrick says sarcastically.) As a high school student in Syracuse, New York, she was, in her words, "a self-absorbed, naive young woman on the go-to-college-and-get-married track." The daughter of a principal (father) and teacher/guidance counselor (mother), Kendrick knew nothing firsthand about poverty and social problems until she was sixteen and became an exchange student. That was, as a novelist might say, her point of insight, when her life changed. That was when her destiny seemed determined by a higher calling.

She had wanted to go to France. Instead she found herself in Guatemala, shaken by the extreme poverty of this Central American nation. In that first month she hated everything about this culture. She had studied French, not Spanish. What was she doing here? She fought the reality of her situation until she tired of her own negative attitude.

Gradually she lowered her resistance and allowed herself to experience this new world. She began to "fall in love" with the destitute Guatemalan people she met. She returned to Syracuse with a different worldview, sensitized to the plight of the poor within her own community.

Her experiences in Guatemala led her to major in Spanish at Trinity College in Washington, D.C. Kendrick's classmates remember her as an exuberant, giving, and unifying leader. She was class president for three years during a time when war protests and race riots raged in the nation's capital. During the summers, Kendrick worked with the poor in Washington, D.C. She also returned to Central America. While she was on a service mission in Honduras, a five-year-old native girl died in her arms. The tragedy crystallized her plans. The twenty-something Kendrick had found her calling: a life of serving others.

After graduating from Trinity in 1966, Kendrick decided to enter the Sisters of Notre Dame de Namur (a religious order founded in France in 1804 and dedicated to "the instruction of the poor"). She had been influenced by the character of the nuns who had taught her at Trinity. She saw them as women of strength, women committed to social action. "I thought the nuns were pretty cool," Kendrick says. "But I didn't have a clue what I was getting into."

Over the next few years, Sister Ann Kendrick earned a master's degree in Latin American literature and taught Spanish at the high school and college levels. But rather than being immersed in social activism, she was stuck in classrooms with bored *gringo* kids. To hold onto her burgeoning liberalism, she spent summers in Spanish Harlem putting on street fairs, working to rehabilitate housing, and helping the low-income residents rebuild a sense of community. Her time on the streets hardened her resolve to not spend a lifetime of service in the classroom. She was searching for a new mission, hoping to find one in the cities of the urban North. That's where she reasoned she could do the most good.

Then came the call from Bishop William Borders of Orlando, Florida, who contacted the Sisters of Notre Dame. He was concerned about the plight of the thousands of farmworkers and their families living in substandard conditions in nearby Apopka. In 1971 Kendrick and fellow SND sister Cathy Gorman flew to Florida to learn about the situation. They made a one-year commitment. Sisters Gail Grimes and Teresa McElwee would follow the pair shortly to Apopka.

Once in Florida, Kendrick discovered scenes of poverty among the African American and Hispanic migrant workers that "just haunted" her, she says. Life turned out quite differently than the headstrong nun from the North had planned. The rural South became her home and the focus of her activism. Now twenty-seven years have passed, and Kendrick is still fighting for the rights of the less fortunate.

* * *

This stifling June afternoon, Sister Ann Kendrick has asked seventeen-year-old Mayra Garcia to stay late and finish the edits on the Pennies for Power brochure that Kendrick wants to take to the Thousand Points of Light conference in New Orleans in two days. She is accepting an award for the work of the OFM. The fact that she and her fellow activists are receiving the award from a group established by Republican President George Bush seems a bit bizarre to Kendrick, who confides that she will have to "clean up her language around all those conservatives."

At 7 P.M., the phones are still ringing, and Kendrick is bustling about, carrying on two conversations at once, proofreading brochure copy, and working on plans for a farmworkers' ceremony next week. The event, which will honor the people who have worked the earth in Apopka for fifty years, will take place in the parking lot outside the OFM's office. Plans call for an altar of prayer, baskets of corn, lettuce, carrots, and celery to be carried by farmworker children, Scripture readings and prayers, chants, and songs. The commemorative ritual will blend Roman Catholic tradition with ethnic customs.

In her stylish white slacks, brightly colored sweater, and penny loafers, Kendrick looks and acts tonight more like an owner of a small ad agency than a Catholic nun. She wears eye shadow, lipstick, perfume, and more jewelry than one might expect—two silver rings, two silver bracelets, a silver watch, and a silver Kokopelli figurine—a Southwestern Native American god that dangles around her neck intertwined with her gold crucifix.

As usual, she was busy all afternoon. She attended the dedication of a new Habitat for Humanity home for a local African American couple and their three small children, the Callahans. Kendrick held the Callahan baby while the parents greeted the mayor and other dignitaries. Then she had a private meeting with some board members of the Apopka Family Health Center, which is being criticized for firing a popular Haitian doctor. Kendrick is one of the community leaders protesting the clinic's policies that threaten the security of low-income patients.

Twenty years ago she had "helped give birth" to this health clinic for farmworkers. Now she has to try to awaken the conscience of the new budget-minded health center administrator, who appears to be shifting the focus of service to a broader base of insured patients.

But first things first. The computer is acting up again. Kendrick has asked old friend and one-time Apopka community organizer Paul Pumphrey to help fix the computer and do some last-minute desktop publishing. Pumphrey had stopped into the OFM offices earlier today while on a trip through Florida.

He didn't plan on staying long, but found himself drafted into helping out around the place that has the look and feel of a shoestring social action office: rummage-sale furniture, mix-and-match file cabinets, colorful posters, handmade signs, a large needlepoint motto ("If you want peace, work for justice."), stacks of books, boxes of paper, framed black-and-white photos and testimonial letters, a large "Notre Dame AmeriCorps" banner, renderings of the Blessed Virgin Mary, and a seven-foot-high wooden cross.

Pumphrey dwarfs the people around him. He wears shorts, sneakers, and a "Campaign for a New Tomorrow" T-shirt promoting his Washington, D.C., organization. When he speaks of Kendrick, he smiles fully and grows nostalgic. As she rushes by, Pumphrey says in a bellowing voice, "You should hear her jokes after she's had a few beers."

At first, Kendrick smiles shyly, and her full Irish-American face turns crimson as she stands near the large lobby tapestry of Our Lady of Guadalupe. The revered image of the olive-skinned Virgin Mary, who reportedly appeared to an Aztec peasant in 1531 and subsequently converted millions of native Mexicans to Catholicism, is the first image visitors see when entering the OFM office. The portrait of the humble, sacred woman who honored a poor people with her presence symbolizes the identity and faith of most of those who come to this office for answers and assistance.

Now Kendrick turns to embrace Pumphrey, and lets go with an old-fashioned belly laugh. In the early 1970s, Pumphrey lived for two months with Kendrick and the three other Apopka "sisters." Can you imagine that? he asks. Four white nuns and one large black man living under the same roof.

Pumphrey and Kendrick chuckle as they recount how the FBI had supposedly bugged the nuns' little rented house on South Central Avenue in the middle of "Lake Jewel," the poor black neighborhood in south Apopka. That was when the union organizing movement was in full swing, back when Chavez and the United Farm Workers (UFW) were taking on Coca-Cola and its Minute Maid orange juice operation in Florida. "They were the first whites to live in that neighborhood," Pumphrey says, praising the four sisters. "That's walking the walk, you know."

Pumphrey explains that the women activists saw themselves as equals to the needy in the community. They were willing to get down and do the work, he says. That work included picking crops in the fields, fixing up dilapidated housing, and serving meals, as well as raising funds to improve living conditions for those who had been powerless for so long.

In 1978 Kendrick and the other SND sisters publicly supported a group of African Americans in their discrimination lawsuit in federal court against the city of Apopka over the lack of water and sewer lines and paved roads in the black community. Five years later, the suit was finally settled.

Also in the late 1970s, the sisters helped open the Justice and Peace Office, which continues to provide residents with job training and adult literacy programs. But the need for education and advocacy remains. Today, Kendrick tells Pumphrey how one of the largest farm owners in the area is trying to get its Lake Apopka farmworkers to say they voluntarily quit rather than admitting the truth, which is that they were fired due to the closing of the farms. If the workers would agree to the voluntary resignation plan, they could access a small retirement fund.

Of course, as Kendrick points out, the wealthy farm owner would save a significant amount of money because of not having to contribute to the unemployment benefits of hundreds of workers. This leads Kendrick to discuss how OFM is getting a "hot-shot" lawyer to go after state and federal funds for retraining the estimated twenty-five hundred workers who are being displaced by the closing of the Apopka-area farms.

Listening to Kendrick and Pumphrey get animated about the ongoing manipulation of low-income workers, it is easy to imagine them in their glory days of activism decades ago. Though the fire still burns, and the spirit still moves them to protest and advocacy, life has changed for the four nuns.

Ann and her fellow sisters, Cathy, Gail, and Teresa, no longer live in the black neighborhood, which was their home for three decades: the scene of cookouts and holiday parties, not to mention hundreds of organizing meetings. And for twenty years, before they opened their storefront operation on South Park Avenue, their home was OFM's headquarters.

But drugs drove the nuns away in 1997. Crack cocaine and the violence it generated became so prevalent in the neighborhood that the sisters feared for their safety. Their home was robbed twice, and Kendrick was mugged during one of the robberies. "There used to be a code on the street: 'You don't do your mama, your grandma, or your aunt. And you don't do no nuns,'" says Kendrick, somberly. But the new breed of street criminal pays no heed to old ways and old rules. So the sisters had to move.

Boy, did they ever. Kendrick admits she and her housemates are having a little trouble adjusting to their "swanky new digs" owned by the Orlando diocese—a six-figure, five-bedroom home, complete with a small swimming pool.

Kendrick is looking forward to going home tonight, but she has hours of work still ahead of her. The copy for the Pennies for Power brochure just isn't right. The punctuation needs fixing throughout. Former teacher Ann Kendrick won't rest until each comma, semicolon, and period is in its proper place.

* * *

The four Sisters of Notre Dame Ann Kendrick, Cathy Gorman, Gail Grimes, and Teresa McElwee have written an essay, "Collaboration in Ministry Challenges the Apopka Four." The piece describes how they came to Florida, discovered their mission, dedicated their lives to service, and found strength through the spirit of their community. But the essay also speaks of the cost of such dedication, of how people of faith can lose their faith and lose their way:

> Religious women, women of the church, are on the front lines of the movement for justice and social change. . . . Unfortunately, trench workers in organizations in which there is serious dysfunction can fall prey to self-destructive lifestyles and become so identified with the cause, so overcome by the problems that their sense of self is lost. Women commit with such heart that they can lose their heart in the process. Frequently, such women can become so busy and caught up in the social struggle that they unconsciously lose the path they are on.

The essay openly discusses the threat of depression, burnout, and withdrawal. It tells of inward journeys and external tensions. And it celebrates the spirit of collaboration with other groups of women.

In a moment of gentle candor, the usually boisterous Ann Kendrick grows reflective. She has lived the essay. She understands the price of intense dedication. She has burned out. During Holy Week in 1990, Kendrick experienced such a crisis of faith that she took a five-month sabbatical. She entered therapy. She explored psychodrama. She prayed. In time she recovered her commitment, but this was only after realizing how her family of origin's problems had followed her years later.

Since childhood she had been the one everyone counted on. Everyone needed her to be fine. She had to be the strong one while her parents coped with their personal struggles.

As an adult Kendrick discovered she was fine fighting for other people's causes, but not her own. Since taking those months away from her mission, Kendrick has continued her quest for self-growth. She has also tried to take better care of herself, including summer vacations to Martha's Vineyard and Christmas breaks back home in Syracuse. She also receives regular pastoral counseling. But Kendrick knows that personal problems can run deep, and true healing takes time.

She was so impressed with the benefits of psychodrama in her own life that she has employed the therapeutic technique with children of farmworkers who are battling their own demons: prejudice, low self-esteem, anger, violence, alcohol, and drugs. In her workshops she tries especially hard to get macho Hispanic teens to display their emotions without fear of ridicule.

Kendrick lives for the children. Watch her taking pictures at a kids' basketball game at the local recreation center. See the children of all colors, shapes, and sizes line up to hug "Sister Ann." Listen to how Kendrick speaks to the children, telling all that she loves them, and that God loves them too. Look at how they go away beaming.

"She draws her energy from the people," says Sara Sullivan, a second-year AmeriCorps volunteer from Colgate University. Sullivan is one of dozens of college students who have traveled to Apopka, Florida, over the years to work with Ann Kendrick and the other nuns. The partnership between the Sisters of Notre Dame and AmeriCorps, the federally funded domestic Peace Corps–type program, began in 1995.

The volunteers serve as in-school tutors and mentors of at-risk children from farmworker, immigrant, and other low-income families. In addition, they teach English as a Second Language (ESL), adult literacy, and citizenship classes, and provide conflict resolution, job, and life skills training.

Kendrick tells of the joy of having these committed young people "getting things done with tremendous heart and soul." But such commitment doesn't come cheap. Each year, Kendrick must raise $50,000 in matching funds to keep AmeriCorps volunteers working in the community. One generous source of annual funding comes from donations of her fellow alumnae at Trinity College in Washington, D.C.

For Kendrick, the AmeriCorps program not only enhances living conditions in the community, but also empowers college students who must confront the harsh realities of poverty, powerlessness, and injustice. It reminds her of how she was transformed by her experience as an exchange student in Guatemala almost forty years ago.

But these days when Kendrick speaks of her mission here, she tends not to dwell on the successes, but on that which remains to be accomplished. The self-described "old workhorse" sounds discouraged and even fatalistic when she says that in many ways, the poor of Apopka are collectively worse off than when she and her sisters began their mission here so long ago. "There's not a public will in this country to care for its poor people," Kendrick says, questioning a system of government that allows hunger, homelessness, and unemployment while others amass such vast wealth.

And the Catholic Church doesn't escape Kendrick's sharp eye and critical tongue. Parishes are often out of touch with the realities of social problems. Why isn't there more compassion shown to people of color? Why aren't more priests activists? How can people of faith not follow the message of the Gospels? Aren't we supposed to be our brother's keeper?

Kendrick's passionate criticism of her church stops well short of rejection. "They've shaped my heart and soul," she says, and others would agree.

Luckner Millien, a Haitian-born immigrant, who has worked with the Farmworker Association since its founding in 1983, speaks of the spiritual kinship he feels toward Ann Kendrick and the other Sisters of Notre Dame. He believes the best way to serve Jesus Christ is to serve others. But Millien says OFM is not an overtly religious organization. The emphasis is not on preaching here, but on offering help, respect, and love to people in need.

Gracelda Payne raises the question that begs to be asked: What will happen when the nuns get too old to work the long hours in their many programs and causes? Who will replace them? Payne confides her fear that the farmworkers' organization will collapse without the strong support of Kendrick and the other sisters.

Kendrick has previously said in media interviews that she will continue working until she has no more energy, and she will likely remain in Apopka until she dies. But such talk seems decades away. The nuns say they gain strength and resilience from the people they serve. They also speak of their bonds of friendship that have sustained them through the years.

* * *

At a farewell dinner with eight of the twelve AmeriCorps volunteers, Ann Kendrick and her "soul-mate sisters" share engaging dinner-table memories: how they once dressed up as giant crayons on Halloween, then realized they could be mistaken for Ku Klux Klan members in their African American neighborhood; how they took Teresa for a birthday to a local disco in the 1970s, only to discover once they were there that it was ladies' night at the club and a male stripper was performing (they claim they didn't look);

34

how they almost capsized in their rented pontoon boat during a storm on the James River, but "captain" Kendrick got them home safely.

Their lives have not been easy. They admit they have not always gotten along so famously. Their worlds have been darkened by loss, grief, and despair. Yet these vigilant women seem blessed. An old newspaper photo shows youthful, dark-haired nuns beside a bumper-stickered VW van. In 1998 they are gray-haired faith activists who drive Ford Escorts and the like. But look in their eyes and see the passion that endures.

[4]

THE REVEREND DR. RICHARD L. TOLLIVER "YOU CAN DO IT, RICHARD"

Photo courtesy of the late Dr. Mack Tanner

The Reverend Dr. Richard L. Tolliver is the rector of St. Edmund's Church, Chicago, Illinois, founding president and CEO of the St. Edmund's Redevelopment Corporation (SERC), and member of countless boards, commissions, and advisory groups. He is an advocate for community revitalization and social justice. He is also a most effective public relations operation. In the four years since I shadowed Reverend Tolliver for a week in May 1999, he has continued to update me regularly with e-mails, letters, press clippings and press releases, photographs, and printed invitations. With these collateral materials and in subsequent telephone conversations, he leaves an indelible impression of a spiritual and spirited man, determined to raise the quality of life in the Washington Park community on the city's South Side. Governmental officials and business, civic, and religious leaders in Chicago and across the country have recognized Tolliver for his trailblazing efforts. The media, including Ebony, the Christian Science Monitor, the Chicago Sun-Times, and the Chicago Tribune continue to run stories, noting the accomplishments of Tolliver and the community development corporation he founded in 1990. (By 2004, SERC will have developed five hundred new or refurbished housing units, an investment of almost $50 million.) Front-page coverage in August 2003 concerned SERC's purchase of abandoned Chicago Housing Authority property, to be rehabilitated as a $9 million mixed-income housing complex (St. Edmund's Meadows) adjacent to Tolliver's Episcopal church. The project, supported with city and federal funding plus private donations, has been deemed a prototype for transforming public housing in Chicago and across the nation. Reverend Tolliver's successful track record of outreach ministry was cited as instrumental to the successful venture. Tolliver remains anchored by his faith and pastoral leadership of the

St. Edmund's congregation. In a February 2003 sermon from the pulpit of his impressive Michigan Avenue church, he spoke of his vision of a just society rooted in acts of helping others. Reverend Richard Tolliver said, "Moral leadership is theology in practice that looks at reality from an involved, committed stance in light of a faith that does justice."

> He that followeth after righteousness and mercy findeth life,
> righteousness, and honour.
>
> —Proverbs 21:21

VISIONARY

Reverend Richard L. Tolliver fights the midday traffic on the Eisenhower Expressway on this deep-sky mid-May afternoon. He also fights the clock on his way to yet another appointment. Always on the clock. Always robbing Peter to pay Paul, or so it seems for this driven man of faith, who shifts between his many roles and responsibilities with Protean zeal.

Tolliver left downtown a little after 1 P.M. after an enjoyable lunch at the Union League Club with *Time* magazine's dapper Midwest bureau chief, Ron Stodghill II. Stodghill met Tolliver three years ago when the former was writing for *Business Week*. In a feature on urban rehab and the role of investment tax credits, he praised the Episcopalian minister as a hope giver who spearheaded the "miracle of Washington Park."

Reverend Tolliver's success story centers on the impressive decade-long housing revitalization he has led on Chicago's South Side. Some say he is erecting his legacy brick by brick, block by block. Much has been written about the dynamic preacher who helped rebuild his aging church and reclaim the neighborhood while serving as president of an aggressive redevelopment corporation.

"You're relentless but not overbearing," a prospective donor said to him recently. Admirers call him a visionary, a prophet of blueprints and master plans, a builder, more Solomon than Moses. He believes he is serving his people by providing new homes and new hope in a community that had been lost decades ago. He believes in living his faith through social activism.

Proud as he is of the positive press his efforts have received, Tolliver becomes prickly when something negative appears in print—even something seemingly minor. He frowns when he recalls being called portly by one writer. Shortly after the story appeared, Tolliver began to diet and exercise regularly, dropping twenty pounds in less than a year. Now on the cusp of his fifty-fourth birthday, Tolliver resembles a streamlined, five-foot-six-inch version of (ex–Chicago Bears linebacker) Mike Singletary.

Tolliver says he is in excellent shape. He had better be, with the exhausting schedule he must maintain as pastor, scholar, executive, and community leader. Like a perfectionist head coach who drives himself and others too hard, Tolliver says he is a prime candidate for burnout. He has a two-month leave of absence coming—if and when he takes it.

"God gives me my marching orders," he says, explaining his energy and tenacity. "I aim to do His will, but sometimes I fall short."

The traffic eases a bit, and Tolliver pulls his gleaming maple-colored Infinity Q45 onto the exit ramp. A Marvin Gaye song plays on his car radio, tuned to 102.7 FM. The car heads south on Michigan Avenue until it reaches 61st Street. He drives past the boarded-up buildings, but his emotions don't betray him.

His small dark eyes take in everything as his mind shifts gears, and he reviews his to-do list. He'll talk to the mayor's office and again ask officials to "brick up" the abandoned public housing units across from his church at 6105 South Michigan Avenue. He's tired of seeing squatters, drug dealers, and gang members near his holy turf. Tolliver won't return to the church until late in the day. First he has to address the senior citizens' group at the recently opened St. Edmund's Towers, a sixty-unit multistory residential dwelling for folks who once lived in the twelve-block Washington Park neighborhood.

They lived here when it was a successful black middle-class enclave. They lived here years before the population plummeted (from 90,000 to 19,000 in two decades), before businesses closed, buildings were ransacked, and a host of social problems descended on this community. About 60 percent of the area's residents still live below the poverty line, and once-impressive brick and stone buildings are hollow, haunting reminders of what once was.

By contrast, St. Edmund's Towers is an impressive new edifice rising above nearby squalor. The building smells of fresh paint and newly laid carpet. The linoleum is polished. The windows are washed. Tolliver marches into the activity room like a drill sergeant on inspection. Everything looks in order. The refreshments have been served, and the clusters of residents, who have come to hear a speaker from city hall and meet Reverend Tolliver, seem content.

Tolliver will keep his remarks short. It's important for him to be at these functions. The people like seeing St. Edmund's rector out in the community, not holed up in the church like some monk. Besides, when you're the president and CEO of the St. Edmund's Redevelopment Corporation you have to demonstrate confident leadership. This is about progress, not pipe dreams: $18 million in SERC projects completed in the 1990s, and $25 million more in progress. For Tolliver the community renaissance plan is equal parts mission and vision.

He discusses this philosophy in a chapter of the book *Urban Churches, Vital Signs: Beyond Charity toward Justice.* Tolliver explains that Christian community development focuses on affordable housing, quality education, economic opportunity, and programs to ensure safe, secure surroundings. He notes that spiritually driven development typically offers more of a holistic long-term approach than purely secular efforts.

"In some of our urban neighborhoods only the church can make this happen," he says, echoing the zeitgeist of the burgeoning faith-based movement.

According to his philosophy, St. Edmund's Church, as the dominant stable institution in the Washington Park community, must take the lead in development efforts. But the church can't do it all. Partnerships with government and private-sector organizations must occur to attract working-class and middle-class families and individuals to move into the area. Certainly there must be low-interest loans, tax abatements, and other financial inducements to spur investment. One such tool is the Low Income Housing Tax Credit (LIHTC), which was enacted as part of the Tax Reform Act of 1986. It offers corporate and individual investors a credit against their federal income taxes for investments directed at acquiring, "rehabbing," or constructing low-income housing.

The Local Initiatives Support Corp. (LISC), the nation's largest non-profit community-development support organization, utilizes the LIHTC to support more than six hundred urban revitalization programs like the St. Edmund's Redevelopment Corporation in more than one hundred U.S. localities. In a dozen years, the LISC (through its affiliate, the National Equity Fund, Inc.) has attracted more than $2 billion in investments from 130 corporations nationwide.

Nile Harper, author of *Urban Churches, Vital Signs,* says that one of the most important products generated by SERC is hope. He writes:

> Entrepreneurial ability, visionary leadership, and long-term pastoral commitment have all come together in the work of St. Edmund's Episcopal Church, SERC, and St. Edmund's Academy. The "miracle in Washington Park" is not a mystery. It is the result of long, persistent, skillful hard work, and the partnership of local people with key financial investors.

> The future is far from certain. There is, however, solid, creative accomplishment and real hope for a positive future in Washington Park.

Before his talk to the senior citizens in the activity room at St. Edmund's Towers, Tolliver enters the first-floor lavatory. He emerges moments later doing a slow burn—his brow creased, his ebony eyes searching the room for the building manager. Tolliver wants the problem addressed NOW.

Without raising his voice, he directs the manager to get a custodian into the restroom immediately. He will not tolerate an unkempt lavatory, and he doesn't accept the lackadaisical attitude of the manager. But he knows how hard it is to get qualified people to come to Washington Park to work. He makes a mental note about recruiting a new building manager.

No time to frown now. He must talk to the congregation of seniors who greet him with polite applause. He steps lightly, clasping his thick fingers at waist level. "I'm Reverend Richard Tolliver from St. Edmund's Church, and I want to welcome you to . . ."

The residents smile along with him. His voice is firm and clear, but not overpowering. He's no hellfire and brimstone preacher, nor a shake-rattle-and-roll evangelist. Yes, he's an African American minister from an inner-city parish, but he is an Episcopalian. He displays a reserved countenance, his dignified demeanor more akin to General Colin Powell's than to Reverend Jesse Jackson's.

Less than twenty minutes after he has arrived at St. Edmund's Towers, he's off again. On this warm and sunny afternoon, he crosses the street to where his Q45 is parked. He hears the distant dialogue and laughter of a group of young black men hanging out half a block away. He glances instinctively at the group, but he doesn't recognize anyone. He has another appointment, and he's pressed for time.

He heads south back onto the expressway, en route to the solidly upper-middle-class black neighborhood of Avalon Park. This is no ordinary social visit. Tolliver will pray with the Finch family, longtime parishioners of St. Edmund's. June, wife of educator Dr. William Finch, is on a respirator. She is dying. Tolliver isn't sure of the reception he'll get when he enters the tidy split-level home.

William Finch was one of Tolliver's earliest critics when he became rector in June 1989. Tolliver says that when he arrived, St. Edmund's was a very staid, conservative church. For several years, Reverend Tolliver has tried to change the church's outlook and move it into "a new paradigm" of service. Some, such as Finch, did not endorse Tolliver's progressive philosophy or personal lifestyle (an affluent bachelor who didn't live in the Washington Park neighborhood).

But today a healing spirit seems to guide the two strong-willed men. Finch, tall and distinguished-looking, embraces Tolliver in the middle of the living room after his daughter has let the good reverend in. Within minutes other family arrive. They will pray in the small bedroom that now serves as June Finch's sick ward. June is alert and smiles when she sees Tolliver. She extends her hand, and he gently grasps it.

With his other hand he holds open the Book of Common Prayer, the book that contains the prayers and order of services of the Episcopal Church. The family prays, holding hands. Tolliver can't explain why this good woman is being called home. Only God knows. He can only comfort and support. He can give hope, not answers.

Minutes later, Tolliver is headed back downtown for a 3 P.M. meeting in the Schiff, Harden, and Waite law firm offices on the sixty-sixth floor of the Sears Tower. On the agenda is bond financing for the St. Edmund's Village project, a twenty-three-story, 230-unit phoenix, soon to rise from the squalor and rubble of Chicago's South Side.

Referring to the partnership he has forged with the city, Tolliver says he is supportive of Mayor Daley because he thinks he is trying to be mayor for all of Chicago's citizens. When Daley last announced his candidacy, Tolliver stood by his side. "He has demonstrated that he cares about the needs of Chicago's minorities, specifically African Americans," says Tolliver, noting that in the most recent mayoral election Daley received 45 percent of black votes, compared with 26 percent and 8 percent of black votes, respectively, in the previous two elections.

As Tolliver prepares to enter his high-powered meeting, he reflects on June Finch's inner strength and deep faith. He also recalls her words of support years earlier when Tolliver was new on the job. "You weren't what we expected, but we're lucky to have you," she had said to him after one Sunday service. "You keep doing what you're doing. You're going places, Reverend Tolliver."

EXECUTIVE

Richard Tolliver sits amidst a room full of "suits," high-priced lawyers, underwriters, city officials, and real estate consultants.

"This looks like a two-thousand-dollar-an-hour meeting," Tolliver says, drawing polite chuckles. "You can double that," says SERC attorney Ray McGaugh.

The nervous energy in this conference room is palpable and expensive. Who's going to get this meeting underway? Who's going to take charge?

The meters are ticking. Let's get going. But, wait, Ron Gatton, SERC's lead consultant is in the restroom.

Gatton, a former U.S. Department of Housing and Urban Development (HUD) official, has been a key advisor since SERC was formed in 1990. The suits will wait on Gatton. A few heads turn to dwell ever so briefly on the picture-perfect scene as sailboats dot deep-blue Lake Michigan.

At 3:20 P.M. the meeting starts, and the numbers keep coming as Ron Gatton tallies away on his calculator. St. Edmund's Village is being given a 5¾ percent interest rate on a twenty-four-year mortgage, assuming the high-rise project can close by September 30, with a $3.4 million payment. What about the $1.5 million principal differentiation line item in the $17 million budget (that will eventually rise to $18.5 million)?

Tolliver looks at Gatton and then sips from his glass of ice water. Gatton returns to his calculator. The suits shuffle their papers and stare straight ahead. Four sides to the conference table, and nary a crossways glance.

Bruce Weisenthal, the lead attorney for the project's bond counsel, resembles another more famous dealmaker: Hollywood super-agent Michael Ovitz. Weisenthal takes charge of the meeting. He's the one asking the questions. He's the one reminding the room of deadlines. He's the one beginning to make Reverend Tolliver look a bit nervous as Tolliver clicks and re-clicks his ballpoint pen, whispers to his attorneys and then to Gatton.

At 3:50 P.M. as the meeting threatens to bog down, dark skies roll across Lake Michigan. Lightning flashes as Weisenthal begins to speak in tongues ... no ... in acronyms. "Will we have CLCs [construction loan certificates] issued by Tri [Capital Corp.] through FHA [Federal Housing Authority]? What about funding the negative 'r' reserve?" he asks with a peculiar half-smile. "Remember we can't have any CLCs on A-7s."

Tolliver swivels slightly in his chair, rubs his eyes, and strokes his chin. He answers one question with one of his own: How do you classify job training at multifamily units where trainees aren't residents?

David Saltzman, a youthful, upbeat administrator representing the Chicago Department of Housing, publicly offers the support of the city in meeting upcoming deadlines: May 26, finance committee; June 9, city council meeting; August 16, the closing. The words fall softly in the room where several side conversations break out. At 4:10 P.M. Weisenthal says, "We have enough to proceed with drafting an indenture." But he reminds others in the room that "the ball's in your court."

Fifteen minutes later, separate conversations are still starting and stopping around the room. Tolliver looks at Gatton. "Can we go?"

"I'm still thinking," says the now red-faced Gatton, studying the pages of printouts before him.

At 4:35 P.M. Weisenthal asks questions that are more like marching orders before dismissal: "Can we identify the next steps to proceed? Can we set a date and time for the next meeting?"

At 4:45 P.M. the large conference room meeting disbands. Tolliver huddles with his "SERC team": Ron Gatton and Tracy Powell, and Susan Leske from the Chicago Department of Housing. They will meet next door in a small conference room to discuss their strategy. In this room, yellow pads sit in gleaming silver trays, and dozens of sharpened green pencils are at the ready. At 5:10 P.M. Rev. Tolliver has his dark suit coat back on, and he's leading the meeting. For two hours he had largely been an observer, listening quietly to the "experts" discuss the project. Now he is driving his own strategy session. "They take their cues from us," he says. "We have to keep proceeding as if it's all going to happen on time."

Yesterday Tolliver had to work to keep another project on track—St. Edmund's Meadows. He and Tracy Powell, SERC director of redevelopment, met with the architect, who seemed confused about just how many three- and four-bedroom units were slated for the buildings being gutted and renovated across from the church. Such a room count was critical to ensure adequate financing. After ninety minutes of pouring over blueprints, making phone calls, and taking faxes, the group still wrestled with the room count. Tolliver ended the meeting insisting there be no more guesswork. "Do another walk-through if that's what it takes."

The last meeting high on the Sears Tower doesn't end until almost 6 P.M. Tolliver barely has time to grab a sandwich for dinner at his neighborhood Boston Market. He squeezes in a quick haircut. Then he spends the next two hours back at St. Edmund's, catching up on paperwork, answering mail, and writing checks. He won't arrive home at his Hyde Park condo until 10 P.M.

He will awake without an alarm at 4:30 A.M. "I am always up by at least 5 [A.M.]," he explains. "Today, I knew I had a lot to do."

At 6:15 A.M., Tolliver takes a call from circuit court judge (and parishioner) Jane Stuart. Can he meet her at the hospital to pray over her mother? This time the doctor says the family matriarch, Mrs. Jane Stuart, is truly at death's door. A few days earlier Tolliver had visited the elder Jane Stuart to say the final prayers. He had expected to find her slipping away. Instead she was alert and eager to chat.

"Father, you look wonderful," came a surprisingly vibrant voice from the darkness of the hospital room. A frail Mrs. Stuart had rebounded briefly with newfound energy. She offered her slender hand to her priest. Tolliver smiled as he chatted softly, amiably, with the eighty-five-year-old woman.

The hospital visit that day had been a false alarm. But despite mother Stuart's remarkable "recovery," Tolliver knew the end was near, and indeed it was. On this morning, death came quietly. The reverend and the loving daughter wept and prayed at bedside. A few minutes later in a waiting room, funeral arrangements were discussed. Then Tolliver had to excuse himself. He had to head downtown to make an 8 A.M. meeting at the Prudential Building.

SON

Richard Tolliver often thinks of his own mother in the early morning hours when he awakes without need of an alarm clock or radio. For as long as he can remember, he has gotten up every day before 5 A.M. That's the time of day when his mother, Evelyn, would leave for work in the darkness in Springfield, Ohio. She would drive twenty-eight miles to the Wright-Patterson Air Force Base in Fairborn, where she worked as a librarian with security clearance in the foreign technology division.

Before she would leave each morning, she would give her only son, Richard, a little nudge. She would sit on the edge of his narrow bed and wait for her son to awaken. He would be up and dressed before his mother kissed him goodbye. He had to get up; he had homework to do. And if he had no homework, he would read every morning before waking up his two younger sisters.

Tolliver always loved books. His third-grade teacher once asked his mother, "Why does he read so much?" Evelyn Tolliver-Woods knew the answer. Books would carry her son to the places in his dreams, like a magic carpet transporting the young scholar as far as he wanted.

In 1954 the U.S. Supreme Court declared segregated schools unconstitutional in its historic *Brown v. Board of Education* decision. In that same year, fourth-grade student Richard Tolliver was helping his teacher, Edith Turner, compile a schoolbook history of his hometown, *It Happened in Springfield*. The book, published in 1958 by the Springfield Tribune Printing Co., contained stories of historical figures and memorable events in the birth and development of this southwestern Ohio town. The young Tolliver provided a child's perspective. In the book's acknowledgments Ms. Turner explained: "The writer also wishes to express indebtedness to . . . Richard Tolliver, an elementary pupil in the Springfield schools, who

44

by reporting several of the stories in a child's language, helped to set the tone for the work."

Forty years later, Tolliver discussed how Mrs. Turner, a white teacher in a largely black classroom, would spend a couple of hours after school helping him write his stories. Then she would drive him home each evening. Tolliver's zeal for a good education continued through the years he spent in the often racially polarized Springfield community. As a student at Springfield South High School, he belonged to a small group of college-bound friends, which included one white boy and two white girls.

What motivated him to eventually secure five academic degrees, including three master's degrees and a doctorate? Tolliver's thick eyebrows danced and a smile spread across his wide face: "I've always liked to read a lot. Why not get credit for it?"

On this damp May morning as on so many others, he thinks of his mother. She was a single mom during most of the years she made the long drive to the air force base. Tolliver recalls how tired she would look when she returned home at suppertime. He remembers how some days she would cry alone in her bedroom before dinner. He would ask her about the tears, and she would tell him of how other women were getting promoted ahead of her. These were women she had trained. These white women with less seniority on the job were getting promoted ahead of her.

Tolliver recalls the sadness he felt at the sound of his mother crying. But he doesn't weep as he recounts the story. His strong jaw is set and his dark eyes are clear and narrowed. His mother didn't raise him to lose hope. She worked hard so that he could dream. When she stopped crying, she would pull him close and tell him whatever he wanted to do, he could do. Whatever his goals, he could achieve them if he was willing to work hard and never quit. "You can do it, Richard," she would often say to him.

A gloriously sunny Mother's Day (May 9, 1999), and the Reverend Richard Tolliver is in the pulpit of St. Edmund's Church. He praises the extraordinary gift of his mother, of all mothers, calling them "elegant warriors, fearless heroes." He quotes the prophet Isaiah (66:13) in speaking of God's unconditional love: "As a mother comforts her child, so will I comfort you; and you will be comforted over Jerusalem."

Today, Reverend Tolliver speaks of the loss of his mother, who died at fifty-six of leukemia in the fall of 1983. "One reason my grief was so profound when my mother died was due to the fact that I knew that I had been loved unconditionally, and I felt that I would never have that experience again." He reminds his congregation that "once a child accepts a mother's love . . . he has a responsibility to return that love."

Each morning when he gets up well before dawn, Richard Tolliver returns his mother's love. He honors Evelyn with his memory. He remains driven by her words: "You can do it, Richard."

DISCIPLE

In his youth, Richard Tolliver's self-confidence was nurtured by the support of his mother and his maternal grandparents, Grace Tolliver and the Reverend Auburn James Tolliver Sr. His Baptist preacher grandfather led by example, gaining the respect of blacks and whites in Springfield, Ohio. Richard was raised by hard-working, clean-living true believers. Decades later, he says little about a father and stepfather who existed in the shadows of his childhood, other than he was not close to these men.

Tolliver built his life on bedrock principles. In doing so, he became a proud young man who knew both the road to success and the way of the Lord. During his senior year at Miami University in Oxford, Ohio, where he majored in religion, Tolliver told his grandfather he was thinking about attending seminary to become an Episcopalian priest.

Reverend Auburn Tolliver's voice was gentle, reassuring: We have known for years that you were going to put on the robe. We have been waiting for you to realize it. The Baptist minister said the denomination wasn't important. What was important was serving God.

The grandson had reservations. He didn't know if he could handle the pressures of religious service. He fretted about the way parishioners talked about their pastors. His grandfather's tone grew sharper. The day you decide to do something with your life, be prepared to be talked about, he said. If you don't want to be talked about, don't do anything in your life.

Richard Tolliver had been confirmed as an Episcopalian during his college years at Miami University. As a freshman he had first attended a local Baptist church, but had been disappointed with the overly fundamentalist nature of the services. In his sophomore year, he was invited by a fellow student to attend an Episcopal church in Oxford, Ohio. Tolliver was impressed with its liturgy, its more liberal atmosphere, and its activism. The congregation was involved in addressing social issues in the mid-1960s, including protesting against the Vietnam War. Tolliver was proud of the church's stance. He also enjoyed the more relaxed attitude the denomination showed toward having a good time socially.

Thanks to a Rockefeller Foundation fellowship, Tolliver entered the Episcopal Divinity School in Cambridge, Massachusetts, in the fall of 1968, months after the assassinations of Dr. Martin Luther King Jr. and Bobby Kennedy, weeks after devastating riots fueled by black rage. But the further Tolliver pursued his spiritual path, the more doubts he confronted. He asked as other disciples had asked two millennia earlier: "Jesus, are you the one, or shall I look for another?"

The former Sunday school teacher and church organist, past president of the Ohio Baptist Youth Conference, and religion major wrestled with his faith. What had sustained him through the years was now being questioned. He wanted to be a leader for his racial community, but was the best route to that leadership through the seminary?

As a divinity student, Tolliver was permitted to take half of his courses in any college at Harvard University. He enrolled in Afro-American Studies and political science courses. He read about the civil rights movement and the apathy of many clergy, including black religious leaders. He learned how Dr. Martin Luther King Jr. had denounced the silence and inaction of the black church during the 1955 Montgomery, Alabama, boycott: "The so-called Negro church has also left men disappointed at midnight."

Tolliver's religious calling was still in flux when, in the summer of 1969, he enrolled in his required six-week clinical pastoral education program in Atlanta. He was assigned to do counseling and crisis intervention at a center for delinquent teenage girls. The social work aspect appealed to him, but he was still debating whether to remain in divinity school. One day he confided his doubts to a chaplain at the center, who told him to read the Scripture passage about Jacob wrestling with God. The chaplain told the perplexed Tolliver, "Perhaps God is trying to speak with you, and you are resisting."

That night Tolliver read Genesis 32:22–29 about Jacob's nightlong struggles with a man.

> When the man saw that he could not overpower him [Jacob], he touched the socket of Jacob's hip so that his hip was wrenched as he wrestled with him. Then the man said, "Let me go, for it is daybreak." But Jacob replied: "I will not let you go unless you bless me." The man asked him, "What is your name?" "Jacob," he answered. Then the man said, "Your name will no longer be Jacob, but Israel, because you have struggled with God and with men and have overcome." Jacob said, "Please tell me your name." But he replied, "Why do you ask my name?" Then he blessed him there.

After reading the passage, Tolliver closed his Bible and slept peacefully for the first time in days. He was able to say in the darkness to his Lord, "Yes, you are the one!"

That fall, Tolliver returned to the seminary, where he was inspired by Dr. James Cone's book *Black Theology and Black Power*. Cone's book about religious social activism gave Tolliver the theological foundation he was seeking for his ministry. It would become the basis for Tolliver's vision of community activism and urban redevelopment that would flourish decades later. The premise was powerful and the message simple: Jesus was on the side of the outsider, marginalized, oppressed, poor, and disenfranchised. Those people of faith who wanted to identify with Jesus and follow his teachings and ministry had to follow in his activist footsteps.

On December 13, 1998, the Reverend Richard Tolliver gave a Sunday sermon in which he recounted his spiritual journey. He told his parishioners of the serious doubts he had as a young divinity student. He spoke of his time in Atlanta, where he had wrestled with his faith. He shared the joy of his summer 1969 epiphany with hundreds of his congregation in his Chicago church on a Sunday in winter almost thirty years later.

ACTIVIST

In 1969, during his second year of seminary studies, Tolliver's pursuit of the social gospel led him to work at a church in Roxbury, Massachusetts, the oft-troubled Boston community. A Harvard classmate who watched Tolliver's immersion in activist causes noted that Tolliver seemed determined to make the black church relevant "even if it kills you."

Tolliver remembers smiling what people called his Cheshire-cat smile. "Yes, that's what I want to be remembered for," he replied to that student and to others. He pushed himself even harder in the classroom and out on the streets. He studied black theology and liberation theology, the model for a growing number of Latin American churches. During this period, Tolliver began feeling an even greater distance from his fellow Episcopalian seminarians.

He was the only African American out of forty second-year students. The ethos of the seminary focused on its Anglican (English) traditions, while Tolliver was more concerned with contemporary civil rights and black activist causes in the United States. Although he admits his dean and some faculty were supportive, Tolliver remembers divinity school as "not a very hospitable place."

"Much of what I was learning felt irrelevant to me as a black man," he says.

While a seminarian in racially tense Boston, Tolliver was more upbeat after a 1969 trip to Chicago with more than a dozen black clergy. They met with Black Muslim leader Elijah Muhammad, who championed their social activism. In a photograph signed, "To my brother Richard Tolliver from . . . E. M.," the divinity student is wearing a dark suit and thick glasses.

Tolliver speaks reverently of his role models ("men who were in charge"). Of all his mentors, none is remembered so fondly as the Reverend Dr. M. Moran Weston, noted rector of Harlem's St. Philip's Episcopal Church. A few months before receiving his master of divinity degree, Tolliver had read in *Ebony* magazine about the work of Reverend Weston. His church was involved in housing and community development programs in New York. Weston, who had a doctorate in social history from Columbia, epitomized the intellectual, activist religious leader Tolliver aspired to become.

In May 1971, a month before graduation from seminary, Tolliver accepted a position as curate (assistant rector) of St. Philip's Church. For the next year, he was Weston's eager protégé. Weston educated Tolliver on community action, and he encouraged his studious assistant to pursue a doctorate. In 1982, Tolliver would earn his Ph.D. in political science from Howard University, Washington, D.C. Years after serving his religious apprenticeship in Harlem, Tolliver would continue to speak and write to Reverend Weston, regularly drawing on the wisdom and guidance of his friend and teacher.

From September 1972 until the fall of 1976, Tolliver was rector of St. Cyprian's Episcopal Church in Boston. His congregation was primarily working-class immigrants from the West Indies. For three of these years, Tolliver also served as graduate advisor to the Divinity School at Harvard University. During his time in Boston, he befriended Cambridge native Dorothy Wallace, a well-known philanthropist.

Tolliver was often a dinner guest at Ms. Wallace's Brookline, Massachusetts, estate. Through the years of friendship, Wallace, a white upper-class Episcopalian with degrees from Vassar and Radcliffe, demonstrated eclectic, cosmopolitan, and ecumenical approaches to social problems. Tolliver cites Wallace as another key person who had a significant impact on his understanding of ministry.

After four years in Boston, Tolliver moved to Washington, D.C., where he initially served six months as administrator and planning consultant to a consortium of ten colleges and universities. In the spring of 1977, he became chief pastor and administrator (rector) of St. Timothy's Episcopal

Church. The majority of the congregants were middle-class black professionals and civil servants, people who were involved professionally and personally in social issues. Reverend Tolliver was the church's first black rector, a post he would hold for seven years. During his time in D.C., he worked as an adjunct instructor in the public affairs department of George Mason University and the department of political science at Howard University, where he earned his doctorate in political science. It appeared that he was establishing roots in the community.

Richard Tolliver was married in 1979, culminating a five-year friendship. His wife was a schoolteacher in Fairfax County, Virginia. Today, Tolliver describes his former marriage as a relationship between two "highly independent, highly individualistic" people. The relationship would be severely tested when, four years after the marriage, Richard Tolliver lost his beloved mother, Evelyn. She died a year after his grandmother Grace. Their deaths were devastating. Tolliver said people didn't understand the depth of his grief. He was emotionally drained. He decided he could no longer serve as rector of St. Timothy's Church. He said he had to find a way to heal, even if it meant leaving the country.

In November 1984 he became associate country director of the United States Peace Corps in Kenya, Africa. For the next twenty months he was responsible for supervising fifty volunteers and for coordinating local planning and economic development programs. Originally, his wife was going to join Tolliver in Kenya at the end of her 1984–85 academic year. But she developed a medical problem that prevented her from moving overseas. As his wife recuperated, she wrote to Tolliver, discussing a divorce. He remained in Africa and she in the United States. In 1986, the couple was divorced. During his tenure in Kenya, Richard Tolliver also had to cope with the pain of losing his grandfather Auburn, who passed away back in Springfield, Ohio.

From July 1986 to April 1988, Tolliver served as country director for the Peace Corps in Mauritania. During that time he experienced the true deprivation of this poverty-stricken desert land. He tried to generate economic development programs by enhancing relations with government officials in Mauritania and America. But he soon realized that none of the urban problems he faced in the United States were as seemingly insurmountable as those being confronted in Third World nations. For example, in Mauritania, getting babies inoculated against disease was an extremely difficult task, compounded by inadequate medical facilities and cultural and religious differences.

Tolliver says that his time spent in this mostly Muslim country taught him much about having patience, living with contradictions, and challenging preconceptions about the dominance of Christianity or any faith in solving problems. He admits that the three major monotheistic religions, Christianity, Judaism, and Islam, are arguably exclusivist in their claims to "the truth." Reverend Richard Tolliver calls himself a pluralist. "No one tradition has the sole answer," he says.

When Tolliver returned home to the United States, he became a lecturer in the political science department at Howard University, the college he once hoped to attend after high school. (His mother had dissuaded him because she thought it was too much of an urban school and too far from home.) While teaching, he waited for the right opportunity to return to serve a church, one that needed strong leadership, vision, and activist spirit.

In June 1989 he became rector of St. Edmund's Episcopal Church in Chicago, Illinois. A year later he would become president and CEO of the St. Edmund's Redevelopment Corp., and he would set a lofty five-year goal: $40 million of investment and five hundred new housing units in the Washington Park neighborhood. Another part of that five-year plan was his goal of reopening a primary school on church property. In 1995 he founded St. Edmund's Academy (reopening the elementary school that had been closed since 1988, after forty-three years of operation). His success has challenged critics and even surprised parishioners who at first doubted he could accomplish so much.

A decade later, on Tolliver's tenth anniversary as rector, hundreds of his St. Edmund's parishioners filled a joyous parish hall to express their appreciation. The large family gathering lasted for hours as the St. Edmund's faithful congratulated their rector on the job he had done as head of their church, president of the redevelopment corporation, and the driving force behind the renaissance of St. Edmund's Academy.

When he looks back on his accomplishments and his ability to persevere through loss, disappointment, and intimidating odds, Tolliver calmly credits his faith and his unshakable trust in God. On this late spring Sunday, the Reverend Dr. Richard Tolliver celebrates a compelling day of worship in his church. He is cloaked in brilliant white vestments, encircled by wisps of pungent incense, and accompanied by the strong, resonant voices of the adult choir. After the service, an elderly St. Edmund's member speaks of how Tolliver helped her to feel the power of the Holy Spirit and to get involved in church affairs after years of inactivity. His faith, she said, "helped her hear the still voice within."

In the sociological stratification of religions, Episcopalians traditionally occupy the higher economic tier. So it has been with the congregation of St. Edmund's. Its parishioners are doctors, lawyers, professors, and other white-collar professionals, long considered among the elite of Chicago's African American community. According to Reverend Tolliver, they expect their rector to reflect their socioeconomic status.

The fact that he drives a late-model luxury car is viewed with respect. After all, he says, a man who earns a six-figure income and serves the church and community in varied capacities certainly deserves a rewarding lifestyle. Tolliver took no vow of poverty. He views himself very much like a corporate executive, compensated fairly for his work, responsibilities, and status.

When questioned about why he doesn't live in the immediate neighborhood of St. Edmund's, Tolliver says firmly that he intentionally chose nearby Hyde Park for his residence. He needs a peaceful place to live so that he may rejuvenate himself ("for solace and refreshment"). His two-story apartment in the Hedgerow Condominiums is his sanctuary, a setting filled with an impressive collection of art, artifacts, literature, and culture.

His residence boasts beautiful paintings, murals, statues, and wall hangings. The most distinctive piece of art is a small statue of a muscular black angel with wings spread, shielding a young black boy and girl. Other furnishings include a three-foot diameter bronze Asian gong and a Baldwin piano, topped by a bust of an African woman in headdress. A black jazz trumpeter statue sits on an end table. Above the mantle is a six-foot-high pastel of ballet dancers, entitled "Pas de deux."

Oriental rugs adorn the polished hardwood floors. The kitchen is equipped with the latest appliances—all in black, designed to complement the large black octagonal kitchen table. On one of the kitchen walls is a charcoal commemorating the 1968 Olympics' protest of John Carlos and Tommy Smith with clenched fists above the clouds. A few feet away is a striking three-dimensional ceramic of a Paris street scene.

A small TV sits on a raised stand above the kitchen table. Tolliver likes to listen to an all-news station while eating his meals. He also enjoys reading while sitting at the table. He devours newspapers, magazines, and nonfiction books. ("Fiction seems like a waste of time because I'm not learning anything.") Two current books on his reading list are *Our Kind of People: Inside America's Black Upper Class* by Lawrence Otis Graham and *Titans of the Black Enterprise 100* by Derek Dingle.

Downstairs in his immaculately maintained residence are two bedrooms and two full bathrooms. A large-screen TV dominates the master bedroom.

The second bedroom serves as an office. A Compaq Presario computer sits on the desk next to phone and fax. His cherished books are shelved around the room. He works here in the early morning and late at night.

Tolliver says that although he is quite comfortable in this condo, he plans on moving into a larger residence in the Hyde Park area, perhaps as early as the end of 1999. He'd like to be closer to Lake Michigan. He has always liked bodies of water; they help restore him. Tolliver knows that the only way he can continue to serve so many people in his varied roles is by taking care of himself. He knows how easy it is to be overextended.

He says he was personally drained a year ago. He drew up plans for his vocational, physical, financial, and spiritual renewal. Those plans included buying a new home, traveling on a sabbatical to Egypt, and earning dual certifications as a Housing Finance Development Professional and an Economic Development Finance Professional from the prestigious National Development Council. He calls the rigorous national certification programs examples of "growth opportunities."

SCHOLAR

Whoever coined the phrase "lifelong learning" should have had Richard Tolliver in mind. He pursues his personal and professional development with insatiable drive. Throughout the last year he has been attending monthly training sessions, sponsored by the BP Amoco Foundation. As a foundation fellow, Tolliver is one of fourteen community organization executives selected for a series of two-day seminars on such nonprofit-sector program issues as personnel relations, marketing, law, and taxation.

Moderators from Chicago-area organizations conduct the seminars. Some are more formal and sit at the head of the room. Others move about and talk with the attending nonprofit execs like roving professors. The information being conveyed is hit or miss, according to Tolliver.

In one session he asks for the spelling of the word "caritas" during a discussion of the English law of charity. He enjoys learning about the evolution of the social welfare of the church, dating back to the almshouses (poor houses) of London. He pays particular attention when the moderator says that nonprofit organizations, such as SERC, are fulfilling roles once expected of government. Tolliver, like several of his colleagues in the room, glances up when the speaker informs them that there are twenty-seven categories of tax-exempt organizations under IRS tax code 501(c)(3).

Tolliver knows that SERC qualifies for low-income housing tax credits; he doesn't have to know the tax code inside and out. On this morning, the day after the meeting in the Sears Tower about the $17 million St. Edmund's Village Project, his mind is on real estate financing issues. At a break, Tolliver walks down the hall with the erect bearing of a military officer. He calls one of his Boulé brothers (from the prominent black social fraternity), who is a director of Harris Bank. Tolliver asks for his insight regarding the buying of tax-exempt bonds to increase the percentage of equity in the project.

Later that day when the talk in the BP Amoco Foundation seminar turns too theoretical to suit Tolliver, he volunteers his opinion. "Let me tell you about the real world of nonprofit operations," he says leaning back in his chair. The rest of the room watches. "When the deal goes down, you cut your own deal. That's how it really is."

Nervous laughter fills the small seminar room as the moderator thanks Tolliver for his comments and moves on with the discussion. Later, Tolliver confides: "These people are on different levels than I am. I'm more involved in political action and economic development issues than in the day-to-day administration kinds of things they're doing. They may think I'm arrogant with my comments, but that's why I don't say much in these meetings."

The next morning, Tolliver arrives looking very sharp in a black suit, purple shirt, midnight blue tie, and black slip-on loafers polished to a high luster. The training session is barely underway when his pager goes off three times in succession, sounding like an electric razor each time he has a message. He leaves the room to answer the calls. A half-hour later he returns, rubbing his eyes. One of the calls had to do with a charter school issue affecting the future of St. Edmund's Academy. Another call is about a sick parishioner who would like him to visit. A third call is from an African American magazine editor, a recent Chicago arrival who is interested in expanding his social contacts in the area.

Tolliver is having a hard time staying focused in the small, increasingly stuffy meeting room. He clicks and re-clicks his ballpoint pen as the speaker rambles on about a taxation issue. He leans back and listens to the chatter from his fellow fellows. He bites on his pen. Perhaps he's wondering about all he could be doing if he weren't committed to being in this seminar. He tries to squeeze lunch in, but while he is eating his clam chowder in the room, his pager goes off again, and he has to leave. A few minutes later, he tries to finish his salad and rolls, but the pager goes off once more.

When the training session resumes, Tolliver and his dozen colleagues are running on fumes. Some people stare off, while others idly take notes.

Tolliver is back to clicking his pen. The moderator decides to wrap up the session a little early, but first she wants some feedback on the monthly sessions held to date.

"I think that was a cute exercise, but too abstract to get anything from it," Tolliver volunteers his opinion on the session on marketing a couple months earlier. "And giving us homework doesn't really work. We're all too exhausted at the end of the day." Others in the room nod as they glance at Tolliver, the self-proclaimed "lone wolf" in the meeting. The moderator draws laughter from the group when she thanks Tolliver.

"Richard has contributed unofficially to the success of this class by telling us what we needed to know about running a successful nonprofit organization." Everyone chuckles, including Tolliver, who puts down his pen and prepares to leave the class en route to his next appointment.

MINISTER

On a bright spring morning, after stopping at the local Dunkin' Donuts for his usual hazelnut coffee to go and a trip to the newsstand for copies of the *Chicago Tribune* and the *Chicago Defender*, Reverend Tolliver arrives at the St. Edmund's Academy parking lot. There he greets a mother, father, and young daughter leaving the building. They are on their way to a doctor's appointment.

"Has anyone signed your cast?" Tolliver asks with a warm smile. The polite laughter is drowned out by the sound of teenage boys yelling from across the street. They are sitting on the steps of the Hull House, the multiservice center founded by legendary social worker Jane Addams. The boys shout to Tolliver: "Hey, why don't you support my mama?"

The rector has more important things to do than answer a group of smart-asses. He has a meeting with a parishioner and plenty of other duties to see to inside. He bids the family adieu and enters the darkened corridor leading from the school into the main church building. Tolliver is still waiting on an electrician to fix the hall lighting problem.

Building expenses are always a concern. The church's annual budget is about $450,000; pledges and tithing account for $300,000. The $150,000 balance must be raised from grants and donations.

At 9:45 A.M., Father John Agbaje, assistant rector, is leading chapel services with about all of the fifty-some St. Edmund's school kids. The boys are dressed in dark slacks, white shirts, and blue ties; the girls wear blue and white skirts and matching blouses. Their young voices are sweet and pleasing to the ear. They fill this beautiful old church with joy.

When Tolliver arrived in 1989, St. Edmund's Church was in a severe state of decline and disrepair. Some thought the church was on the verge of closing. Virtually all of its longtime parishioners had moved to the suburbs. As the Washington Park neighborhood continued to decline, so did St. Edmund's. The roof leaked, routine maintenance slacked off, and vandalism had become more common.

Like so many historical architectural gems in America's inner cities, St. Edmund's was on the verge of being lost. The 1927 building, which reflected Italian Renaissance and Byzantine influences, had formerly been the site of Saints Constantine and Helen Greek Orthodox Church. The church was across the street from St. Anselm's Catholic Church, which had served as the model for St. Patrick's in James T. Farrell's 1930s novel, *Studs Lonigan*.

St. Edmund's Church, named for a martyred Christian English king (700 A.D.), was founded in 1905 in another South Side location. It moved to its present location in 1946, and membership soon swelled to more than two thousand members by the 1950s and 1960s.

"God didn't just reserve the Baptist Church for black Americans," Tolliver said in a May 20, 1996, *Chicago Sun-Times* article by Andrew Herrmann, referring to the predominance of professionals in black American Anglican Protestant churches such as St. Edmund's. The article reported that in 1999 about 5 percent of the nation's two-and-a-half million Episcopalians were black, and in the Chicago diocese, 10 of the 141 congregations were largely African American.

Building on the support of longtime members as well as the strength of the Greater Chicago Episcopalian community, Tolliver sought donations to fund a $1.2 million renovation and restoration of St. Edmund's. Tolliver wanted to preserve such unique features as the long altar rail, copied from the one in St. Sophia's Church in Istanbul, Turkey, and the beautiful murals depicting the Nativity, Crucifixion, and Resurrection of Christ. But he also wanted to promote a strong, vibrant African and African American presence in the church. In 1995 he commissioned an artist to draw black spiritual icons and a new celestial painting for the church's majestic domed ceiling.

Tolliver's decision to replace the church's traditional thirty-five stained-glass windows of saints and martyrs with depictions of heroic figures from African and African American history seems inspired. He has said that he wanted parishioners to glance up and be motivated by role models such as Dr. Martin Luther King Jr., Rosa Parks, Nelson Mandela, Thurgood Marshall, Archbishop Desmond Tutu, Frederick Douglass, St. Augustine, and Simon of Cyrene (the black man who, according to legend, helped Jesus carry his cross to Calgary).

The restoration of the church, the reopening of St. Edmund's Academy (kindergarten through sixth grade), and the neighborhood revitalization efforts evolved to become part of Tolliver's master plan in the early 1990s. Yet he admitted that visions of housing rehab and economic development were not what originally drew him to St. Edmund's. And many parishioners, according to Tolliver, were at first opposed to his involvement in community issues. They wanted their rector to run their church and see to their pastoral and spiritual needs.

Shortly after he arrived in Washington Park in June 1989, Tolliver realized that the future of the neighborhood and the future of his church were intertwined. He sought to balance his two roles: ensuring both the pastoral care of his parishioners and the social gospel needs of the community. Forming the St. Edmund's Redevelopment Corporation (SERC) in the winter of 1990 was a bold step. But it would soon be embraced by such residents as Margean Jackson, who told visiting French journalists years later: "I wish more ministers would take on that responsibility."

In the video produced by CAPA Presse TV (September 1996), Tolliver spoke of how he was working to change people's opinions of the value of neighborhood involvement. "I have built a new sense of hope," he said, pointing to buildings that had been gutted and remodeled within blocks of his church. "But the residents won't believe it until they see more. That will change people's attitudes."

City officials had already taken notice. Chicago Department of Housing Commissioner Marina Carroll was quoted in a July 25, 1992, *Chicago Defender* article: "The heroes of community development include Father Tolliver and his congregation who have organized to reverse the tide of disinvestment in the church's back yard." Reverend Tolliver and his church garnered international attention in fall 1996 when *Anglican World* magazine, commenting on a (May 1996) visit to Chicago by Archbishop of Canterbury George L. Carey, wrote about "St. Edmund's Episcopal Church on the southside, where incredible work is being done with housing rehabilitation in the area surrounding the large and stately St. Edmund's Church. . . . The rector, Reverend Richard Tolliver, is doing a great job of bringing the church back into the center of the community as well."

Though pleased with the positive publicity he and St. Edmund's have received, Tolliver readily credits the work of the laypeople of his parish. He believes that most of God's work is performed by members of the congregation, people such as Bernard Spillman, president of the St. Edmund's Academy Board of Directors. "They're just very hard workers," Tolliver says. "They free me up to concentrate on activities like fund raising."

Tolliver uses the analogy of a corporate organizational structure when describing the many committees and groups operating under the auspices of the church, the academy, and the redevelopment corporation. He believes in delegating and empowering. He speaks of paradigm shifts and mission statements. He asks staff and volunteers to provide him with meeting summaries and project status reports. He sounds very much like a new-millennium exec when he says, "You have to listen and take your cues from people."

Today he takes his cues from assistant rector Father John Agbaje, a native of Nigeria who has been at St. Edmund's since 1997. Tolliver assigns much of the pastoral care duties (such as visiting sick parishioners) to Agbaje, a broad-shouldered man with a contagious smile and comforting manner. Tolliver knows that Agbaje is seeking a rectorship of his own, and will likely leave St. Edmund's within the year. But there's much work to be done now and no time to worry about what-ifs and when.

When the two ministers meet in Tolliver's office it reminds one of a scene from the TV series *M.A.S.H.*, with Radar O'Reilly reporting to Colonel Blake. Each man tends to finish the other's sentences as they discuss the state of outreach services. One parishioner is grieving for her late husband. A retired member of the congregation is depressed about his serious illness. A middle-aged parishioner has been rushed to the hospital with panic attacks. Agbaje hands Tolliver handwritten notes on each of his pastoral visits. At the end of the meeting, Agbaje asks when he can speak with Tolliver about some of his plans. Tolliver says he will have to let him know because his calendar is so busy for the next few days. He can't speak any longer this afternoon because he has a parishioner in crisis waiting to see him.

Moments after Father John has left Tolliver's office, an anxious-looking matronly woman enters her minister's office seeking comfort and counsel. A veteran crisis counselor, starting with his seminary days thirty years earlier, Tolliver sits and listens patiently as the woman describes the bitter feud she has been having with an old friend and fellow St. Edmund's member. Ever since a time-share condo deal fell apart, the two women have been fighting. There have been cross words exchanged, nasty letters, and mean phone calls. The bitterness culminated with an incident on a recent Sunday during the communion ceremony.

Tolliver nods knowingly as she speaks. He tells her that he cannot permit any such actions to interfere with the sanctity of the passing of the Eucharist in church. He asks her what she plans to do to forgive her old friend, if she can forgive her. He reminds of her of his sermon on "hate," which he recently delivered from the pulpit.

As the woman sits on the plush red leather couch listening to the comforting voice of her pastor, she looks at him behind his desk, flanked by his file cabinets. Next to her is a long wooden table with photos of Tolliver with dignitaries: President Clinton, Archbishop Tutu, former president Jimmy Carter, Rosa Parks, and others. Across from the table of photos is a bookshelf with more framed photos, a small statue of a black rhino, a *Collins Robert French Dictionary,* the *Oxford Dictionary of the Christian Church,* an Episcopal Church annual, hymn books, and two King James Version Bibles.

Rather than trying to solve her problem, Tolliver puts the course of her action in her hands. He encourages her to find her own solution. He does urge her to "take the high road" in her actions. She thanks him with tears in her eyes and tells him how she will pray for him when she prays tonight for strength, for answers, for forgiveness.

Tolliver knows how difficult it can be, even for a Christian and a minister, to forgive. On the subject of racism in America, he says, "What has kept me sane are the good experiences I've had with whites." He notes that in October 1996, when he received his alma mater's (Miami University) distinguished achievement award, the school's highest honor for alumni, he told the largely white audience at the reception that it was "bittersweet accepting the award."

What he didn't share with the crowd were his memories of prejudice on the bucolic southern Ohio campus in the mid-1960s: the French professor who gave him lower grades for the same quality work as white students; students in his dorm who would greet him one on one, but ignore him when their parents came to visit; a dean who told him that blacks typically weren't suited to majoring in math or the sciences; a girlfriend who transferred because of bias she encountered. Yes, it was bittersweet to accept the award. "But when people hear you talk like that," he says, "they accuse you of being an angry black man."

Through all the years Tolliver has had a guiding formula for dealing with problems and setbacks: He outworks anything that stands in his way. Most of the time he succeeds. His record of success has earned him recognition and the respect of powerful people in politics, business, and civic affairs throughout Greater Chicago.

At the end of this work week in mid-May, he has been asked to give the opening prayer at the annual dinner of the "100 Black Men of Chicago," a high-profile peer-mentoring program for African American children ages ten to eighteen. Former Atlanta mayor Maynard Jackson will be the keynote speaker at this prestigious event in the opulent ballroom of the Chicago Hilton Hotel.

Tolliver resembles an ambassador in his tuxedo and gold vest as he glides between handshakes and hellos in a room full of hundreds of formally dressed men and women—the crème de la crème of Chicago's African American community. Men seek Tolliver out to introduce themselves and their wives. Some ask about the progress of redevelopment projects. Others recall names of St. Edmund's parishioners and school graduates. Tolliver mentions the journalist Margo Jefferson, a cultural critic for *The New York Times*. She is the daughter of parishioner Irma Jefferson. More anecdotes are swapped amidst the greetings and hors d'oeuvres.

Tolliver is comfortable with the power brokers and VIPs. He must be. He never knows when he'll meet a head of community relations or an executive with a foundation interested in urban problems. Tolliver jokes with James Compton, head of the Urban League, and shares a few moments with former Atlanta mayor Jackson before it is time for dinner.

The Hilton ballroom is ornate in gold, white, and cream-colored décor. Victorian décor: huge chandeliers, overhanging balconies, table after table with crisp white linen cloths and sparkling place settings. Tuxedoes and evening gowns fill the room with an air of regal anticipation and celebration. This is a special night to recognize people who are giving something back to their community.

The master of ceremonies introduces Tolliver, and he strides confidently to the podium to deliver the night's invocation. He looks out on the audience, and once again he is in the pulpit seeking to enlighten and inspire with Scripture. "To whom much is given, much is expected," he says in a clear, melodious voice that fills the now quiet ballroom as heads are bowed. He knows these words. He lives by these words. These are the words that keep him going, keep him striving to do even more. These are the words that awaken Richard Tolliver when most of the world is still asleep.

[5]

DOUG AND JUDY HALL "BOSTON'S SERVANT LEADERS"

Photos courtesy of Emmanuel Gospel Center, Inc.

For a couple rooted in inner-city Boston for almost forty years, Doug and Judy Hall love to travel. In June 2003 they went to Scotland and the United Kingdom for a three-week vacation. While there, the Halls met with European evangelical Christian organizations to explain their doctoral ministry training in complex urban systems. The Halls believe there may be consulting opportunities abroad in the future. Before they left, Doug and Judy had two reasons to celebrate. In May 2003, 150 people attended an open house to mark the grand opening of the new Emmanuel Gospel Center (EGC) headquarters on Shawmut Avenue. A few days later, a banquet was held in honor of ten urban students (with full tuition scholarships) who would be attending Gordon College, Wenham, Massachusetts, in the fall. These students were the first cohort of New City Scholars, part of the EGC College Success Initiative. Doug Hall is proud of the progress the EGC is making on many fronts, but he is never one to grow complacent. His mindset is best expressed in his proactive philosophy toward urban problems: "All who know me well know what often drives my approach to social action—and virtually any form of ministry in which I am involved—is the sense that I can be counter-productive." Hall says that anticipating what can go wrong pushes him to prepare long-term responsive strategies. Colleagues and peers say this strategic thinking has anchored the Halls' success through the decades, and is guiding new generations of social activists throughout the Greater Boston area.

The many people that they have blessed have turned around and supported their work, served on their many boards, and advocated for them all over the world.

—PASTOR BRUCE H. WALL, Dorchester (Massachusetts) Temple Baptist Church

On this, the last Saturday of June 2002, Doug and Judy Hall are showing off. Showing off? Not a chance. The Halls are models of Christian humility, self-effacing perhaps to a fault. They have built their reputation as religious visionaries and social activists by hard work, sacrifice, and perseverance. They would never flaunt their success.

But perhaps they have a right to show off just a bit. For on this day they are giving a tour of their new, lovely nine-hundred-square-foot loft apartment in a converted Wareham Street warehouse in Boston's South End. After spending their early years in substandard housing and hovering for decades at or below the poverty line, the couple finally caught a break. They received waiting-list priority status from the City of Boston because they had been displaced by the Redevelopment Authority back in 1971 when urban renewal leveled entire city blocks. Thanks to their priority (set-aside) status, the Halls bought their new condo for about a third of its market value.

Doug is beaming as he shakes hands at the door. His thick pewter-gray hair and moustache have recently been trimmed. The sixty-five-year-old Hall looks hip in his colorful "Oslo" (Norway) tee shirt, black jeans, and black 804 Nike running shoes. Judy appears momentarily, her voice as lyrical as it is welcoming. Like her husband, she wears oversize glasses. And, like her husband's, her gaze is friendly but focused, as they like to maintain eye contact. She is auburn-haired and half a head shorter than Doug, but she is quicker on her feet than her loping husband. In her white tennis shoes, white slacks, and red-and-white-striped pullover, she seems ready for a sailboat ride on the Charles River.

On this weekend afternoon the Halls look rested and as freshly scrubbed as their spic-and-span condominium in the summer sunlight. They are proud because they are first-time homeowners as a pair in their sixties. And if you knew the Halls and their years of selfless, sacrificial living, you would say they have earned the privilege of pride.

Although it is only two blocks from the Emmanuel (means "God is with us") Gospel Center (EGC), the innovative urban ministry they have led since 1964, this new condo on Wareham Street seems light years away.

From 1977 until 2002, Doug and Judy lived adjacent to the Center in a nineteenth-century, five-bedroom townhouse (parsonage) they had gut-level rehabbed. The former burned-out building was cozy, but old. It had a narrow, rickety staircase, crumbling interior brick walls, and noisy plumbing. Over the years it was the residence for not only Doug and Judy and their children, Rebecca and Kenneth, but for an estimated fifteen hundred people. Some stayed for a weekend, others lived with the Halls for a year or more. The Shawmut Avenue home was lovingly dubbed "the Hall Hotel" by their guests.

The tour of the Halls' new Wareham Street abode begins on beautiful hardwood floors. Plants flourish throughout the apartment. The interior is tasteful: a new floral print loveseat, couch, and chair, antiques, and French doors. The eye is drawn to bookshelves that "handyman" Doug Hall has installed above their wooden desk.

Books range from religion and philosophy to psychology and social work. There are tomes one would expect—*The New National Baptist Hymnal, Managing the Congregation,* and *Integrative Theology.* But there are also vintage editions of *Treasure Island* and *The Flying Norseman.* Artifacts on the shelves reveal more about the Halls through the years: figurines, pottery, Doug's handmade wooden toys and his replica of a nineteenth-century clipper ship, plus the gathered reminiscences from their travels and those of friends from such destinations as Norway, India, Haiti, Kenya, and the Philippines.

The household walls are lined with paintings (an Impressionist landscape, a farm scene, a black Jesus), memorabilia, and family photos. If every picture tells a story, then there are hundreds here and in the scrapbooks that appear in a flash from Judy's ever-busy hands. Doug is of sturdy Norwegian descent. His father and five uncles were all professional ski jumpers. They had emigrated from Scandinavia to Michigan's Upper Peninsula. Judy is of Germanic heritage, and like Doug she has Midwestern roots.

Sitting in their new condo, the Halls seem genuinely humbled by their recent good fortune and that of the Emmanuel Gospel Center. In the last two years, the EGC capital fund-raising campaign has raised more than half of its $2.4 million goal. The funds will be used to renovate the three-story Shawmut Avenue building, around the corner from the former San Juan Street location, to serve as EGC's new headquarters, offering expanded room for several of its ministries, new training and meeting facilities, and an enhanced library. The capital campaign will also establish an endowment to provide support for building upkeep and staff development.

The Halls report other promising news: a six-figure two-year grant from the Boston Foundation to the EGC to conduct a major research study of the city's neighborhoods. As of June 2002, grants from the Lilly Endowment and the U.S. Department of Health and Human Services are pending to the EGC in a consortium with other community groups. A large fall 2002 conference (Multicultural Leaders Consultation) is being planned by the EGC to bring two hundred representatives from sixteen different racial/ethnic groups ("a mini Christian United Nations") in Greater Boston to discuss church issues such as serving second- and third-generation immigrants, dealing with financially strained social service systems, and addressing youth violence, education, and homelessness.

Today the nonprofit Emmanuel Gospel Center's annual operating budget exceeds $3 million, and there are more than forty staffers to serve the needs of its twelve ministries (including services for the homeless, economic development and educational support programs, youth ministry, and research and consulting). All this success suggests a couple questions: How did the Halls accomplish so much? How did the EGC evolve from a storefront rescue mission into a multifaceted, internationally renowned parachurch organization?

Friends and colleagues praise the Halls' faith, intelligence, integrity, commitment, and quiet strength of character. They say the Halls are special people who have spent their adult lives in Boston's South End ministering "with," not "to," the poorest of the inner city.

"The Halls are unsung heroes in the fight for social justice," says Dr. Eldin Villafane, founding director of the Gordon-Conwell Theological Seminary's Center for Urban Ministerial Education (CUME). Villafane, who has known Doug and Judy since 1973, credits their deferential attitude in working successfully with minority groups in Boston through five difficult decades. He cites Scripture when he refers to Doug Hall as a contemporary Epaphroditus: "my brother, fellow worker, and fellow soldier" (Philippians 2:25).

The Reverend Dr. Michael Haynes, senior minister of Boston's historic Twelfth Baptist Church and one of Doug's mentors from the turbulent 1960s, wrote in the fall 1995 edition of the *Urban Update* newsletter that the Halls are reaping the benefits and blessings from a lifetime of faithfulness to God and their mission. The Halls, as evangelical Christians, explain their life's work in terms of a spiritual "calling."

"If we had been civil servants or social workers in the conventional, secular sense, we never could have lasted all these years," says Doug, sharing their story en route to the Victoria Diner, which sits at the crossroads of three Boston neighborhoods: Roxbury, Dorchester, and the South End. The diner was an island of calm during the violence that erupted over the court-ordered school busing/desegregation in 1974. The Halls worked with churches and community organizations back then to help restore peace to the streets of their adopted hometown. That was one of many occasions when Doug and Judy preached prophetically about the role of the urban churches as "healing communities" to counter social problems.

"Such churches . . . develop because such problems exist. They are meeting significant social needs and demonstrating that the city needs the church," Doug would later write in one of countless papers and book chapters on EGC's holistic approach to urban needs and multiethnic church startups (i.e., church planting). The Halls were "talking the talk and walking the walk" about faith-based initiatives long before they were in vogue.

But, as they will attest, their visionary status was years in the making. When they first came to the Boston area in 1964 in their black Ford Fairlane, they didn't even plan on staying. Doug was enrolled in divinity school, and the Halls intended to become missionaries to India upon his graduation. They were also expecting their first child. Doug had been working as a janitor; Judy was a substitute teacher. They heard about a job in inner-city Boston that offered a free apartment and a salary of $2,400 a year. Doug says he took the position "that no one else wanted" as superintendent of the Emmanuel Gospel Center. His annual operating budget was $3,000. Judy served as Doug's unpaid assistant, a title she still carries to this day.

When the Halls arrived, the EGC was a neighborhood mission with a twenty-seven-year history of ministering to the South End's working poor. Doug Hall was hired to preach, run Sunday school classes, and counsel street alcoholics and other disadvantaged people. Local residents expected him to continue the old ways of serving the largely immigrant population that had settled in the South End for generations.

But Doug Hall wasn't an evangelist or an ordained minister. In the early days he seemed much more comfortable as the EGC's resident repairman. Staffers share stories of him often looking more like the Center's janitor than its superintendent.

* * *

A large cloth banner high on the walls of the Center's San Juan Street location quotes the prophet Jeremiah (29:7): "Seek the peace and prosperity of the city." Doug doesn't remember his journey to Boston in quite such prophetic terms. In a 1995 commemorative newsletter edition, he noted: "We came to the city with not a lot of faith. I worry a lot. And I don't have a lot of obvious gifts."

The man who would one day be praised for his progressive systems thinking, countless achievements, and contributions to enhancing the quality of life for thousands in Boston began his urban ministry with a fair share of doubts and what-ifs. His humility and self-deprecating style served him well in masking his insecurity. But such fretting had been woven into the fabric of his life from boyhood, when he strived to be the "good son" in a blue-collar family in Farmington, Michigan.

As a teen in the 1950s, Doug was a "vokie," a vocational education student, who spent the first two years out of high school working twelve-hour days at a machine shop. Both Doug and Judy talk about difficult family times during their upbringing: money problems, relocations, alcoholism, break-downs, and terminal illness. They say they tried to do what was right. But that wasn't enough to bring peace to their lives. It took something quite profound to alter their existence. That something was a religious transformation. They were both converted to evangelical Christianity in 1955. Doug was eighteen; Judy was seventeen. Two years later they would meet as students at the Moody Bible Institute in Chicago, Illinois.

Doug, a bright student who had always been curious about "the technical side of things," was now deeply interested in missionary work and in broadening his intellectual pursuits into history, foreign language, research, and writing.

In 1960 the Halls married and enrolled at Michigan State University (MSU), where Doug earned a degree in sociology/anthropology and Judy a bachelor's degree in elementary education. In 1963 Doug began his graduate work at MSU in counseling and guidance. But grad school would be put on hold, as the Lord had other plans for this comely, likable couple from the nation's heartland. They were coming East, and they didn't know what they were getting into.

In his 1995 testimonial commemorating the Halls' then thirty years of service to EGC and the city of Boston, the Reverend Dr. Michael Haynes noted how Doug and Judy came to a South End "that was decaying, being abandoned, being written off. . . . And they came, remarkably, with the love of Jesus Christ." Doug says that in the mid-1960s preachers were not very popular. He recalls driving his car once with a neighborhood resident who remarked, "You know, we ought to burn down every church in the city and leave the preachers inside." Welcome to Boston, Doug and Judy Hall!

As a pair of transplanted small-town white Christians, the Halls would confront a host of urban problems in the South End, including racial hostility, the plague of drugs and alcohol, and countless lost lives. They would survive assaults both verbal and physical and overcome crippling illness, and Doug would even escape serious injury (by virtue of a rehearsed shoulder roll) when struck in a crosswalk by a speeding cab. Yet the Halls would keep on keeping on.

Yes, they are true believers and community activists, who have protested over issues such as better housing for low-income residents of the South End. They are credited with empowering hundreds of individuals and helping to foster and support dozens of urban organizations over the last forty years. But they are human. You won't hear of any St. Augustine–like confessions, but you will learn how in the early years, Doug doubted himself even as the EGC flatbed trailer rolled through Boston's inner-city neighborhoods trying to bring a message of hope, love, and salvation.

When those mean streets erupted in chaos, violence, and despair, Doug questioned his role. He wondered how life in the poor neighborhoods could ever improve. He worried about burning out from his long hours at EGC and in finishing his master's degree by completing five hundred hours of client counseling at a state mental hospital in Greater Boston. While Doug battled negative thinking, Judy admitted to feeling overwhelmed at times and mediocre in her efforts. But the Halls stayed, endured, and sacrificed.

More than just persevere, the Halls reinvented themselves and the mission of EGC. Along the way they brought systems thinking and organizational development to Christian urban ministry. The social gospel of Jesus was about to earn its doctorate.

* * *

During the difficult early years, Doug and Judy became convinced that the Emmanuel Gospel Center needed to redefine its mission. If it was to survive, the EGC had to become connected to the broader, interrelated Christian community in Boston. They realized that an indigenous, interdenominational religious organization could provide more effective urban ministry than a neighborhood rescue mission.

Working with colleagues, such as the late Reverend Chet Young, the Halls changed their strategy from one-on-one ministering to supporting the work of other urban churches and community organizations. "We became facilitators and enablers, helping others to do the works that result in long-term benefits for the city," says Doug. According to the Halls, their holistic approach is based on understanding the city as a large, highly interrelated social/spiritual system, which, when nurtured properly, is capable of supporting the positive development of all individuals.

Dr. Villafane, a fellow urban ministry educator, says that Doug Hall's systemic approach sees the complexity and interaction of different churches, programs, and ministries. In similar fashion, he says, the Halls' interpretation of the gospel is not just to save souls, but also to transform institutions and society by enhancing the lives of individuals and the work of community organizations.

Sociologists as well as savvy politicians have long recognized the urban churches, especially in the African American community, as vital neighborhood institutions. The EGC built its outreach approach on the enduring strength of the traditional black church and on the flourishing of new (often Pentecostal) churches from the influx of immigrants in the late twentieth century. In what the Center's research would later call the "Quiet Revival" in Boston, the number of Christian churches doubled during the years 1975 to 2000. (Currently, the EGC claims that there are more than 600 churches in Boston and Cambridge, representing more than 110 denominations and 33 different languages.)

Such growth has offered the EGC expanded opportunities for networking and collaboration, applied research, and development of new ministries. Doug's long-held vision has been to maximize the churches' grassroots ties to the community in order to generate new social, educational, and economic development, as well as spiritual leadership. Case in point has been the Emmanuel Gospel Center's relationship with the Boston TenPoint Coalition.

The Coalition, an ecumenical group of clergy and lay urban leaders, including Pastor Bruce H. Wall, a loyal friend and colleague of EGC and the Halls since the mid-1960s, has worked to mobilize Boston's Christian community around issues affecting black and Latino youth. It originated in the 1990s as a response to urban gang violence and a host of social problems facing the young minority population of Boston. The ambitious faith-based effort included such programs as evangelizing youth in gangs, providing advocacy for underprivileged juveniles in the courts, and ensuring enhanced economic development opportunities for the poor and disadvantaged. In 1995 the Emmanuel Gospel Center conducted a research study on youth ministry in Boston. The research showed that there was only one full-time church-based youth worker in all of Boston and Cambridge dedicated to outreach activities. The study also revealed how part-time and volunteer youth workers were burning out because of stress and insufficient support systems. As a result, the Youth Ministry Development Project was launched with the goal of raising funds so that twenty urban churches could hire youth workers over the next ten years. The Halls are pleased to report the project is making steady progress.

Another cooperative ministry launched by EGC in the 1990s was the Boston Education Collaborative (BEC). The BEC is a community-based urban alliance that gives Boston's minority population avenues for post-secondary training and education. Since 1999 the BEC has established Higher Education Resource Centers in the South End, Brockton, Dorchester, Lawrence, and Worcester. The centers provide SAT test preparation, tutoring, and mentoring to help students enhance their academic performance. The BEC's mission was a direct result of the Emmanuel Gospel Center's applied research that found that while 75 percent of Christians in Boston were people of color, fewer than 5 percent of the students in area Christian colleges were students of color.

In typical fashion, Doug Hall downplays his social activist role in these and other programs over the years. He defines an activist as someone who "forces things to happen." Doug believes that if you "push too hard, you can screw things up." He relies on his faith to determine how and when he gets involved. "God will somehow make it happen," he says.

Longtime friends are proud to call Doug and Judy Hall activists. They cite their significant efforts in community organizing from the late 1960s until the mid-1970s to protest redevelopment plans in the South End, to secure low-income housing, and to help create an attractive urban plaza (Villa Victoria) for area residents.

Ministers and laypeople alike recall how Doug and Judy and the Emmanuel Gospel Center assisted churches that had joined together in the summer of 1972 to stem the violence in Boston's Hispanic neighborhoods. An evangelistic crusade was held with clergy, gang members, and young and old area residents praying for a peaceful resolution to days of rioting in and around Blackstone Park. Judy Hall remembers how the community affairs director for the Boston Police Department referred to the prayer service as a miracle in calming the community's tensions. "Perhaps for the first time the community came to appreciate the important part the church plays in ministering to people under the most severe social situations," Judy Hall recalls thirty years later.

Doug Hall will acknowledge utilizing the techniques of 1960s activists, such as Saul Alinsky, through the years, but he will quickly add that rarely have he and his wife employed solely secular community organizing methods. "Without any redemptive process, the society will fall apart," he says, citing the influence of such early Christian evangelists as Paul the Apostle.

* * *

One of Doug Hall's enduring legacies is his advocacy for urban ministerial education in Boston. In 1969 he wrote a detailed proposal to what was then the Gordon Divinity School (today: Gordon-Conwell Theological Seminary, G-CTS). Among the suggested strategies: Establish an "urban year" program for seminary graduate students. By 1973, such an immersion program was in place for seminary students to live, minister, and study in the inner city and in working-class sections of metro Boston.

Doug taught classes at the Emmanuel Gospel Center as part of the urban year program, and developed and refined his systems thinking. He also collaborated with Dr. Eldin Villafane, who lived with his family near the Halls in the Villa Victoria plaza area. In 1976 Dr. Villafane became the founding director of the Center for Urban Ministerial Education (CUME). In 1981 Doug Hall received an honorary doctorate from the Seminary for his contributions to CUME.

Today, both master's and doctoral students at Gordon-Conwell learn principles of urban ministerial education espoused by Doug Hall. They listen to lectures on linear versus systems thinking, "hexagoning," and causal loop diagrams. They smile as Doug uses the metaphor of a cat (a systemic, organic creation) and a toaster (a linear product of components). He features the cat as the model for Christian-based community outreach to help students learn "how God works in large interrelated systems." The urban ministers try to pay attention as Doug, the "absent-minded" adjunct faculty member, drifts off course or drones on in his nasal Midwestern accent while discussing his theories and admonitions. For example: "We must be aware of the counter-intuitive nature of complex social systems. . . . We could be promoting the wrong factors of the model as the ones to be emulated."

"Doug does tend to wander sometimes in his presentations," says Ron Ruthrliff, a minister from Seattle, one of sixteen clergy and Gordon-Conwell doctoral students from states such as Washington, Texas, Ohio, Florida, Pennsylvania, and Massachusetts, who are back in Boston in June 2002 for two weeks of on-campus residency.

Half of the class are men and women of color; the other half are white males. They represent a range of several Christian denominations, notably

Baptist, Methodist, Pentecostal (Assembly of God), and Greek-Orthodox. The Gordon-Conwell three-year professional (versus academic) doctor of urban ministry degree requires these preachers and pastors to make the annual two-week trek to Boston for intensive study, with the remaining doctoral requirements conducted in their home communities, culminating in a dissertation.

In 2002 the summer residency is based at the Walker Center, a religious conference and retreat center in Newton, Massachusetts, established as a home for missionary children in 1910. But this doctoral program isn't conducted in traditional classroom style. Doug and Judy Hall and Ron Griffin, chairman of the EGC board, have planned an ambitious schedule of visits to see models of urban ministry in action. Most of the ministers ride to the destinations in and around Boston in a rented sixteen-passenger white Dodge Ram van, piloted by Griffin, with Judy Hall serving as navigator. ("Doug," she says, "is terrible with directions.")

One afternoon stop is at the Judge Connelly Youth Correctional Center. At this juvenile detention facility, Scott Larson, founding director of Straight Ahead Ministries, speaks on the mission of his fifteen-year-old organization, which is active in twelve states and dedicated to ministering to juvenile offenders while they are incarcerated and upon their release. According to Doug and Judy Hall, Straight Ahead Ministries has compiled an impressive record by providing positive adult (Christian) role models to serve troubled youth, enabling a high percentage to complete their high school education and attend college.

Larson, a tall, athletic-looking former stockbroker in blue jeans and gold sport shirt, talks comfortably to the gathering in the correctional facility chapel. As he speaks about the spiritual development of at-risk youth, Father Joe, a Catholic priest and Department of Youth Services chaplain, looks on. Father Joe bears a striking resemblance to the actor who played diner-owner Al Delvecchio in the TV sitcom "Happy Days." He nods as Larson, who has written books and designed courses for social workers, fills a washable chalkboard with crime statistics and other percentages related to the woeful state of services for youth offenders.

Larson also writes catchy statements on the board: "Rules without relationships = Rebellion" and "Glance at weakness. Gaze at strengths." He shares case histories, including his own troubled youth, discusses fund-raising efforts, and advocates for national juvenile justice ministries. His remarks appear well received by the doctoral students before him.

Doug takes occasional notes in a two-by-four-inch black and white "nickel" memo pad. He says he has stacks of the little notebooks gathered over the years, and he often rereads them while on long meditative walks. Judy takes copious notes, filling line after line of her yellow legal pad with small, neat handwriting. While Doug stretches his legs, rests his hands on his chest, and yawns occasionally, Judy doesn't break stride. She writes constantly, as if unable to take a break until the session concludes.

The presentation by Larson ends after about ninety minutes. The urban ministers stand arm in arm to offer a closing prayer. Then Larson shifts gears and becomes a smiling entrepreneur hawking his wares. He puts his black credit card machine on the chapel altar next to a stack of his books and CDs and readily issues receipts to his audience-turned-customers. One wonders how Father Joe feels about Larson conducting business on the same altar where the priest consecrates bread and wine during Holy Communion in his weekly Masses.

Later that night, Doug Hall and the class of urban ministers begin to debrief about Scott Larson and Straight Ahead Ministries. But too much good food at the Mandarin Gourmet restaurant and a humid evening back at the stuffy Walker Center's upstairs parlor-conference-room cause the discussion to veer from the intended systemic analysis. Instead the group engages in interesting dialogue on racism, the state of the criminal justice system, and the need for expanded youth ministry.

But Doug returns to his analytical agenda the following night. He stands at his overhead projector at the head of the tables where the urban ministers sit with Palm Pilots, laptops, and old-fashioned pen and paper. The cat and the toaster are back up on the screen, representing systemic and linear designs. "Is Larson a cat or a toaster?" Doug asks the group. The responses are less than enthusiastic. Doug answers his own question: "He's a cat on my rating sheet."

Then he moves into an analysis of *primary* culture, achieved through human relational networks, and *secondary* culture, accomplished through direct use of financial resources. Doug concludes that Straight Ahead Ministries scores high as an organization committed to primary cultural relationships, much like that of the Emmanuel Gospel Center.

Such systems thinking, Doug explains, is more than fifty years old, and has long been applied to research in the physical and social sciences. Systems dynamic engineering is a more mature, modern expression of such analytical thought, he says. In his writing he often cites the influence of author Peter Senge and his book *The Fifth Discipline*.

Although Doug is in his comfort zone discussing the theories of Senge and other researchers, his credibility results from the Emmanuel Gospel

Center's applied research and its record of establishing deep, lasting relationships with individuals and organizations throughout the community.

Doctoral student Ray Wilshire, a pastor, Boston probation officer, and native of Panama, says, "The Halls and EGC have an impeccable record and consistency of service that transcends race." Another member of the class is Bruce H. Wall, pastor of the Dorchester Temple Baptist Church. Wall is even more emphatic about the influence of Doug and Judy. "The Halls and my senior pastor have had the most influence on my community activism, political involvement in the city, and my willingness to die for the causes that are dear to my heart," Wall says fervently.

In the case of the EGC, its strong primary culture has generated benefits at the secondary culture level, in the way of attracting foundation grants and other "secular" financial resources. But Doug has cautioned ministers about potential risks in engaging in faith-based initiatives, such as those endorsed by the current Bush administration. He says that one real danger in church/state or secular/Christian cooperation in such programs is that churches could lose their ability to do effective social ministry because their theological belief system may be weakened at a subconscious, indirect level. In other words, the secular world may compromise the sacred.

One of the doctoral students, Reverend Rodney Hart, has more than twenty-five years' experience working with a well-known faith-based program. Hart is executive director of Teen Challenge, New England, Inc., part of an international organization dedicated to physical and spiritual rehabilitation and renewal for people with drug and alcohol addictions. Reverend Hart's own story is one of remarkable human transcendence, for he overcame teenage years of drug and alcohol abuse, crime, and self-destructive behavior before he was "saved by God, through the work of Teen Challenge" in the mid-1970s.

Hart jokes that he sometimes finds it hard to grasp all of Doug's message as he waxes and wanes on systems thinking in theology and urban ministry. But his respect for Doug and Judy Hall's conviction and compassion is unshakeable. He first met them in 1980, when they looked "like a couple of hippies in the South End." Over the next twenty years, Hart would learn much more about the Halls and their work at the EGC.

"They have what Eldin Villafane calls 'a burning patience,'" says Reverend Hart, noting that Doug and Judy won't go into a community or visit an organization unless they are invited. As Doug Hall explains in one of his white papers, "We only begin such projects when we are significantly asked in some way to do them, and then only when they are significant to other players that will work with us on them, especially the people most involved in the social needs."

* * *

Of all those who hold Doug and Judy Hall in high esteem—and there are legions of supporters—none can compare with nor claim the unique perspective of their thirty-two-year-old son, Kenneth (Kenny). The Halls adopted Kenny, who is African American, when he was a five-month-old baby in 1971. How did the Halls' son feel about being raised by white parents? "God wanted me in that family," he says proudly. "Because of my special background—a black child in a white family in a Puerto Rican neighborhood—I felt that I could fit in anywhere. I was also fortunate because I had plenty of strong black role models growing up."

Today, Kenny is youth coordinator for the Greater Boston Baptist Association, an organization of seventy churches, serving an area with more than thirty thousand youths from a myriad of cultures. "How I was raised prepared me well for my work in a multicultural world," he says. "I'm comfortable in all racial environments."

Kenny says he and his sister, Rebecca, were involved in their parents' ministry since they were young children. They didn't have much of a choice because their mom and dad went to work where they lived—right next door to the Emmanuel Gospel Center. Their home life was also shaped by their parents' social activism, for their residence was also home for any number of people, sometimes entire families for months at a time.

"When I was a teenager, I found it hard to cope at times with all the people coming and going," says Kenny. "Selfishly, I wanted my parents to myself. But I outgrew those attitudes." Kenny also admits that he had to outgrow his parents' shadow and secure his own name, which wasn't easy because of the great reputation of his parents, particularly among members of Boston's black and Hispanic communities. "I used to wonder if I got hired because I was Doug and Judy's son. For a time I tried to break away from that. But now I say it with reverence, that I am their son."

Kenny Hall understands the essence of his parents' success. "They love life, and they love what they do. They accept their calling as servant leaders to the poor and needy of Boston." The proud son can talk easily and at length about the Emmanuel Gospel Center's track record of nurturing ("planting") new churches and collaborating with community organizations in launching innovative social programs. But he would prefer to chat about his parents' devotion to each other, the sacrifices they made for their children, and their enduring close family ties. (He speaks fondly of his older sister, Rebecca, who is married and lives in New York City.) "My parents' love, faith, and years of service have inspired me to succeed," says Kenny, one of a new generation of Boston faith activists who will help ensure that the legacy of Doug and Judy Hall continues.

That legacy was on the mind of Doug Hall during a reflective moment at the Walker Center late one evening in late June 2002. He propped his legs up on the edge of a conference table, while Judy helped one of the doctoral students with some paperwork. "If there is no generation of social activists to follow us and others like us, then we've been unsuccessful in our mission," says Doug, who took steps in the last few years to plan for his succession.

In 1999 the EGC Board named Doug's protégé, Jeff Bass, as executive director. Doug was named president, which he said would enable him to focus on "vision bearing," refining the EGC as a learning organization and enlarging the process of applied research needed to "nurture city-wide Kingdom growth."

Doug says he feels more radical now than back in the 1960s, when he was "one of the weirdos" hanging out with the militants. He says that such radical thinking will be needed in the years ahead. A decade ago, Doug wrote rather prophetically that "changing economic and political climates will call the church to greater levels of social action."

More recently he outlined the role for the Emmanuel Gospel Center in achieving systemic change over the long term: working cooperatively and strategically, using applied research to produce effective community intervention, and uniting the resources of churches and individuals. The Hall plan for the future of the EGC is an ambitious faith-driven manifesto that addresses several lofty goals:

- Reducing crime and addictions
- Expanding available affordable housing for low- and medium-income people
- Compiling new in-depth research on the homeless
- Increasing the role of social ministry to address community problems
- Enhancing people's understanding of racism
- Breaking the cycle of family dysfunctionality
- Curtailing youth violence
- Addressing inequities in education
- Serving new immigrant populations

If you didn't know Doug and Judy Hall, you might be skeptical of their chances for achieving these objectives. But after the Halls' nearly forty years of successful social activism, only a serious nonbeliever would underestimate the power of commitment in the hands of these veteran Christian "do-gooders."

Decades ago a young man named Doug Hall came to Boston to answer a calling. He was filled with doubts and questions. He wondered if he could achieve what was being asked of him. Could he fulfill his mission? Along the way, he found his answer. He summed it up a few years ago when he wrote: "I believe that Judy and I—who have always worked as a team—are uniquely gifted to carry out the job we need to do. . . . We're in it for the long run."

[6]

FATHER ROY BOURGEOIS "THE COURAGE OF CONVICTIONS"

Photo by Mark H. Massé

When I spoke to Father Roy Bourgeois in June 2003, he was enjoying some summer R&R, a rare respite from his busy schedule. He had just returned from a reunion in Lutcher, Louisiana, where his mother, Grace, eighty-seven, and his father, Roy Sr., ninety, still host family gatherings. But later that month he was back on the road, representing the School of the Americas Watch (SOAW), the organization he founded in 1990. He was warmly received by a large United Auto Workers (UAW) convention in Pittsburgh, Pennsylvania. Bourgeois shared stories of violence against union workers in Colombia. He encouraged UAW representatives to attend this year's vigil at the gates of Fort Benning in Columbus, Georgia. The vigil attracts thousands who are protesting the presence of a U.S. Army facility that continues to train Latin American military, security, and police squads despite documented human rights violations and atrocities committed by School of the Americas graduates. Bourgeois was encouraged by word that anti–capital punishment activist and old friend Sister Helen Prejean would be among the notables attending the November vigil. Before then Father Roy's calendar would be filled with more than thirty speaking engagements on campuses, before church groups, and with community organizations, in some thirteen states. People from coast to coast would have a chance to hear the words of one of activism's most enthusiastic and charismatic messengers.

We must learn to welcome and not to fear the voices of dissent.

—J. WILLIAM FULBRIGHT

At 9:45 A.M. on a chilly Sunday morning, a handsome priest prepares to address his congregation in the streets of Columbus, Georgia. Father Roy Bourgeois leaves his small apartment by the gates of Fort Benning and makes his way to the stage where he will officially open the annual vigil of the School of the Americas Watch. November 17, 2002, is a brisk autumn day—football weather. Bourgeois, the former running back and captain of his high school team, moves swiftly as he once did on the gridiron in his native Louisiana. Today, instead of a football uniform or a priest's collar, he wears black jeans, a dark sweatshirt, and a turtleneck under his familiar faded blue button-down shirt and a navy three-quarter-length lined jacket.

He scans the scene before him. Some twenty yards from his front door are barricades guarded by local police officers and county sheriff deputies. Another twenty yards beyond these somber-looking black-uniformed men and women is the main gate of Fort Benning Military Reservation. The entrance and exit to the fort are protected by a twelve-foot-high chain-link fence. A sign on the fence reads: "Warning. Restricted Area." Behind the fence are a cluster of soldiers and military police; a few more military and municipal officials are in a tall, yellow hydraulic "cherry-picker" lift. One man in the lift is videotaping today's event. In front of those gates is a mass of humanity stretching for at least a quarter mile on Fort Benning Drive. Thousands of enthusiastic protesters, both young and old, are waiting to hear Father Roy.

Before he makes contact with anyone, he instinctively spits on the ground. It's a gesture typically made by athletes and soldiers before entering a field of play or battle. Bourgeois has seen both in his richly textured life, and today he will experience them again in Columbus, Georgia, at the vigil that is part commemoration, part confrontation, and part activists' encounter session.

Bourgeois looks much younger than his sixty-four years, with a full head of light brown hair and striking blue eyes. He bears a close resemblance to pro golfer Retief Goosen. Nostalgic movie buffs say he looks like Danny Kaye, the late comedic actor. Bourgeois is a trim five feet nine inches. He walks deftly, his work boots gliding along the damp ground.

Before he reaches the stage, which is rock-concert size, complete with giant black speakers, musical instruments, and several microphones, an admirer and his wife stop him and ask for a posed photo. Bourgeois obliges, and his face lights up in a warm smile as the first of dozens of cameras capture the image of this Maryknoll priest, Vietnam War veteran, and leader of a national movement called SOA Watch. From the website (www.soaw.org):

> SOA Watch (SOAW) is an independent organization that seeks to close the U.S. Army School of the Americas, under whatever name it is called, through vigils and fasts, demonstrations and nonviolent protest, as well as media and legislative work.

The SOAW logo is a skull topped by a mortarboard with a noose instead of a tassel.

There have been several "warm-up acts" this morning before Father Roy's opening remarks: Buddhist drumming and chanting, a Mayan blessing, and a welcome from Jeff Winder, SOAW program director ("I see a beautiful living river of people coming forward to confront the violence that happens on the other side of this fence.").

Maryknoll Sister Jean Fallon says: "Raise your crosses high. It is in their name that we are here." Detroit Bishop Thomas Gumbleton, founder of Pax Christi, urges the crowd to "say no to the nuclear weapons of the United States of America." Others on the agenda include Rebecca Kanner of the Ann Arbor (Mich.) Reconstructionists Havurah and Barbara Graham from the Pagan Cluster. A letter from Ibrahim Ramey of the Muslim Peace Fellowship is read: "We salute the courage and peaceful vision of you who are protesting the SOA." The comments seem particularly compelling as talk of war against Iraq is in the air and on the lips of countless protesters here today.

Other remarks are read to the gathering this morning. Actress Susan Sarandon, who has narrated SOAW videos, has written: "Thank you for doing what I cannot do today." Musician-activists, including Jackson Browne, Graham Nash, and Bonnie Raitt, have sent a statement of support for the SOAW rally and protest: "Today, as we stand in front of this abominable institution, we see a nation poised to start yet another war for oil. . . . But there is no greater insult to these freedoms . . . than the continued existence of this terrible training ground for global terrorists."

Massachusetts Congressman James P. McGovern, who has cosponsored legislation to close the SOA, sends his greetings to the demonstrators: "We shall continue this fight. And we shall ultimately prevail."

Now on stage, Father Roy Bourgeois stands comfortably at the microphone. He acknowledges the applause that greets him and speaks for several minutes sans notes or script. He looks Kennedyesque on stage, but his accent is from the Bayou, not Boston. His voice is gentle and somewhat high-pitched; his words flow as in a homily:

> This is a very special and a very solemn moment in our struggle to close down this school that is so connected to violence, death, and suffering. It is solemn and special because we are gathered here today to keep alive the memory of our sisters and brothers in Latin America who have been the victims of graduates of this school. We are here today to confront this violence. To say: This must stop.
>
> When we first gathered at this gate years ago, and as our movement took root, it had to be rooted in nonviolence. Early on we drew on the wisdom and the experience of people like Dr. Martin Luther King Jr., Mahatma Gandhi, Dorothy Day, Cesar Chavez. Their ways were going to be our way, the way of nonviolence. There is a lot of anger that many of us feel because of the violence, the suffering, and death that our country is causing throughout Latin America, the Middle East, and throughout the developing world. We have to be careful so this anger does not consume us. Our movement is about hope and about joy. It is about peace, and this is what we must hold on to. We are peacemakers. The challenge is to keep that peace within each of our hearts because we have come to discover that we cannot have peace out there in our world unless there is peace within our own lives, peace within our hearts.

Bourgeois sounds tired. His voice is reminiscent of the early political party speakers at a presidential convention. The fatigue is understandable. He has been putting in twenty-hour days in advance of the annual protest. He is lead organizer as well as the spiritual leader of SOAW. That means countless details are his responsibility, from booking rooms at dozens of hotels in the area to arranging for twenty-one Port-a-Potties along the protest route, from conducting countless media interviews to hiring a handful of off-duty cops for extra security, from the signing of contracts to the securing of tents, stages, microphones, and, yes, even supervising the hanging of an eight-by-twelve-foot banner ("Welcome Peace Makers. Close the School of Assassins") from the tall Georgia pines near the Fort Benning gates.

Last night, he took calls until quite late, got a few hours of restless sleep, then awoke about 3 A.M. to take yet more notes. His only respite was his beloved Psalms, which he reads each morning during his contemplative time. Bourgeois won't let the fatigue stop him. He will dig deep, relying on the discipline he honed during his years of competitive athletics.

On this Sunday morning, Father Roy's sermon isn't finished. He has more to say to the crowd, which is becoming animated, peppering his remarks with applause.

"And so this is a very sacred time for us as we gather once again as peacemakers, as people from all over the country, from all walks of life to

80

speak in one voice to say: 'Not in our name.' I would now like to read a short statement from the president of the United States, the president as portrayed on 'West Wing.'" Rousing applause rings out on Fort Benning Drive.

"As many of you know, Martin Sheen has been with us in years past. He regrets to say that he cannot be with us today, but he sent a statement to be read. Martin says: 'Now more than ever, we must stand with the marginalized. We must give voice to the voiceless and be true to ourselves. For it may appear that our country is running the world, but there is a higher power leading it. And when we rely on that higher power, peace and justice will prevail.'" Applause is now followed by Andean music and a song in honor of victims of Latin American violence ("No Mas, No More").

On the street, people assemble in rows of ten across. Teams of high school and college students, veterans' organizations, several religious denominations, and many "affinity groups" prepare for the solemn vigil at the gates of Fort Benning. The crowd, estimated at between sixty-five hundred (by police and media) and ten thousand–plus (by SOAW), is asked to recite the SOAW pledge of nonviolence. Hundreds carry two-foot-high white crosses with the names of human rights victims from several Latin American nations. An older man in a knit crimson-and-gold Loyola cap and bright green jacket carries the cross of the "martyr and prophet" Archbishop Oscar Romero of El Salvador.

Father Roy's words echo in the air as he takes his place at the head of the march: "Let the solemn funeral procession begin." Bourgeois is in the first group of protesters holding crosses. They walk a few paces behind eight black-cloaked mourners carrying eight symbolic coffins, honoring the murdered Jesuit priests and the two other victims from November 1989. As the people march slowly, names of hundreds of victims are recited reverently and alternately by a man and woman on stage. The names are chanted, and after each name all those gathered on the stage and thousands in the procession say in unison: *"Presente."*

The dead are not forgotten; they are present in the loving memory of all those gathered today. As the Indigo Girls (Georgia natives) sing on stage, the giant SOAW speakers drown out an Army officer with a bullhorn on the other side of the fence. He warns protesters about the consequences of crossing over onto the grounds of Fort Benning ("a violation of federal property").

When the lines of people reach the fence, some pause to pray; some kneel; others sit on the street or nearby grass. Most stick their white wooden crosses (and a random Star of David) into the chain-link and barbed wire fence, transforming a manmade barrier into a temporary shrine. *¡Presente!*

Father Roy Bourgeois is proud of his congregation today. He speaks of the grace that has blessed his ministry for more than a decade. He prays that this year his efforts and those of so many will be successful. He recalls the journey that started so humbly here a dozen years ago.

* * *

> Truth never damages a cause that is just.
>
> —MOHANDAS (MAHATMA) K. GANDHI

Father Roy Bourgeois founded SOA Watch in 1990, less than a year after the murder of six Jesuit priests, their housekeeper, and her daughter by Salvadoran soldiers on the grounds of Central American University in El Salvador. Investigations into the killings revealed that several of the soldiers involved in the incident had been trained in the United States on the grounds of Fort Benning at an institution called the School of the Americas (SOA).

The school, a combat training facility where soldiers learned commando and counter-insurgency tactics, counter-narcotics operations, mine warfare, and military intelligence, was a vestige of the Cold War. It had been started in 1946 in Panama to train Latin American military to halt the spread of communism. In 1984 it was moved to Fort Benning as part of the Panama Canal Treaties.

During its almost sixty-year history, the SOA has trained an estimated sixty thousand Latin American soldiers at a cost to U.S. taxpayers in the hundreds of millions of dollars. But the financial implications pale in comparison to the human toll associated with the School of the Americas during several bloody decades. Graduates of the SOA program have been linked to kidnappings, torture, murders, massacres, and other atrocities and human rights violations in their native countries, including El Salvador, Nicaragua, Guatemala, Colombia, and Bolivia.

In addition to the Jesuit priest murders in 1989, Latin American soldiers and their commanding officers trained at the SOA were tied to two highly publicized crimes in El Salvador in 1980: the assassination of Archbishop Oscar Romero as he was celebrating Mass and the rape and murder of four U.S. churchwomen. The deaths of nine hundred civilians in the Salvadoran village of El Mozote were also allegedly committed by many SOA-trained officers. Death squad leaders, such as Roberto D'Aubisson, and dictators, including Manuel Noriega, have been trained at the SOA.

In a National Public Radio broadcast on March 24, 2000, on the twenti-eth anniversary of the death of Archbishop Romero, Robert White, former U.S. ambassador to El Salvador and Paraguay, and today president of the Center for International Policy in Washington, D.C., spoke about the unholy alliance between the U.S. and Latin American military: "And it was the American trained military units, such as the Atlacetl Battalion, that compiled the worst human rights records, wiping out entire villages and then denying their responsibility with the help of U.S. officials."

In January 2001, the SOA was replaced by the Western Hemisphere Institute for Security Cooperation (WHINSEC). Same operation, same location, same mission, basically just a name change—courtesy of a De-partment of Defense proposal, following a failed Congressional effort to close the SOA and conduct an investigation. Bourgeois was unimpressed by the name change and the claims of a new and revised curriculum at the former SOA. "This is still a combat school to provide the muscle to protect the economic interests of America's corporations."

While the Pentagon has issued denials of accusations by critics such as Father Roy Bourgeois and has called the SOA an instrument of democracy, organizations such as Amnesty International (AI) have begged to differ. In a 2002 publication, *Unmatched Power, Unmet Principles,* Amnesty Interna-tional USA described the work of Bourgeois and SOA Watch as "an effec-tive reform movement," while calling on the U.S. government to:

- Investigate and suspend the School of the Americas/WHINSEC and introduce strong human rights safeguards in all U.S. military, security, and police training schools (an estimated 275 of which exist in the U.S. today, training some 100,000 foreign police and soldiers).
- Take immediate steps to establish an independent commission to inves-tigate the past activities of SOA and its graduates, particularly the use of "these manuals" in SOA training and the impact of such training.

  [Note: In September 1996, after years of lobbying by SOA Watch and other grassroots and religious organizations, the Pentagon declassi-fied a report revealing that several training manuals had been used at the SOA during the 1980s that had advocated blackmail, beatings, torture, false imprisonment, executions, and payment of bounties for enemy dead.]

- Pending the publication of the findings of the above-mentioned inde-pendent commission of inquiry, training at the WHINSEC-SOA should be suspended.

Bourgeois says SOAW waited three years for the AI report. He is buoyed by the stern language of the report and an accompanying letter that describes "serious human rights consequences" of U.S. training programs of foreign military and police, which is "consistent with much of what SOAW has boldly proclaimed for years."

"This report will help us tremendously in our legislative lobbying," Bourgeois adds, reflecting on upcoming meetings in Washington, D.C.

Father Roy often repeats a phrase that could be the mantra for SOAW: "They cannot silence the truth." Arrests and prison sentences certainly haven't silenced the movement. Bourgeois has served four federal prison sentences, totaling forty-four months, many in solitary confinement.

By late 2002, more than one hundred "prisoners of conscience" (ranging in age from eighteen to the late eighties) had joined Father Roy. These men and women had served a combined fifty-plus years of jail sentences at federal institutions across the United States. More than two dozen were in prison as of November 2002. Their crime? Trespassing onto the grounds of Fort Benning and symbolic acts of civil disobedience. Their penalty for this misdemeanor? Typically six months in prison and a $5,000 fine.

"The closer we get, the meaner they get. They're always looking for ways to intimidate us, to try to clamp down on any kind of protest. They haven't learned that we can take it. Anything they dish out, we can handle," says Bourgeois, a self-described stubborn Cajun. Bourgeois also points out that each time a SOAW supporter is sent to prison, it helps to energize the movement by attracting more supporters and generating coverage in both hometown papers and national media. He estimates that during his four prison sentences, he has probably participated in more than fifty major media interviews, educating countless Americans on the cause.

Newsweek magazine dedicated two pages in its August 9, 1993, issue to the School of the Americas. The article by Douglas Waller examined SOA's human rights record and the government's rationale for its continued operation. Waller wrote that SOA's graduates "include some of the region's most despicable military strongmen." He described murders and human-rights violations that could be traced to Latin American military who had received training at the school; one such report charged violations by 246 Colombian officers, 105 of whom were SOA alumni.

In response to such accusations, Waller quoted then SOA commandant Colonel Jose Alvarez, who asked if the Wharton School had taken the blame for one of its notorious graduates, Michael Milken? Alvarez later remarked, "What this school does is give you a seat at the table with the armies of Latin America." Perhaps the most compelling excerpt from the feature story was the question posed by Waller: "But can a year at Fort Benning make Jeffersonian democrats out of Latin American soldiers, many of whom have been accustomed since childhood to view priests and social workers as subversives?"

The Washington Post has run extensive articles on the School of the Americas and Father Roy Bourgeois's campaign to shut it down. A front-page story by Dana Priest on September 21, 1996, reported the existence of the U.S. Army intelligence manuals used from 1982 to 1991 at the SOA that advocated executions, torture, blackmail, and other forms of coercion against insurgents. On November 29, 1998, Peter Carlson wrote an in-depth profile of Father Roy Bourgeois ("The Priest Who Waged a War"). The article quoted then Rep. Joseph P. Kennedy II (D-Mass.): "Father Roy is one of the most decent, committed individuals I've ever met. . . . He's a solid individual with a great sense of humor, a great smile, and a sense of perspective about himself. And deep down, he's a rock of integrity." Carlson noted that on September 18, 1998, the day Bourgeois was released from his fourth federal prison sentence, congressional critics came within eleven votes of cutting off funds for the school; the bill was sponsored by Rep. Kennedy.

The New York Times's lead editorial ("School of the Dictators") on September 28, 1996, concluded: "An institution so clearly out of tune with American values and so stubbornly immune to reform should be shut down without further delay." A *Chicago Tribune* editorial ("Lights out at School of the Americas") on April 16, 1999, listed a number of arguments for shutting down the school. "Most of Latin America has entered an era of peace and civilian rule. . . . Closing the book on the School of the Americas would be an important endorsement by the U.S. of such hopeful developments."

The *Los Angeles Times* wrote in its editorial ("Bury This Relic") on May 21, 1999: "The program also aimed to instill democratic values in rising military officers. In many cases, that's not the way it worked out. . . . The time has come to remove this Cold War relic and pass a bill by Rep. John Joseph Moakley (D-Mass.) and more than 100 co-sponsors to direct the secretary of the Army to shut down this school." However, despite the support of major media and elected officials, Father Roy and SOAW have come up just short of needed votes in Congress to close the WHINSEC-SOA.

Over the years, the SOAW movement has garnered some of its most impressive support from decorated war veterans. Charlie Liteky received the Congressional Medal of Honor in 1968 for his valor under fire as a chaplain in Vietnam who rescued more than twenty soldiers. He has been an activist blood brother with Father Roy since 1990. Like Bourgeois, Liteky has served multiple prison terms for the courage of his convictions. Retired Major Joseph Blair, a twenty-year Army veteran, was also decorated for his service in the Vietnam War. Blair is a powerful SOAW ally because of his former connection to the School of the Americas. From 1986 to 1989 Blair served as an instructor at the SOA.

In a 1998 video, funded by the Veterans for Peace, Inc., Minnesota chapter, Blair explains his indictment of the combat training school:

> I became an outspoken critic of the School of the Americas when I began reading in local newspapers repeated denials that the United States Army and the School of the Americas knew anything about the atrocities and murders that the graduates of the School of the Americas were committing in Latin America.
>
> The continued existence of the Army's School of the Americas serves one single purpose and that is to sustain and promote a wealthy, elite ruling class as the dominant players in their own countries, in control of their social structure, their economies, and their international relations. The masses of people essentially live in poverty.

* * *

> Blessed is he that considereth the poor: the Lord
> will deliver him in time of trouble.
>
> —Psalm 41:1 (KJV)

Father Roy Bourgeois has seen firsthand the plight of the Latin American poor and suffering. His first assignment after being ordained a Catholic priest in the Maryknoll Order in 1972 was a barrio outside La Paz, Bolivia. For the next five years, this slum was his home. He lived in a small room without running water and with only a hotplate to cook his meals. He said Mass in a vacant lot. But he was happy; his life had meaning. He helped establish a medical clinic, a day-care center, and a community center for the poor of La Paz, who had become his teachers.

In a 2002 publication, *From Warriors to Resisters,* containing profiles of Bourgeois and other veterans-turned-activists, Father Roy recalled lessons learned as a young priest in Latin America:

> Bolivia's poor taught me about the human condition of suffering. The majority of the people don't receive a just wage for their labor—and they struggle for survival. They live in shacks without running water. They don't have schools for their children, and when they get sick there are no medicines to heal them. In short, the poor of Latin America die before their time. They are hungry for food—and they are hungry for justice.

Bourgeois also experienced the bravery of the poor who were organizing and speaking out for more equitable distribution of wealth and resources. He had learned of Latin America's liberation theology in the Maryknoll Seminary when he read the works of Gustavo Gutierrez, an indigenous Peruvian activist, and Paulo Freire, a Brazilian advocate for the poor and author of *Pedagogy of the Oppressed*. Gutierrez and Freire helped teach the poor to form a critical consciousness and become agents of change. Such advocacy was dangerous in countries where education for all but the elite is seen as subversive.

In Bolivia, Bourgeois began visiting political prisoners who had been jailed for their outspoken views. He met with tin miners, factory workers, university students and their professors, and he learned of their mistreatment. He was arrested along with other church leaders and people of faith who were trying to bring about human rights reform. Upon his release he notified officials in the United States about conditions in Bolivia. To this day he believes that such correspondence resulted in his subsequent interrogation by members of the Bolivian military, death threats, and deportation with his passport stamped "persona non grata."

He would never be allowed to return to Bolivia. He would also never allow himself to return to a once held worldview of capitalism, democracy, and U.S. foreign policy.

* * *

Growing up in a small town in the bayous of Louisiana,
I was taught to be patriotic.

—Roy Bourgeois, quoted in *From Warriors to Resisters*

Bourgeois's journey to the priesthood and social activism began under very secular circumstances. He was born in 1938 and raised in the bayou country of southern Louisiana in the Mississippi River town of Lutcher (est. four thousand population). As a boy in a close-knit, blue-collar family (the second of four children), Roy enjoyed playing all sports, hunting for rabbits and doves, and fishing for bass. He was raised Catholic, but his aspirations weren't church-directed. He planned on getting married, raising a family, and getting rich in the oil business. In 1962 he graduated from the University of Southwestern Louisiana with a bachelor's in geology. But his ambitions were put on hold by the Vietnam War.

Like many Americans with conservative, patriotic roots, Bourgeois believed it was his duty to enter the military and fight the spread of communism. He was a U.S. Navy officer for four years. ("My ticket out of

Louisiana.") After two years at sea, bachelor Roy enjoyed the good life when stationed for a year in Athens, Greece. In 1965 he volunteered for shore duty in Vietnam. He received special (survival) training, but that didn't prepare him for "the kind of violence, the kind of poverty" he would experience in a country wracked by war.

Bourgeois saw his friends die, and he was wounded by shrapnel when his officers' barracks in Saigon was bombed. Fourteen men died. Bourgeois received the Purple Heart. While recuperating from his wounds, Bourgeois began to reexamine his beliefs, his values, and his faith. His positive spirit, which had fueled his drive throughout his life, was challenged. He wondered about his future. Should he go to graduate school? Should he make a career out of the military?

Then in 1966, with five months to go on his tour of duty, Roy Bourgeois met a Canadian missionary from Quebec named Father Lucien Olivier at a Mass in Saigon. Father Olivier talked about his nearby orphanage for some three hundred Vietnamese children, many of whom had been wounded by American bombs and napalm. He invited Bourgeois to make a visit. The visit would transform the naval officer's life.

"I fell in love with these kids," Bourgeois recalls in a lilting voice. He started getting his buddies to volunteer at the orphanage when off-duty. He brought supplies and clothing from the base. He asked his family back home to send donations. Father Olivier became a saintly role model. "He was a healer, a peacemaker trying to heal the suffering of others," Bourgeois says. "He was doing what Jesus intended us to do."

Before Bourgeois left Vietnam, he had decided to become a priest. His chaplain recommended the Maryknoll Order: They're the Marines of the Catholic Church. They work with the poorest of the poor. The "macho" Bourgeois was intrigued. He had no interest in being a conventional priest, working in a parish, and serving "spiritual lollipops" to people.

He visited a group of Maryknoll clergy in Hong Kong while on R&R, and that convinced him. He returned to the United States in late 1966 and spent a month with his family, fishing, jogging on the levee, and relaxing. Then he entered the seminary of the Maryknoll Missionary Order.

He spent a year in the Chicago area, where he studied philosophy and religion, worked in poor neighborhoods, and met community organizers and activists such as Saul Alinsky and Monsignor John Egan. Bourgeois was becoming more enlightened, but his liberal protest days were still years away. In fact he boycotted an appearance by Jesuit priest Daniel Berrigan, a prominent anti–Vietnam War critic. As Bourgeois recalls: "It wasn't that simple for me. I was against the violence (of Vietnam), but what about friends who had given their lives for a cause they believed in?"

In 1969 Bourgeois joined in his first antiwar protest. He traveled to Washington, D.C., and marched with Vietnam War veterans outside the White House. He would later return his Purple Heart along with other veterans who were trying to awaken the American conscience with their words and symbolic gestures.

In 1972 Roy Bourgeois was ordained a Catholic priest. He was sent to Bolivia. As had occurred in Vietnam, Bourgeois would be transformed by his experiences, working for five years with the "poor and suffering of Latin America." Upon his return to the United States, Father Roy Bourgeois became involved in several activist causes, including the nuclear arms race, the international peace movement, and antipoverty programs. He moved into a Catholic Worker house in Chicago and worked in the soup kitchen and provided other services to inner-city poor.

He participated in a weeklong protest at the Pentagon as part of the Jonah House's yearlong presence. (The Jonah House had been established by Phil Berrigan, Daniel's brother, Liz McAllister, and other peacemakers.) Bourgeois traveled across the country, giving talks on campuses and to church groups about the nuclear arms race, military spending, and their relationship to acts of repression in Latin America.

When Archbishop Romero and the four U.S. churchwomen (two of whom were Maryknoll nuns and friends of Bourgeois) were murdered in 1980, Father Roy became intimately involved in events unfolding in El Salvador. He went to the country as a translator for a TV crew. Then, as recounted in the November 29, 1998, article in *The Washington Post*, Bourgeois became "radicalized." He discovered that many of the victims of the Salvadoran death squads were clergy and laity who were embracing liberation theology, the egalitarian Christian movement that Bourgeois had read about in the seminary. But now he was on the frontlines. He toured the country interviewing witnesses to the atrocities. According to the article, "In April 1981 he hiked into the mountains controlled by leftist guerillas, leaving behind a letter saying, 'I have decided to join the poor of El Salvador in their struggle,' though adding, 'I personally will not and cannot bear arms.'"

Despite fears for his life, Father Roy returned two weeks later. He denounced the U.S. support of the Salvadoran military junta. His outspoken views had put him in harm's way. U.S. embassy officials informed him that he was now a target of death squads. He returned to Chicago, where he continued speaking out against the repressive regime in El Salvador. He also criticized the Catholic Church's reticence in addressing the conditions in Latin America. Years later his railings against the Church hierarchy would continue unabated: "Many bishops today are like corporate executives . . . cheerleaders for Caesar. We've gone wrong someplace. We've watered down the (social gospel) message of Jesus."

In 1982–83 Bourgeois channeled his activism into a yearlong project of writing and producing a documentary on the nuclear arms race for Maryknoll World Productions. The film, *Gods of Metal*, was nominated for an Academy Award. After completing work on the documentary in New York City, Bourgeois read a short newspaper article about 525 Salvadoran soldiers receiving combat training at Fort Benning. He received permission from the Maryknoll Order to move to Columbus, Georgia, to speak out about the presence of Latin American troops at Fort Benning. After months of community organizing and an aggressive public information campaign, Father Roy decided to take his message directly to the Salvadoran troops. Once again he was making a life-altering decision to do what he believed was right.

* * *

> And they shall beat their swords into plowshares, and their spears into pruning hooks: nation shall not lift up sword against nation, neither shall they learn war anymore.
>
> —Isaiah 2:4 (KJV)

Seven years before he founded SOA Watch, Father Roy Bourgeois committed his boldest act of nonviolent civil disobedience. In late 1983, Bourgeois, Larry Rosebaugh, an Oblate priest who had worked in Brazil, and U.S. Army reservist Linda Ventimiglia dressed as high-ranking military officers and entered Fort Benning late at night. They had a large boom box, a tape of the last sermon Archbishop Romero gave before being gunned down, and tree climbers. They worked their way high up on a Georgia pine tree, adjacent to the barracks housing the Salvadoran troops. They waited until all was quiet; then Romero's words awakened the nearby soldiers: "In the name of God, in the name of the suffering people whose laments rise to the heaven each day more tumultuous, I beg you, I ask you, I order you, in the name of God, stop the repression."

Mike Wilson, author of the 2002 Bourgeois biography, *The Warrior Priest,* describes what happened next as the words of Romero cut through the night air:

> The Salvadoran soldiers ran out of the barracks, looking up at the sky toward the voice. They probably knew Bishop Romero's voice and were frightened. They couldn't see Father Roy and his friends because it was dark, but the soldiers started shooting toward the voice, trying to shoot

down whoever it was. Within minutes sirens sounded in the distance and armed military police and instructors with dogs arrived in jeeps and trucks. They ordered Father Roy and his friends down from the tree, saying they would be shot if they refused. They handcuffed the three protesters, put them on the ground and, according to Father Roy, kicked them and strip-searched them. Then the three were brought in for questioning and the FBI was called. They were charged with criminal trespass and with impersonating U.S. Army officers.

The case was heard by federal judge J. Robert Elliott, described in the July/August 1983 issue of *The American Lawyer* magazine as "an old-line segregationist who flaunts his deep-rooted prejudices against blacks, unions, and criminal defendants." In 1974 Elliott had reversed the court-martial conviction of Lt. William Calley, who had been jailed for his role in the My Lai massacre. (The article notes, "One year later, the Fifth Circuit court found Judge Elliott in error on all grounds and ordered Calley back to prison.")

Bourgeois was sentenced to eighteen months in prison by the judge he called "Maximum Bob." His first stop was the prison in Terre Haute, Indiana (where Timothy McVeigh served his final days). Once there, Bourgeois spent forty-five days in solitary confinement for refusing a work order. The long days (twenty-three out of twenty-four hours in isolation) took their toll on Father Roy. He began to doubt whether his activism had accomplished anything. He spent many "dark nights of the soul" being tested in his seclusion.

To cope with the depressing conditions, Bourgeois read voraciously—the writings of Trappist monk Thomas Merton, the meditations of the "desert fathers" from the third and fourth centuries A.D., and passages by the cofounder of the Catholic Worker Movement, Dorothy Day. Bourgeois found special solace in Day's reflections. She said not to worry about how effective you are. Worry about how faithful you are, and be faithful to what you know in your heart is true. As he read those words, he began to feel a burden being lifted. "It was a moment of grace and insight," he says. "I now felt free. I felt God's presence. I felt freer than I had ever felt."

Bourgeois asked the warden if he could spend his remaining seventeen months in solitary confinement. The warden refused, and Bourgeois was transferred to a federal prison in Sandstone, Minnesota, where he served the remainder of his sentence teaching English as a Second Language (ESL) classes to Hispanic inmates.

Upon his release from prison, Bourgeois moved to a Trappist monastery in Conyers, Georgia. He spent five months living as a contemplative with other monks. He found healing in the monastery, but he also discovered that he wasn't called to be a full-time monk. However, he realized the need to integrate solitude and reflection with his active life of working for peace and justice. In the years to come, Bourgeois would make regular retreats to the Trappist monastery.

In spring 1990 Father Roy, with the support of the Maryknoll Order, returned to Columbus, Georgia, and rented a small one-bedroom apartment, a football toss away from the main gates of Fort Benning. Bourgeois had come back after learning of the November 1989 murders of the six Jesuit priests, their housekeeper, and her daughter in El Salvador. What had triggered his return was the report of a U.S. congressional task force that had investigated the killings and confirmed that several of those responsible had been trained at the School of the Americas. Bourgeois moved steadily to establish the School of the Americas Watch organization, headquartered in his apartment.

Friends and supporters arrived. In September 1990, joined by Charlie Liteky, his brother Patrick, Kathy Kelly (who would later cofound Voices in the Wilderness), and others, Bourgeois camped at the main gate of Fort Benning and went on a water-only fast for thirty-five days. A total of ten people participated in the fast, including Vietnam veterans, clergy, and a schoolteacher. After the fast, Bourgeois and his colleagues used the Freedom of Information Act to begin researching human rights reports and other documentation to examine the role of SOA graduates in crimes in countries such as El Salvador, Nicaragua, Colombia, Bolivia, and Guatemala.

On the first anniversary of the Jesuit priest murders, Bourgeois and the Liteky brothers decided to take further action against the School of the Americas. They poured vials of their own blood on the SOA headquarters sign and on photographs that lined the walls of the school. Once again Judge "Maximum Bob" Elliott sentenced Father Roy. This time the sentence was fourteen months in a federal prison.

During the 1990s Bourgeois would receive two more prison sentences of six months each for "crossing the line" onto Fort Benning property during the SOAW November vigils. There would also be lengthy fasts and protests at the Capitol in Washington, D.C. The SOAW struggle for social justice would gather significant momentum thanks to media attention, legislative support, a growing national organization (now including a Washington, D.C., office), and Bourgeois's charisma and the message that he brought to audiences across the country.

One measure of the success of the SOAW message was the increasing size of the annual protests at Fort Benning. Within a couple years of the initial ten-person fast and protest in 1990, hundreds came to Columbus, Georgia. By 1997, an estimated 2,000 protesters arrived, and 601 were arrested for marching onto the base. Among those sent to prison for the 1997 protests were: Reverend Nicholas Cardell, 72, a Unitarian minister and World War II veteran who had fought in the Battle of the Bulge and had served time in a German POW camp; Carol Richardson, 53, a United Methodist pastor and mother of two teenagers; Father Bill Bichsel, 69, a Jesuit priest from Tacoma, Washington, and former dean of students at Gonzaga University; Sister Rita Steinhagen, 70, a medical technologist and Sister of St. Joseph who worked with the homeless in Minneapolis; and Father Roy Bourgeois, 59, founder and codirector of SOAW.

In his fourth prison sentence, Bourgeois was again sent to solitary confinement for refusing to work. He spoke publicly about using this time to think, pray, and study. "I hope this will purify my heart and bring me closer to God." Privately, he wondered (as he confided to friends in letters) whether his ego rather than God's love was motivating his actions. Was he on a power trip? Was he acting out of arrogance, or for other selfish reasons? As time passed, he found solace and renewed hope. He was convinced now more than ever that, as St. James wrote in the Bible, he had to integrate his faith with actions. He had to keep "walking the walk" and continue to inspire others to do the same (*The Warrior Priest*).

In mid-November 1998, a couple thousand more people came to the gates of Fort Benning, including actor-activist Martin Sheen. (Sheen would return again in 1999 and march with Daniel Berrigan.) On "Vigil Sunday" more than 2,300 protesters "crossed the line"—too many for the military police to process, so the demonstrators were turned loose. In November 2000 the media reported that more than 6,000 people attended the vigil. In 2001, SOAW estimated that more than 10,000 were part of the solidarity effort. The number of protesters who crossed the line onto base property was down from previous years, due largely to the long, high fence that was erected at the entrance to the military reservation.

What hadn't changed over the years was the resolve of a committed cadre of people, led by Father Roy, who were determined to protest until the School of the Americas, under whatever name it was called, was closed for good. "A few years ago, we began to realize," Bourgeois says, "that this [movement] was bigger than the school and closing it down. The school has simply become a symbol in a way of U.S. foreign policy."

* * *

In every country where man is free to think and to speak,
differences of opinion will arise from differences of perception,
and the perfection of reason.

—THOMAS JEFFERSON, 1801

On Wednesday night, November 6, 2002, about four hundred of the good people of Columbus, Georgia, came to hear a debate between Father Roy Bourgeois and Colonel Richard Downie, commandant of the Western Hemisphere Institute for Security Cooperation (WHINSEC). According to the November 7 issue of the *Columbus* (Georgia) *Ledger-Enquirer* newspaper: "Bourgeois found himself in a lion's den of cordial opposition. . . . Columbus and Fort Benning residents lined up to ask Bourgeois: Why doesn't the group take its 'offensive' protest to Washington, D.C., and leave Fort Benning alone?"

Newspaper staff writer S. Thorne Harper observed that Father Roy remained composed. He explained to the crowd, "Civil disobedience is a difficult thing to understand." (Bourgeois had said much the same thing to his parents, Roy Sr. and Grace, and siblings years earlier when they had questioned his actions and the resultant prison sentences.) Bourgeois clarified: "We're not trying to shut down Fort Benning. We're trying to shut down this school that's causing shame to our country and bringing death to Latin America."

Colonel Downie, a twenty-six-year Army veteran and West Point graduate who holds a doctorate in international relations, was welcomed warmly, at one point receiving a standing ovation. He said that the institute had placed greater emphasis on human rights training and that it was instrumental in providing "inter-agency operations," while establishing vital military contacts. "You will hear Rev. Bourgeois say that the military and police can't teach democracy," Downie said. "I disagree. Who better to teach those things? What better role model can you think of other than our police and military?"

Bourgeois and Downie would square off a few days later over breakfast at a local family restaurant, Ruth Ann's, in downtown Columbus. They would be joined by Major General Paul Eaton, commanding general of Fort Benning, Eaton's wife, and the SOAW communications director, Matthew Smucker. The breakfast meeting was Downie and Eaton's idea.

"It was a good opportunity to meet and do a little intelligence gathering," Bourgeois recalls. "I believe in dialogue, in meeting face-to-face, in sharing a meal." The pleasantries lasted a while. Then, according to Bourgeois, Major General Eaton expressed his concern over the potential for violence at the 2002 annual vigil. Bourgeois instinctively chuckled. He briefly explained the tradition of nonviolence surrounding the peaceful protests at Fort Benning. Then Father Roy said that he was a little taken aback by the general's concern. He said that if he were really concerned about violence, he would look at what was going on at the school and its graduates.

Bourgeois's comments went over about as well as several cups of cold coffee on an empty stomach. Downie tried to shift the conversation. He said his task was to reform the school. Bourgeois countered that his task was to shut the school down. The breakfast gathering ended after less than an hour. Days later, reflecting on the meeting, Bourgeois wondered aloud a question he has asked so many times before: "How can you teach democracy through the barrel of a gun?"

Not long after the breakfast meeting, Bourgeois was notified by the Columbus Police Department of its intent to set up check points on Fort Benning Drive and to search all individuals at the Saturday and Sunday SOAW events with handheld metal detectors (magnetometers). The rationale was to protect public safety and the protesters from "provocateurs." On Wednesday, November 13, SOAW and the ACLU replied by filing an injunction lawsuit and a motion for a temporary restraining order in federal court against the mayor and police chief. Bourgeois and the other SOAW plaintiffs said their First (e.g., freedom of assembly and speech) and Fourth (e.g., freedom from unreasonable searches) Amendment rights were at stake if "unprecedented mass searches" were carried out.

On a pleasant, sunny Thursday afternoon, November 14, as Bourgeois busies himself with arrangements and greets early arrivals outside his apartment, he receives a phone call from attorney Bill Quigley. "We're going to trial," Father Roy says matter-of-factly as head of an organization that has spent much of its history in the courtroom. "Tomorrow (Friday) at one o'clock." He refuses to be deterred about the trial or any obstacles in the way. "This is a marathon; we're in this for the long haul."

That evening, Bourgeois drives his tidy mid-1990s white Ford Escort to Lee's Golden China restaurant, where he will have dinner with several of the prisoners of conscience from years past. These are people who have served time in prison for their civil disobedience and for their "realizations connected to justice and to confronting violence that many came to late in their lives," according to Bourgeois.

Father Roy's mood brightens when he greets the twenty-plus folks in the buffet-style restaurant. The group is a mix of retirees, middle-agers, and college-student protesters. "The people here think this is just a nice reunion," says Bourgeois, breaking into an infectious grin. "They don't know we're a bunch of ex-cons."

Dinner talk includes reminiscence, discussion of plans for the days ahead, and hope for the future of the movement. Those here believe the activist spirit is alive and in good hands with the younger generation. Bourgeois and others are encouraged by the connections the young activists are making between foreign policy, military action, and globalization.

On Friday night Father Roy's faith in the young is rewarded a thousand-fold by busloads of enthusiastic Catholic students from universities across the country at the Jesuit tent on the banks of the Chattahoochee River. Students from Notre Dame, Marquette, Gonzaga, Boston College, Loyola, University of Dayton, Ursuline College, and others have packed the seats under the large white tent in downtown Columbus, Georgia. Bourgeois takes the stage at about 7:30 P.M. and speaks extemporaneously for fifteen minutes about the mission of SOAW.

His words warm the crowd: "What an honor and joy to welcome you. Your presence is such a blessing for us. You bring us a lot of hope. Thank you." Thunderous applause greets Father Roy as he steps from the podium. It's hard to imagine even Martin Sheen getting a better reception.

Bourgeois seemed to draw a little extra satisfaction from the warm reception. Just a couple hours earlier he got the news of U.S. district judge Clay Land's decision allowing the city of Columbus to proceed with the magnetometer searches of people attending the SOAW vigil. The trial lasted four hours. The most engaging part of the testimony came from a police officer who voiced his concern over the potential for "frenzy" at the SOAW gathering. He cited last year's event when four women bared their breasts. Such actions, he indicated, could incite dangerous crowd behavior. In his decision the judge didn't refer to topless women, but he noted the conflict between the compelling government interest in public safety and individual rights. He denied the SOAW motion and dismissed the case.

Someone browsing an article in the *Columbus Ledger-Enquirer* on Saturday morning (November 16) in the local Denny's, where SOAW demonstrators outnumbered the locals by at least twelve to one, might have been struck by the irony of The Associated Press story. Dateline BOGOTA, Colombia—"Colombian army troops *rescued* one of Latin American's [*sic*] leading Roman Catholic bishops and another priest Friday after a gunbattle with their rebel captors in an Andean mountain region." Latin American soldiers rescuing clergy? One wonders if this good news will be on the agenda at the SOAW protest today.

Father Roy doesn't mention that news story in today's paper. He refers to the headline on page one: "Search On. Judge Dismisses SOA Watch Claims."

"It's disappointing, but it's going to be OK," Bourgeois says as a chilling rain falls on the Saturday crowd. He wears a red poncho and a blue-and-white Maryknoll World Productions cap. He seems to be constantly surrounded by friends and admirers. Two of these are an engaging older couple: Bob and Tess Koenig from Los Angeles. He is eighty, a retired Los Angeles firefighter and a World War II veteran. She is in her late seventies, and she too served in World War II, in the Army Nurse Corps. Bob has a salt-and-pepper beard and matching ponytail. He is about six feet tall, walks with military bearing, and offers a firm handshake and a hearty laugh. Tess is a shade over five feet, with lively bespectacled eyes and a bright smile. They first heard Bourgeois speak in the mid-1980s. At that time they were actively involved in the Los Angeles Catholic Worker organization. Later, they heard of Father Roy's thirty-five-day fast in 1990. By then they had started their years of nonviolent protests that would include demonstrations against the U.S.-sponsored Contra War in Nicaragua, the actions of the death squads in El Salvador, the Panama invasion, the Gulf War, the Weapons in Space program, and the U.S. invasion of Afghanistan. They have been coming to Columbus, Georgia, to support the closing of the School of the Americas since 1993. They will keep coming until it is closed. They say they owe that to Father Roy, who has empowered so many people.

The Saturday gathering is titled "A Celebration of Hope and Commitment." From 11 A.M. until 5 P.M., more than thirty speakers, musical acts, demonstrations, and festivities are presented to an appreciative crowd of some four thousand (as estimated by police) on rainy Fort Benning Drive. The processing of people with magnetometers has gone smoothly, with few complaints, though one man was arrested for refusing to submit to what he deemed an unconstitutional search.

The day's events range from the serious (speakers from groups such as Prisoners of Conscience, Torture Abolition and Survivors Support Coalition, United Students Against Sweatshops) to the arguably silly (samba bands, a walking Statue of Liberty on stilts, hundreds of colorfully dressed drywall "mud" bucket drummers, and flag carriers with Grateful Dead smiles, accompanying giant yellow, red, and blue puppets). Several organizations have information tables, and their members carry signs and banners: Mennonites for Peace, Voices in the Wilderness, Episcopal Peace Fellowship, Baptist Peace Fellowship, Franciscans for Peace and Justice. Vendors promote their causes and hawk books, CDs, and T-shirts (most original: "Agitated, Agitator, Agitating"). The smell of hamburgers, hot dogs, and steaming coffee fills the air. The day has the look and feel of a big street fair.

But the police presence is very evident, from the endless line of orange and white barrels and wooden barricades to the miles of yellow "Don't Cross" police tape. Handfuls of Army Rangers mingle with the crowd, along with city police and county sheriff deputies. The most intimidating sight is the cream-colored "Sky Watch" lift anchored in the parking lot of the K. W. Tailor Shop, adjacent to Father Roy's apartment building. The black-tinted windows have an eagle's nest view of the proceedings today and tomorrow. Veterans of the annual protest here at Fort Benning say there is likely a police sniper in the lift.

On this day before the vigil, Father Roy speaks solemnly when needed and laughs and dances on stage when the spirit moves him. He waves to his younger brother and sister, Dan and Ann, who have been coming to Fort Benning now for years to show solidarity for their brother. He hugs old and new friends, smiles and poses for enough pictures to fill plenty of activist scrapbooks. At day's end, the mood of the crowd isn't dampened by the rain that falls with the temperature. A long night awaits Bourgeois: a Mass at the Jesuit tent by the river, orientation and logistics sessions, affinity group meetings, and a benefit concert. He has to decide what to attend and for how long. Others on this night are deciding whether to "cross the line" tomorrow and risk arrest and imprisonment.

* * *

Our greatest enemy is ignorance. Our sword must be wisdom.

—Buddhist monk to Father Roy Bourgeois
on his return to Vietnam, summer 2001

"Daddy, don't go to the white line," says a little girl riding on her father's shoulders Sunday morning near the gates of Fort Benning.

At 11:45 A.M. cheers go up as the first protesters have made it through or around the fence onto the fort's property. A few minutes later, the cheering increases as small groups of people are seen in the distance scurrying up the grassy knolls and waving back to the protesters on the other side of the fence. By 12:30 P.M., Gerry Waite, an anthropology instructor from Ball State University and former U.S. Army enlistee, Vietnam veteran, and frequent SOAW event attendee, reports that "the MP bus has made several trips down the road; so there must be a lot of protesters crossing the line."

At 1 P.M. Father Roy hugs his family goodbye in the small parking lot near his apartment. He will see them soon back in Lutcher, Louisiana, during the holidays. Then Bourgeois resumes his position behind the stage and watches the procession of people that flows past the gates of Fort Benning. His hands are clasped in front of him. He acknowledges people with a smile and a nod of his head as the names of victims continue to be announced. *Presente.*

The autumn wind rustles the leaves in the many trees on the beautiful Fort Benning grounds. The wind also causes the fort's large American flag to wave. No one in the crowd is seen saluting this blue-sky flag today, but it still waves proudly as so many on the ground voice their democratic right to dissent.

SOAW staffers Eric LeCompte and Jeff Winder are on stage to report on those who have crossed the line. Among the first to be arrested today were five nuns, one of whom called on her cell phone. Eric and Jeff work the crowd, guiding people to the "Follow Me" signs that show where they can get through the fence onto the fort property.

"We've had fifteen or sixteen waves of people cross over."

"Anyone interested in crossing the line, please come to the stage."

"Remember, everyone risks prison who crosses over."

Protesters contemplating the walk onto Fort Benning property have been directed to attend weekend orientation sessions, to talk with SOAW staff or volunteers, and to read the three-by-four-inch "Know Your Rights" card that has been widely distributed in the days leading up to the Sunday Vigil. Still one wonders if, as Bob and Tess Koenig have noted, "Sometimes the crowd makes you do things you normally wouldn't do." They share an anecdote from a recent SOAW protest about a nineteen-year-old college student who got caught up in the excitement of the events, crossed over, and received a prison sentence.

According to Father Roy, Eric LeCompte and Jeff Winder have been tempted to "cross the line" in years' past, but they never made the walk. They were never arrested; nor have they served prison time for acts of civil disobedience at Fort Benning. Bourgeois says they believe they are of greater value to the movement to stay put and to work for social justice at the national SOAW office in Washington, D.C.

"We don't want anyone going off to prison if they haven't worked through the process, unless they're really at peace with it. Unless they feel they've been called," Bourgeois says, discussing the discernment process confronting people who struggle with the weighty decision to commit acts of civil disobedience. "We're not into numbers."

By mid-afternoon on Sunday, November 17, Jeff Winder announces that more than ninety people have "crossed over." This is more than last year. People who have searched their conscience and are prepared to act are still being encouraged to go through or around the fence.

Those in the crowd are also solicited to make a contribution to the cause by putting money in the brown shopping bags being distributed by identified SOAW staffers. The movement's organization is impressive. Hundreds of people with color-coded plastic nametags move freely—SOAW peacekeepers, SOAW advisory group, SOAW speakers, SOAW medics. Several of these SOAW workers chat amiably with police officers and sheriff deputies.

By 3:30 P.M., Father Roy looks relaxed. He is smiling and hugging away. One of his longest hugs comes from a bearded man with a "Veterans for Peace" T-shirt. Another holds a sign, "If you aren't a veteran for peace, what are you a veteran for?"

As the day winds down, older protesters stand and watch, while the high school- and college-age members of the crowd move close to the fence; several sit defiantly on the stone sign at the entrance to Fort Benning. An Atlanta TV crew arrives to film the monument of white crosses wedged into the fence. Earlier another crew captured footage of a young-looking protester who crossed over, turned his back, and peacefully submitted to the plastic handcuffs put on by a military police officer. That action, which will be shown later on *CNN Headline News,* was not witnessed by the large crowd still milling about on the street.

At 4 P.M. Father Roy bounds on stage with renewed resolve. He is beaming as he looks out at the sea of people by the stage and along Fort Benning Drive as shadows lengthen. His voice is strong and clear.

> This wonderful, incredible celebration of hope is now ended for this weekend at the main gate of Fort Benning. We now return to our home communities, our loved ones, our friends, our high schools, our colleges, our workplaces. Let us take this energy, this life, this hope we have experienced over the last two days back to our friends and our communities. Let's hold on to this because it is so important now in the midst of all this violence.
>
> We will be back here next November. We are not going away until this school is shut down! So let us go back now and spread the word, bring back this hope and life that we have experienced here. Bring your friends, your loved ones, your *companeros* and *companeras,* and we will see you at the main gate next November. Thank you. We love you. Thank you.

* * *

> Nowhere can man find a quieter or more untroubled retreat
> than in his own soul.
>
> —MARCUS AURELIUS

On Monday, November 18, a number of SOAW staff and supporters gather for a modest continental breakfast at the Day's Inn on Victory Drive in Columbus, Georgia. The talk is of media coverage (CNN, USA Today, NPR . . .), this morning's arraignments of the ninety-plus who "crossed over," and travel plans ("Who's going to the airport?").

Bob and Tess Koenig are packed and ready to go. They will return to Los Angeles. But they plan to reunite with Father Roy and other SOAW activists in April at the annual protest on the steps of the Capitol. They hope that someday soon they may return to Columbus, Georgia, not for a protest or a vigil, but for a celebration. "When the legislation almost passed in Congress a couple years ago," Tess says, "I thought the SOA would be closed. I remember saying to Father Roy that November, 'I thought this would be the year for our celebration.' He said: 'I did too. Maybe next year.'"

Two weeks later, Father Roy Bourgeois sits in his quiet $240-a-month apartment and reflects on the November 2002 protest and the state of SOAW. When at his desk in the small but clean and well-organized living room/office, he is surrounded by books, stacks of paperwork, and rows of photographs on the walls from past protests in Columbus, Georgia, and Washington, D.C. Behind him are a Latin American cross and a small bookshelf Buddha. In front of him is a bust of Archbishop Oscar Romero. On a facing wall is a large framed drawing of the four churchwomen from El Salvador. Their smiling faces are captured in a timeless image of joy.

"We're at a good moment," Father Roy says, sounding like a man at peace. He speaks of the overwhelming positive feedback he has received from this year's event. He talks of the impact such an event has in peoples' lives. He shares insights into the activist spirit:

> When we come to a rally like the vigil . . . we discover that this brings to our lives a certain amount of hope and joy when we walk in solidarity with others. We start discovering ourselves at a deeper level, and that's how a movement grows.
>
> When we start using our voices for the voiceless, we feel we are doing something for the world. Our lives take on new meaning, greater meaning. We can no longer go back to the person we used to be.

[7]

MARION MALCOLM "JUSTICE FOR ALL SEASONS"

Photo by Mark H. Massé

Marion Malcolm e-mailed her reply to my request for new information eight months after my visit to Oregon: "I don't really feel a need to send updates. There'd be no end to that." She did tell me about the local drama surrounding the renaming of a major thoroughfare to commemorate Dr. Martin Luther King Jr. According to Malcolm, the city council handled the matter "ever so badly," stumbling its way through a drawn-out process, including a reversal of its original decision, before honoring King with a changed street name. Subsequently, Malcolm and other community leaders organized a march and public program on the fortieth anniversary of the famous August 1963 civil rights march on Washington, D.C. On a personal note, Malcolm welcomed another member of the family to labor movement advocacy as her daughter, Bayla, a recent University of Oregon graduate, entered the work force. Bayla joins her father, Stefan, and brother Andrew as union representatives. Mother Marion Malcolm's legacy of social activism appears well secured in the lives of her children.

> Social progress never rolls in on the wheels of inevitability. It comes through the tireless effort and the persistent work of dedicated individuals.
>
> —Dr. Martin Luther King Jr. (June 6, 1961)

On a damp, chilly January morning in Eugene, Oregon, Marion Malcolm greets old friends in Martin Luther King Jr. Park. Old friends and fellow activists. Their names are Alan, Leslie, Dwight, and countless more, but they might as well be known by the causes they have shared, the projects they have

102

worked on, and the battles they have fought together through the decades: civil rights, human rights, antiwar, antipoverty. These and other social justice issues have defined their lives and their community for years.

They have gathered with their children, friends, and neighbors on this particular Monday, January 20, 2003, to march in honor of Dr. Martin Luther King Jr. More than two hundred people walk nine blocks in about twenty minutes to the city's new Police and Fire Training Center. Some carry signs and placards for peace, for tolerance, for human dignity. One Hispanic man holds a beautiful poster-size black-and-white photograph of the late Dr. King. Most in the crowd are middle-class, middle-aged whites; they wear University of Oregon caps, knit hats, and hiking boots. They march steadily and reverently, forming a three-block-long colorful serpentine of people along the sidewalks of west Eugene.

Malcolm wears a hooded forest-green parka and black leather gloves. She carries a laminated poster proclaiming the Martin Luther King Jr. Contest and Celebration, a kindergarten- through twelfth-grade-student art, essay, and poetry competition, which will be held this afternoon from 2 to 4 P.M. in the adjacent city of Springfield. She smiles easily and laughs often on the brisk walk to the training center. At sixty-four, she is sturdily built and fit, having spent much of her life enjoying hikes, canoeing, and other outdoor pursuits, when not engaged in the demanding, often round-the-clock life of a community activist.

She says she is "semi-retired," but that is merely her official explanation. She remains very busy and very much a leader, teacher, organizer, spokesperson, and visionary for progressives in Oregon and across the Northwest. She has compiled an impressive record since she arrived in Eugene in the mid-1960s.

"Over the years I'd see her on the front lines of every important social justice cause the newspaper covered: civil rights, peace, religious tolerance, care of the homeless and needy, volunteerism," says Jim Godbold, executive editor of *The Register-Guard* newspaper. "Heck, she was in the news again this past week, speaking out at a rally against the war in Iraq. . . . That's the Marion Malcolm I know in a nutshell—passionate, unafraid, articulate, and always willing to speak out for what she believes in, even if the message is unpopular. Perhaps especially if the message is unpopular. She is a great gift to this community, part of its heart and soul."

At today's MLK Jr. rally in the crowded atrium of the Police and Fire Training Center, Malcolm is content to stand amidst the crowd and listen to speakers bring both the "bad news"—the rise in hate crimes in Oregon—and the "good news"—local officials will proceed with plans to rename

Centennial Boulevard, a major thoroughfare, to Martin Luther King Jr. Boulevard. Malcolm smiles knowingly, and her green bespectacled eyes brighten when a young girl barely able to see over the lectern speaks of how she learned activism from her parents, from distributing leaflets and press releases to doing grassroots networking. Malcolm's two sons, David and Andrew, and daughter, Bayla, were exposed to social justice issues from an early age. Bayla led her first boycott (grapes) in third grade in her school cafeteria.

"Marion has made an enormous contribution to the younger generation of activists in the Northwest," says longtime friend Carol Van Houten, who first worked with Malcolm as an anti–Vietnam War protester in Eugene.

Malcolm's faith in and mentoring of young people of strength and conviction is a hallmark. ("One of the true joys of my work," she says, referring to programs she inspired such as Youth for Justice.) While others speak of MTV-generation anomie or a pop cultural malaise, Malcolm believes in the promise of youth to ensure a more enlightened future. She has steadfastly held that belief since her own introduction to social activism as a college student at Cornell University more than forty years ago.

* * *

When Bergen County, New Jersey, native Malcolm attended Cornell in Ithaca, New York, the "silent" 1950s were giving way to the 1960s. She was pursuing a literature degree, with plans to become a teacher. In the early college years, she was not a politically involved student. But she had been raised in a family of Scottish-English descent with a strong social conscience. Her grandparents and parents had been Christian missionaries to India. Malcolm had grown up with the understanding that she was responsible for more than just herself, that she was part of a larger "human family." Although the actions of her fellow students would start her on the path to a lifetime of activism, Malcolm credits her parents with "igniting the passion."

In college she had been at the fringe of socially engaged students. She attended some campus rallies and marched in sympathy with civil rights sit-ins underway in the segregated South. But she hadn't put herself on the line.

In an oft-repeated anecdote, Malcolm tells of lying for several days in a campus infirmary bed during finals week, June 1961. She had contracted measles, followed by pneumonia. At that same time, some of her friends were among the first northerners to join the "Freedom Riders" in battling racial segregation down South.

These fellow Cornell students had attempted to integrate the Greyhound waiting rooms in Jackson, Mississippi. They ended up serving time in the Parchment State Penitentiary. They were arrested and jailed while Malcolm confronted herself in that infirmary bed.

"It became stunningly clear that my friends were in jail for values with which I was raised and claimed to hold, and that if I did not apply my values to the social issues, if I did not live out my values, then they were empty words, and I could not claim them," she recalls, describing the realization that was to change her life. She made a vow to act on her beliefs, her values. She knew her Scripture well: "Faith without works is dead."

Malcolm became part of a burgeoning civil rights protest movement. She also went to Washington, D.C., to demonstrate for nuclear disarmament as a grad student at Brown University in 1962. The more she was involved in activism, the further she drifted from organized religion. Although she had attended both Presbyterian and Methodist churches while growing up, as a college student she began to question Christian theology's "monopoly on the truth." She was also troubled by the passivity of her congregation toward causes such as civil rights. Malcolm says in those years she was more comfortable with her Jewish and nonreligious friends, who had more passion for social issues.

Her break with formal religion was to be the first of several milestones as her character and commitment to activism were being shaped. Her parents didn't confront her about her decisions, though her mother suggested that she investigate other denominations. Malcolm respectfully declined and pursued her faith and spirituality in her own way, in her own time.

After a year of graduate school at Brown University, Malcolm followed her family tradition and traveled to India, where she taught at a private school. In 1964 she returned to the United States and married her first husband, Bruce Barnes, who had been friends with her and the "Freedom Rider" crowd at Cornell years earlier. Barnes and Malcolm headed to Berkeley, where he taught and she worked for a year in an Oakland daycare center, before entering a master's program in South Asian Studies. Malcolm would revel in the free speech movement on the University of California–Berkeley campus. Her activist apprenticeship was underway, and she was about to fulfill her vow made in that infirmary bed in Ithaca, New York.

* * *

In 1966 Malcolm and her husband moved to Eugene, Oregon. He was hired as an assistant professor in the mathematics department. She was seeking out venues to protest the Vietnam War. It didn't take long to connect with the antiwar community in Eugene. Within a week of arriving, Malcolm was at the University of Oregon (UO) demonstrating against a speech by then U.S. vice president Hubert Humphrey.

For much of the decade between 1965 and 1975, Malcolm was committed to the antiwar movement. She organized vigils and marches, gave speeches, wrote articles, lobbied with elected officials, participated in poetry readings, and staged "die-ins" and benefit events. Her colleagues considered her a gifted, eloquent, and convincing speaker who could motivate people to join the cause. But she was also praised for building relationships and using reason and reasonableness rather than rhetoric and rancor.

"You can't organize from a place of contempt," says Malcolm.

During the antiwar years, Malcolm was active in the local chapter of the Women's International League for Peace and Freedom. One of her cohorts was Carol Van Houten, who was also the spouse of a UO faculty member. Van Houten and Malcolm weren't merely interested in protest; they examined underlying issues surrounding the Vietnam War, such as militarism, racism, and social justice. Van Houten recalls that Malcolm was unusually insightful and perceptive, "able to see what was important." But the assertive Malcolm didn't try to alienate people. She preferred to rally them to her side.

Two of those close by her side in the early 1970s were her sons, David (born in 1969) and Andrew (born in 1971). The kids would come to the marches and protests and play with the children of other activists. Malcolm loved raising a family, and she appreciated that her parents, retired chemist Gordon and retired homemaker and music teacher Jean, had relocated from the Northeast to Eugene. Malcolm enjoyed her sense of balance, of being grounded in her home and life's work.

But as the war years dragged on, her marriage began to slip away. In retrospect, Malcolm says that her husband "wasn't interested in or affirming of me as a person, and certainly not affirming of my sense of vocation or the value of the antiwar work I was doing. This is my perspective, of course." In 1975 after a dozen years of marriage, Malcolm was divorced. She and Barnes agreed to joint custody of the children, and have since maintained a decent, civil relationship.

"In general, my activism has cost me very little," says Malcolm. "For the same kind of activism in many countries, or even in this country with a different skin color, I might have been dead by now, or at least jailed or tortured. I'm very conscious of this, of the fact that I've been protected by racial and class privilege and by living in a relatively free and open society."

Malcolm makes that point often when talking to young audiences about the lessons of the Vietnam War. She continues to give talks to schoolchildren throughout Eugene and Lane County, Oregon. In an April 1999 talk to Jefferson Middle School entitled "A Perspective from an Antiwar Activist," Malcolm said: "Those who were sent to fight, including those who volunteered and went with a patriotic belief in America's war, were not the ones who involved us in the war. They were not the ones making the decisions or telling the lies that kept it going. And most of us in the peace movement knew that all along." She reminds her audiences of the crucial role Vietnam War veterans played in the protest movement, how they protested in Washington, D.C., and how so many returned their medals of distinction to the government as symbols of their opposition to the continuing war.

Through her years in the antiwar movement, Malcolm learned to be a persistent skeptic, to research deeply, to ask tough questions and demand answers, to probe more carefully to learn what is really happening, and to not rely on "official" explanations. Malcolm also realized during those years that she was well suited to be an activist and organizer. She knew protesters who in the mid-1970s "breathed a huge sigh of relief at the end of the war" and never again were politically engaged. Malcolm says these people were often involved out of a sense of urgency or obligation, but hated the detail work—the phone calls, meetings, and grassroots organizing. But she thrived on it and still does.

"As long as we have some fun while we are doing it," she says, her voice husky with a trace of ex-smoker's cough. "There has to be something to replenish the spirit—laughter, music, poetry, food. We are serious, but we can be 'lively' serious instead of 'deadly' serious."

Malcolm also considers herself fortunate to have been a child of the 1950s. For one thing, she thought the music from that era was wonderful. But from an activist's perspective, she says that unlike many who came of age in the 1960s, she didn't bank on revolutionary change to transform society. "I never thought change was going to be easy," she says. "So I didn't get discouraged. I knew it was going to be a long haul."

As a result of Malcolm's reputation in the antiwar effort, she was offered a part-time job (fifteen hours a week for $150 per month) in 1974 to run the Eugene branch of the national Clergy and Laity Concerned (CALC) movement, whose main focus was on antimilitarism and international human rights. The position later became full-time. For the next twenty-five years she would serve CALC (earning under $10 per hour for most years).

She would also serve for several years as co-chairperson of the national CALC organization. In the late 1980s and early 1990s, she would oversee Lane County (Oregon) CALC's mission change from focusing on such global issues as Vietnam, nuclear disarmament, Central American repression, and South African apartheid to local concerns: homelessness in Lane County, farmworker rights, gay rights, anti-bigotry, and youth empowerment. Along the way, CALC would change its name to Community Alliance of Lane County.

Although its mission would evolve, CALC's impact on changing people's lives would remain steadfast through the years. Case in point: Dr. Irwin Noparstak, a now retired Eugene-based psychiatrist. He met Marion Malcolm in 1985 at a CALC-sponsored symposium on the ten-year anniversary of the fall of Saigon.

Noparstak had been sent to Vietnam during the war as a division psychiatrist. There he had a "rude awakening to social-political awareness" and left Vietnam in shock. He settled in Eugene in 1971 and confronted his need for therapy and healing. By 1985, one-fourth of his private practice was counseling Vietnam veterans. It made sense for him to go to the CALC symposium, which would be attended by many vets. What he didn't realize was how CALC and Marion Malcolm would enrich his life by challenging him to engage in social activism.

"I got it that just as we were horribly misled about Vietnam, and intervened to the utter destruction of that country, we were horribly misled about Nicaragua and El Salvador and were utterly destructive to both countries, in different ways," he says, describing how with Malcolm's urging he joined a CALC subcommittee. In time he would become a member of the organization's steering committee and participate in all levels of community action. "I was able to admire her, be inspired by her, and be led by her."

* * *

The 1980s would alter the course of Marion Malcolm's activism as well as her personal life. The start of the decade had brought both joy and despair. She was happily remarried to Stefan Ostrach, a union business representative. They had a new daughter. And they were living with other activists in a large, bustling circa-1915 bungalow, part of a housing collective on tree-lined Mayfair Lane, on the outskirts of Eugene.

But in El Salvador, 1980 was the year of two high-profile tragedies: the assassination of Archbishop Oscar Romero and the rape and murder of four U.S. churchwomen. As she had done in her anti–Vietnam War activism, Malcolm probed beneath the surface reports of the crimes. She began to learn more about the repressive regimes, the poverty, and the violence rampant in Central America. Over the years she would also learn of the U.S. military's role in the region through the training of Latin American soldiers and officers at the School of the Americas facility on the grounds of Fort Benning in Columbus, Georgia.

"The best antidote to despair is to take action." The quote is attributed to Marion Malcolm by Ronna Friend, a longtime colleague, who has worked with Malcolm for more than twenty years on issues such as antimilitarism.

In the 1980s Malcolm took action by immersing herself in the human rights and refugee crises in Central America. She became directly involved in the sanctuary movement. She not only worked to bring refugees to the United States, she also traveled to Nicaragua during the Sandinista-Contra civil war. There, amidst the poverty and violence, she discovered the hope and faith that were alive through the vibrant, activist Christianity of liberation theology.

In presentations to Trinity Methodist Church in March 1989 and Central Presbyterian Church in December 1992, Malcolm explained how her work in Central America helped her come to terms with her faith and spirituality. Though she still could not call herself a member of any congregation because of the complacency of most U.S. churches, she told the audiences that she considered herself a person of faith who was trying "quite imperfectly" to be a follower of Jesus. She credited the deeply religious poor of the region for bringing her into this renewed relationship:

> For Central American Christians there's nothing abstract about the person, the ministry, the death, or the resurrection of Jesus. North American Christians worship Christ, especially on Sunday mornings. Central American Christians identify with Jesus, the circumstances of his birth, the political context of his ministry, the power structures which conspired against him, his suffering and death, his resurrection—all are familiar to believers in Central America.

Malcolm befriended refugees. She read the correspondence of those who had later been killed either in war or in human rights atrocities. She heard the poems of contemporary Central Americans, and she reflected on the Scripture (particularly the Gospel of St. Mark) she had read as both child and adult.

Liberation theology was the heart of the social gospel—the words of Jesus, the revolutionary, telling the poor and oppressed that they could have a better life. But such thinking was a threat to the established order, and it could cost the poor their lives. Malcolm learned that the symbol of crucifixion was all too real for oppressed Central Americans whose suffering was commonplace. But so was the theme of resurrection. Malcolm came to understand the power of the resurrected human spirit.

"In Central America people answer the naming of the dead with the cry, 'Presente,'" she says. "The word *Presente* is a pledge to remember those who died, but it is also a vow to carry forth the work and commitment of the dead, to pick up the cross, to accept the risks, to carry the struggle forward."

* * *

Under Marion Malcolm's leadership, CALC transformed itself into a vehicle for grassroots social change. A new mission statement was adopted: "CALC's Mission is to work for a society free of bigotry, upholding human rights and human dignity. CALC seeks to educate, promote and mobilize individuals, groups and movements who are committed to peace and justice. CALC works to promote public policies based on social and economic justice."

Malcolm took lessons she and others learned in Central America and applied those to conditions in Lane County and Oregon. She would continue to be respectful in her dealings with people, but she would be relentless in seeking ways to improve living conditions for the indigent and disenfranchised. "Working in solidarity with Central Americans in the '80s and working in solidarity with farmworkers from then until now has given me much more than I have contributed, because it has shown me the human capacity for resistance and resilience," says Malcolm, whose eyes narrow and voice rises, becoming East Coast rapid when she gets excited about a subject. She admits with a wry grin: "I'm a Jersey girl. I talk a bit too loud, too fast, maybe too much."

Malcolm's co-workers say that her actions speak louder than her passionate words. In a December 20, 1999, article in *The Register-Guard* newspaper, Paul Neville cites Erik Nicholson, chief bargainer for the state farmworkers' union known as PCUN (Pineros y Campesinos Unidos del Noroeste—Northwest Treeplanters and Farmworkers United):

> Malcolm often leaves Eugene at 2 A.M., arriving in Woodburn at dawn to visit migrant farmworkers in their camps or to join their picketing at local farms. Nicholson recalls one such visit to a farm camp in 1997 after police had arrested two people for making similar visits. With police officers and police dogs hovering nearby, Nicholson says he watched Malcolm and the rest of her group join in praying and singing with the camp's residents.

Nicholson was moved by Malcolm's actions that day. Malcolm tends to shrug off such comments. She is prone to explain that she comes from a long line of stubborn individuals. "I'm an instigator; I cop to that," she says, breaking into an infectious laugh. "It's fun. I did it as a kid back in my neighborhood, and I'm still doing it."

What Malcolm is proud of are the years spent exposing countless people, including clergy and youth delegations, to the realities of the lives of Oregon farmworkers with visits to the fields and migrant labor camps. She has been a tireless advocate for PCUN since it was established in 1985. Her son Andrew and daughter, Bayla, have worked summers with the farmworkers' union. Today, Andrew is a union organizer. Bayla will soon graduate from the University of Oregon. Malcolm's eldest son, David, is a middle-school teacher.

Malcolm has appeared before civic, professional, and religious organizations over the years to heighten awareness of the plight of the farmworkers. Though she acknowledges that there are many honest, hardworking farmers in the Willamette Valley who treat their employees decently, she focuses on the growers in the region who exploit their workers. She reports her own eyewitness accounts of thousands of farmworkers living and working under dreadful and degrading conditions. She argues for the unionization of these workers. In the spirit of one of her heroes, Cesar Chavez, on behalf of CALC she has called for boycotts of targeted farm products, frozen foods, and canned goods.

The words of Marion Malcolm have also filled many a classroom, conference room, and town hall for decades, telling of the plight of immigrants to the United States, and to Oregon in particular. This consciousness-raising began during her years working with the sanctuary movement. In recent times, her advocacy has been aligned with the Network for Immigrant Justice, another CALC program. She tries to educate people on the role of macro-economic issues, such as foreign debt and free trade agreements, as the reason why people in Mexico, for example, come to the United States, seeking a better way of life.

Often Malcolm's activism consists of "grunt work," the glue for most campaigns. On a Friday morning in late January 2003, Malcolm sits at her large dining room table, folding more than one hundred flyers and addressing an equal number of envelopes. A Neil Young *Heart of Gold* tape is cranked up as Malcolm works on her pile of "Justice on the Table" flyers, promoting a new documentary about the current struggle for farmworker justice in Oregon. "I try to educate and mobilize people who have humanitarian values. If they apply those values to the political situation, they're going to come out in the right place."

Most believe the key to Malcolm's success is her skill in out-organizing the opposition. Friends talk of her discipline and ability to plan, anticipate, and strategize.

On the table is her trusty black address book and ever-present red pocket calendar. She is constantly checking one or the other, crossing items off one list, starting a new list, or adding yet another meeting or event to attend. Later, after her farmworkers flyers have been mailed, Malcolm waxes philosophical about the risks that face successful activists. "The line between an organizer and a manipulator is razor thin," she says. "If you are an organizer and you have these skills, then you have to watch yourself. You have the capacity to manipulate. Then you're no longer trustworthy."

* * *

"Marion is so trusted in this community. She is a tuning fork on so many issues," says Rabbi Yitzhak of Temple Beth Israel in Eugene. He calls Malcolm a "godly person with a beautiful spirit. I want her to be Jewish." The rabbi, who befriended Malcolm in the early 1970s, laughs heartily as he continues to praise her work in combating bigotry and discrimination of any kind in the community.

In the summer of 2001, anti-Semitic literature was mailed to Lane County residents. Malcolm helped CALC representatives and other religious leaders stage a press conference to decry the bigotry that continues to surface in the so-called liberal college town of Eugene. Malcolm made sure that Tammam Adi of the Islamic Cultural Center was an integral part of the press conference. She also helped foster an emerging friendship between Rabbi Yitzhak and Adi.

After September 11, 2001, when threats were made against Eugene's Muslim community, Malcolm again worked to provide an interfaith response. Members of the Temple Beth Israel congregation and other Eugene church members staged vigils outside the Eugene mosque during Friday prayers. In November 2002, when stones painted with swastikas were hurled against the walls and windows of Temple Beth Israel, the Jewish and Islamic communities of Eugene united in another demonstration of support against hate crimes. Their unity was illustrated by the public embrace of Rabbi Yitzhak and Tammam Adi.

When asked about her commitment to combating bigotry, hatred, racism, and all the other "isms" afflicting society, Malcolm responds with steely resolve: "I will choose where I want to stand and what I want to stand for, and I will not endorse by my silence anything that degrades humanity." Above her desk in the converted attic space that she uses as a home office hangs a teaching from the Talmud, from the Ethics of the Fathers: "It is not incumbent upon you to complete the work. But neither are you free to desist from it." Temple Beth Israel plays an important part in Marion Malcolm's life. Malcolm hasn't converted to Judaism, but she regularly attends Friday Shabbat services, which she calls "spiritually relaxing." Her husband, Stefan, is Jewish, and they raised their daughter, Bayla, in the faith.

While Bayla proudly wears her Star of David on a chain around her neck, her mother, Marion, talks of getting her old silver peace symbol necklace repaired. The veteran antiwar activist is now back protesting in front of the federal building as she did decades ago. Then it was the war in Vietnam. Today in January 2003 it is the pending war in Iraq.

Malcolm hurries to make it downtown in time for the hour-long vigil. She adds a few more miles to the 140,000-plus on her blue 1992 Olds Cutlass. She rushes to this antiwar protest and chats with a small group of people holding placards and waving to those drivers who honk in support of their message.

Afterward Malcolm walks a couple blocks to city hall to show her support for a "living wage standard" currently being debated by city council. En route she is stopped by a young woman with a backpack, heading to the living wage meeting. "Are you in charge?" she asks Malcolm, who politely defers. No, this time Marion Malcolm is not in charge. But her presence seems to encourage those who have come to argue their support for action on the issue. Several individuals make impassioned presentations to city officials for a progressive response to challenging economic conditions. After the meeting, Malcolm once again greets old friends, fellow activists, and those she has mentored along the way.

One of the last items on Malcolm's agenda this week is perhaps the most low-key, but hardly insignificant. She and representatives of SAFER, the Springfield (Oregon) Alliance for Equality and Respect, have a get-acquainted meeting scheduled with the interim superintendent of Springfield Public Schools. SAFER was created by Malcolm and other CALC representatives in the 1990s, in response to a growing climate of dissension and intolerance between the white, working-class majority and the growing minority population (mostly Hispanic) of Springfield, a traditional lumber mill town adjacent to Eugene. SAFER's mission: to build community awareness about human rights and to promote grassroots leadership to advance social justice.

Twenty minutes before the 5:15 P.M. meeting is to start, Malcolm is still printing out the agenda. "I'm such a last-minute Liz," she says with a nervous chuckle.

The file cabinet next to her desk is lined with family photos. Nearby are plaques and posters from past campaigns, protests, and boycotts: "The Wrath of Grapes," "Stop Sweatshops in the Fields. Support Oregon Farmworkers," "Asian Women's Human Rights Council," "Anne Frank in the World, International Exhibition." The room is lined with bookshelves on all sides, including nooks and crannies. Small plants and pottery adorn windowsills. Bright watercolors and photographed sunsets and seascapes decorate the walls.

Malcolm changes from her jeans, turtleneck, and hiking sandals to a more "professional" appearance at the school meeting: wool slacks, a light green turtleneck and matching green shell necklace, a multicolored knit vest, and casual shoes. She talks on the cell phone as she dresses. Malcolm is a notorious multitasker. Earlier in the day in her large eat-in kitchen, she had two large cast-iron skillets blazing away—one full of scrambled eggs for an impromptu lunch for her and a visiting professor from Indiana, the other filled with sizzling beef for a dinner stew with Stefan and perhaps one of her kids who might drop by. "One more thing I can cross off my to-do list," Malcolm says, reciting one of her favorite mantras.

The SAFER/CALC folks, Elaine, Laurie, Guadalupe, and Michael, are waiting for Marion in the superintendent's office. Steve Barrett is on the phone, which gives Malcolm time to distribute the agenda. The primary purpose of the meeting is to hear about the district's ongoing commitment to diversity and to foster positive race relations in the midst of the challenging budget situation facing Springfield and arguably all school districts in Oregon.

But there are other issues to get on the table tonight: harassment policy and procedures, staff diversity (recruitment, retention, training), discipline policies (racial disparity concerns), and programs for immigrant students. Interim superintendent Barrett is cordial as he greets the group gathered around the small circular table in the corner of his near-stifling office. His white shirt is damp and rumpled, and he has dark circles under his eyes, but he appears engaged in the conversation. He talks about the difficulties of cutting $2 million from his budget, with more budget cuts pending. He uses phrases such as "[we must] keep the embers burning" when Malcolm and the group emphasize their dedication to human rights in the school district. The other SAFER/CALC representatives are more animated in their discussion with Barrett. But Malcolm's voice comes through most clearly at the end of the meeting when Barrett says, "We want you to hold us accountable." Malcolm responds, "We will."

* * *

These days, Malcolm uses the word "ally" in many of her conversations and her presentations. There is yet another CALC-inspired group active in the community: Allies for Human Dignity. In one of her talks at a workshop for youth in January 2002, Malcolm explained her job as a "useful ally." She told these future activists that it isn't her job (or theirs) to necessarily "organize," but to serve as allies for others, to work *with*, not *for*, people, who have the right to empower themselves. She cautioned the audience about undertaking social justice work for the wrong reasons, such as ego gratification or an impersonal sense of duty. That can lead to telling people how they ought to conduct their struggle for change. Doing justice, Malcolm said, means accompanying people who are defining their own path.

Kelley Weigel, field director of Western States Center, a social change organization, is one of several twenty- and thirty-something activists who were mentored by Marion Malcolm. In Weigel's case, she was a recent college graduate, newly hired by CALC. She recalls Malcolm's "boundless commitment to equality" and her teaching that progressive reform always comes from the actions of small groups of believers. Weigel remembers Malcolm speaking emphatically to her and others: "You just can't make people believe what is right. You must show them through your work and actions. Otherwise we are just like what we are trying to change."

More than forty years ago, Marion Malcolm lay in an infirmary bed at Cornell University and made a vow to put her faith, beliefs, and values into action to work for a more just and humane society. These days, Malcolm continues to fulfill that vow. She believes that what she and others strive for does make a difference in bettering people's lives. She remains firm in where she stands: "I'm on the left because of the values I was raised in within my religious tradition—because I believe in human dignity and freedom and democracy."

In the years ahead, even Marion Malcolm will slow down, though she reminds people that her mother, Jean, was active in CALC and community activism well into her nineties. Malcolm wants to enjoy some "downtime," hiking, canoeing, and traveling with her husband and children to favorite destinations like Mexico and her beloved India, where so much of her family history exists. She looks forward to being a grandmother. She hopes to host even more South Asian dinners for friends and guests.

Even Marion Malcolm will eventually lose the energy that has driven her many causes for so many years. But Malcolm assures friends, colleagues, and admirers that she will never lose her "real stubborn hope" and her faith in the "incredible human capacity for resistance and resilience. Nobody can take that away from me."

[8]

MARY NELSON "REBUILDING WITH HOPE"

Mary Nelson's message in the Summer 2003 Bethel New Life, Inc. (BNL) newsletter was somber. She spoke of financial struggles and adjustments: eliminating seven positions, reducing operating expenses, and consolidating programs. She cited government deficits, resulting in slashed services and future budget cuts. She asked BNL supporters to contact the President and members of Congress to urge them to provide the child tax credit for the working poor. Nelson also encouraged donations to BNL to "make a difference helping our matched savings accounts for education and housing, enabling job placement, quality child development."

There was good news to share as well. The front page of the newsletter announced the BNL partnership with the (Chicago) Field Museum in creating an inspirational multimedia exhibition showcasing stories of transformation. These accounts were culled from personal narratives of community members and local and national leaders. The stories in "Steppin' Up: Journeys from the Soul" focus on themes central to the organization Nelson helped establish almost twenty-five years ago: courage, creativity, education, faith, and social justice. Funds raised from a series of exhibition events would help support the ongoing work of Bethel Cultural Arts, one of many community-based programs fostered by the resilient Mary Nelson.

Bethel New Life, Inc., Mission Statement:

If you put an end to oppression, to every gesture of contempt, and to every evil word; if you give food to the hungry and satisfy those who are in need, then the darkness around you will turn to the brightness of noon. I will always guide you and satisfy you with good things.

I will keep you strong and well. You will be like a garden that has plenty
of water, like a spring of water that never goes dry. Your people will
rebuild what has been in ruins, building again on the
old foundations. You will be known as the people who rebuilt the walls,
who restored the ruined foundations.

—Isaiah 58:9–12

Mary Nelson has lost her keys again. She realizes this at the end of
another twelve-hour workday as she roots through her purse by her dinged
and dented 1995 Nissan Stanza in the parking lot of the Beth-Anne Life
Center Campus. At about 7 P.M. on a cold midweek night in early February,
Mary sighs as she returns to her office in the former St. Anne's Hospital
building on Chicago's West Side. Will she find her keys on her desk,
credenza, or file cabinets, amidst the piles of papers, files, binders, and
reports? Does she have her spare keys? Will she have to call her old friend
Kate Lane for help? The more things change, the more they remain the
same for Nelson, the dynamic, at times absent-minded, neighborhood
rebuilder from West Garfield Park.

Mary Nelson and Kate Lane were two of the founders of Bethel New
Life, Inc., the community development corporation (CDC) established in
1979 with the financial and spiritual backing of Bethel Lutheran Church.
Nelson's late brother, David, longtime pastor of the church, was one of the
other original visionaries, dedicated to transforming the depressed, poverty-
stricken neighborhood into a place of hope and a place of God (i.e.,
"Bethel"). For the last twenty-four years Mary Nelson has made Bethel New
Life her life's work. Some say she has been married to the organization that
began as an urban housing ministry and has evolved into a multi-million-
dollar national model of holistic, sustainable community development,
providing thousands of people with homes, jobs, education, health care,
and social services. Still others wonder how a sixty-three-year-old white
woman with Scandinavian roots and Mrs. Claus looks could have accomplished so much for so long in a place decimated by riots, crime, unemployment, and despair.

To answer that question requires a history lesson, a biography, and a
course encompassing city politics, race relations, grassroots organizing,
and asset-based, faith-driven social activism. Or one can spend several days
shadowing Mary Nelson, reading volumes of documents and press clippings, and talking with friends, associates, and colleagues. That journey

begins in the archives of Nelson's large executive office, the very office where she hopes to find her keys on this chilly midwinter evening.

Bethel New Life, Inc., is organized into several program areas: Housing and Real Estate Development, Employment and Economic Development, Services for Seniors, Community Building, Family Support, and Cultural Arts. Each of these areas is subdivided into operational categories and individual projects. For every area, category, and project, there is a file— make that several files. They all appear to be in and around Mary Nelson's office. Metal and plastic file holders, file crates, and large brown multi-file envelopes are on the desk, credenza, and file cabinets (where hundreds more files are lurking). Files are on chairs and side tables, and dozens are on the floor, along with large binders, storage boxes, a couple briefcases, a carry-on airline bag, paper shopping bags, and a pair of dark casual shoes.

As Nelson searches her office, she mutters to herself while classical music plays on the radio. Where could those keys be? She retraces her steps from her usual 7 A.M. arrival. Ah-ha. She had stopped at Dunkin' Donuts this morning to bring sustenance for the senior management team conducting all-day midyear personnel reviews. She had the keys in her hands while carrying the boxes of donuts and, of course, files. Nelson stops looking above ground and glances about on the carpet. Keys found. Problem solved. If only all of her and Bethel New Life's problems (or opportunities in disguise) could be solved this easily. But, then again, Mary Nelson never sought nor expected an easy life.

1950s–1960s

"Well, what are you going to do about it?"

She was born in Duluth, Minnesota, as the youngest of four children of Clarence and Ruth Youngdahl Nelson. Her uncle, Luther Youngdahl, had been a two-term governor of Minnesota. Politics ran deep in the family, but religion ran deeper. Her father, a Lutheran minister, was transferred to an inner-city Washington, D.C., church in the late 1940s. He was an urban pastor in a black neighborhood in the age of segregation.

The children, David, Jonathan, Lorraine, and Mary, would walk through the community with their parents trying to "gather a congregation." Mary and her siblings were expected to work hard in and out of school and not complain. Her mother, Ruth, would challenge her children to become self-reliant and to confront their problems. Her words still drive Mary Nelson to this day when she faces an obstacle: "Well, what are you going to do about it?"

119

The Nelson family had a long tradition of concern for the underdog. Her mother was described as a tireless advocate for social justice. Mary was raised in a home where guests could include poor immigrants, people released from jail, and those struggling to find a better life. They all became part of Mary Nelson's "human family."

She left her urban multicultural world in the late 1950s to return to her Swedish Midwestern roots and attend Gustavus Adolphus College in Saint Peter, Minnesota, where she was an English-German major. Upon graduation she worked for the Lutheran Church in America, which sent her to a girl's secondary school in Tanzania, in what was then the nation of East Africa. She taught English literature to students in a beautiful setting on the slopes of Mount Kilimanjaro.

One of her high school students with whom she would forge a lifelong bond was Kaaneli ("Kaana") Makundi. "Most of the other teachers were older missionaries," Makundi recalls. "Mary Nelson was one of the younger generation. She was a religious and spiritual person with a sense of humor. She told us it was OK to dance and socialize."

But Nelson would teach her students much more than that it was appropriate for Lutherans to have fun. She instilled in Makundi and others the responsibilities they had as Christians to serve their community, especially the poor and distressed. "Mary Nelson became a role model for faith in action," Makundi says. "She was patient in teaching us values. She made us feel blessed."

Makundi would later attend college in the United States and spend her summers vacationing with the Nelsons at their cabin on a lake in north central Minnesota. The family vacation spot remains a "great healing place" for Mary Nelson, who treasures the memories of hiking, swimming, and sailing with her two Lutheran minister brothers, David and Jonathan.

Makundi returned to Tanzania and directed social service and welfare programs for seventeen years before joining the Lutheran World Federation, based in Geneva, Switzerland. For the next thirteen years she was deputy director for the Federation's worldwide disaster relief programs. Then in 2000 came a call from her old friend and mentor, Mary Nelson.

Nelson asked Makundi if she would come to Chicago to work with Bethel New Life, Inc., as director of supportive housing, the transitional program for formerly homeless women. Makundi decided that if Nelson could come to teach in Tanzania years earlier, she could move to Chicago and serve the Lord. What a journey it has been.

Makundi left the idyllic environs of Switzerland for the streets of an oft-described urban wasteland, where the landscape is littered with aban-

120

doned hulks of cars, shuttered and barricaded storefronts, abandoned homes, and vacant "brownfield" lots. Makundi's office in the former Saint Mel Grade School is a cramped, cluttered workspace where the air conditioning unit is covered by a trash bag and duct tape.

But as a protégé of Mary Nelson, Makundi sees beyond the problems to the hope she gives to women and their children striving to return to mainstream society. On this sunny but frigid winter day, Makundi's world is beautiful. She is surrounded by grateful faces of mothers and children receiving a rainbow of hats, gloves, and scarves. This African-born woman, who resembles the late actress Esther Rolle, is beaming as she cradles a small black boy in her arms. "Here I work one on one with people, hearing their life stories. I've seen miracles happen here," Makundi says. "I'm grateful to Mary for that."

Mary Nelson has touched so many lives, but she deflects any praise, giving God the glory. She is both humbled and inspired by the success of people such as Kaana Makundi. How is Nelson such a good judge of talent and potential?

She explained the source of her spiritual strength and personal/professional vision in a video produced in 2002 by The Annie E. Casey Foundation, which had recently given BNL a $500,000 unrestricted "Families Count" award: "Coming out of our faith perspective, you see the person that God made possible, and you see the possibilities."

Seeing possibilities in the midst of devastation could summarize the unexpected challenge facing Mary Nelson when she came to Chicago in the summer of 1965 on a brief visit to help her brother David settle in as pastor of Bethel Lutheran Church, a 1903 edifice in the heart of West Garfield Park. Mary had a master's degree in teaching from Brown University. What she didn't have was a clear sense of her mission—where she would go, where she would work. The answer would come in the form of a race riot in August 1965.

The first of several riots to hit Chicago's West Side during the next five years began with the death of a young black mother, killed by a fire truck driven by a white crew. The National Guard was called in to calm the streets of West Garfield Park and adjoining neighborhoods. Reverend David Nelson and his sister Mary waited for the crisis to pass. But the anger and destruction continued. In the days that followed, the Nelsons' car was pelted with bricks while they drove the mean streets.

Mary Nelson decided she had to stay a while to support her brother. She didn't envision that she was making a life-altering decision. She didn't realize then that she was being called to a ministry that would extend

121

through five decades. "I like to say it's been a riot ever since," Nelson jokes, slipping into her patented hearty laughter that has shielded this tall, robust woman through self-described years of "agony and ecstasy."

Following the riot of 1965, the warm, outgoing Reverend Nelson went door-to-door in his effort to build his congregation with the increasing numbers of black families now living in the community. The African American church members would transform the evangelical Lutheran institution over the years until it would one day be known as "that Lutheran-Baptist Church," complete with exuberant twenty-five-member blue-robed choir, accompanied by organ, piano, and sometimes African drums—all part of a rousing, embracing two-plus-hour Sunday service, with plenty of altar calls.

In late 1965 Reverend Nelson joined with clergy from a dozen other local churches, forming an ecumenical association called Christian Action Ministry (CAM) to address community needs, particularly those of disenfranchised, disconnected area youth. Nelson's outspoken, hard-charging sister, Mary, became program coordinator. Over the next thirteen years she would help establish and operate an employment center and a network of day-care centers. For ten of those years she would also serve as founding principal of the CAM Academy (today: Christian Community Alternative Academy), an alternative high school for dropouts.

The riot following the assassination of Dr. Martin Luther King Jr. in April 1968 was the most violent and caused the most long-term damage to West Garfield Park's housing and commercial stock, its economic viability, and its community psyche. White flight continued. The traditional European-immigrant base of residents abandoned the community in droves.

Businesses closed down. Jobs disappeared. Houses and apartment buildings were abandoned, left to be vandalized and later demolished. The neighborhood was disappearing, and it would take more than faith to save it. But it couldn't be saved without the core faith of those stubborn church-going folk who remained.

1970s–1980s

"We're going to do affordable housing because no one else is doing it."

In the twenty-year period following the riots, the one-square-mile West Garfield Park neighborhood population declined from an estimated seventy thousand to about twenty-four thousand. By the end of the 1970s, an average of two hundred housing units a year were being demolished or abandoned. Crime and social problems were increasing. Young men were dying violently on West Side streets year after year; the neighborhood's infant mortality rate was almost three times the national average; and the large senior population lacked proper housing and support services.

David and Mary Nelson and other concerned residents realized something had to be done to save and reclaim the community, or Bethel Lutheran Church would be an island in a sea of despair. In Mary Nelson's words, "God commands us to be about this stuff." Bethel Lutheran Church contacted the other churches that had formed the ecumenical Christian Action Ministry (now: Christian Community Services) to see if they wanted to join in an urban housing ministry. In an August 7, 1994, article by Tom Seibel in the *Chicago Sun-Times,* Mary Nelson explained the churches' reaction and what ensued: "According to Nelson, other churches in the ecumenical effort didn't want to touch the task, maintaining that 'Housing is too complicated, capital intensive and that's not something churches should be involved in.' So they opted out."

Reverend Nelson appealed to his 150 congregants, and they responded patiently, faithfully. Each person was asked to donate $5 or $10 a week toward a goal of $5,000. In a few months the money was raised, and Bethel Housing (later Bethel New Life, Inc.) was established. Mary Nelson and Kate Lane were among the handful of volunteer staff for the organization, whose first project was the purchase and "gut rehab" of a three-flat building on Karlov Avenue, two blocks from Bethel Lutheran Church. "Back then we were a couple of ragamuffins sitting on the curb," Lane recalls.

The dilapidated shell of the Karlov Avenue building was purchased from the U.S. Department of Housing and Urban Development (HUD) for a mere $275. But the rehab project would require more than $35,000, plus plenty of "sweat equity" (translation: donated labor of future tenants or homeowners, plus volunteers). "This community was redlined; so there was no loan from the bank," Mary Nelson said in the August 7, 1994, *Sun-Times* article. "They said, 'Are you crazy, this is an abandoned building.'"

David and Mary Nelson pooled their personal lines of credit for the first building rehab. Bethel Lutheran Church would later secure additional mortgages as collateral for three larger community housing projects completed in the 1980s. The commitment of the church led to the successful renovation of Anathoth Place—a symbol of hope in the midst of uncertainty and destruction, as noted in the first of several BNL scrapbooks in Nelson's office.

The successful completion of the Anathoth Place project in fall 1980 gave Bethel Housing a foothold, a track record with a local bank. Mary Nelson was no Pollyanna, but she was determined to keep hope alive. She told her brother and anyone else who would listen: "We're going to do affordable housing because no one else is doing it."

By mid-1981, two more family housing projects were completed, and Bethel's annual budget had climbed to more than $150,000, largely the result of government funding. The organization also had established a food co-op, a sewing cooperative, and a senior housing repair and weatherization program. In 1982 a sixteen-unit building was renovated and marketed as a housing cooperative; new townhouses were being built on Washington Boulevard; dozens of area apartment units were now under the auspices of Bethel's property management; and ambitious plans were underway for the construction of a new $2.6 million, forty-unit senior apartment building (Anathoth Gardens). The building's first floor would include a holistic health center, offering area residents preventive health services, in cooperation with the Chicago Board of Health.

Another program launched in the early 1980s was Bethel's training and certification of homecare providers (housekeepers) to serve West Garfield Park's large senior population. Job training and development was now integral to the Bethel mission of not only providing affordable housing, but also offering the means to attain that housing. By 1982 the board approved a name change to Bethel New Life, Inc.

The outside community started taking notice of efforts underway in West Garfield Park. Stories appeared in major publications. In 1982 BNL received the TRUST (To Reshape Urban Systems Together) Neighborhood Award for its successful completion of a housing cooperative, enabling low-income residents to gain access to home ownership and honoring its goal of "development without displacement." A year later, Bethel received its first major foundation funding, a $250,000 loan from the Enterprise Foundation and a grant from the Continental Bank Foundation. The financing was provided to Bethel New Life, Inc., for its renovation of Douglas Villa, a twenty-four-unit transitional (supportive) housing cooperative, providing formerly homeless families with access to decent, low-cost housing.

By 1986, when former president Jimmy Carter and his wife, Rosalynn, came to West Garfield Park to build Habitat for Humanity housing, Bethel New Life, Inc.'s annual budget had climbed higher than $2.5 million, and more than two hundred full- and part-time staff were on the payroll. Later that year, the Living-Learning Center (renamed the Family Wellness Center), a multiuse building, featuring twenty-six two- and three-bedroom apartments, classrooms for grades five through eight of the Bethel Christian School, and facilities for an after-school program, was opened. The project was praised for its "adaptive reuse" of a former elementary school building. Then Chicago mayor Harold Washington, a friend and ally of Mary Nelson and BNL for years before his untimely death from a heart attack in 1987, presided at the dedication of the new Center.

By this point, financial institutions such as Harris Bank were supporting Bethel New Life, Inc., projects. But, according to Nelson, the banks hadn't been willing lenders until Mary Nelson and BNL teamed up with the Woodstock Institute and the National Training and Information Center as part of the Community Reinvestment Alliance. The coalition, which had researched the lending practices of Chicago-area banks, informed the banks that they would be challenged for not complying with the federal Community Reinvestment Act of 1977, which required financial institutions to reinvest in the areas they served.

During negotiations, Mary Nelson would tell the bankers, "You want us with you, not on your back." Nelson's comrade-in-arms, Kate Lane, recalls another favorite expression from their confrontational activist days: "Don't tell us no. Tell us how we can get it done." Nelson's and Lane's persistence was well known in and around Chicagoland. Just ask the suburban bank president who was called at home by Bethel's "dynamic duo" during dinner, and who couldn't get off the phone until he had agreed to hold a meeting with "his people" and the Bethel New Life team. Or ask those attending a reception at former mayor Jane Byrne's home when Kate Lane "crashed" the party to make a point about one of BNL's projects. Over the years, Nelson and Lane would be arrested for acts of nonviolent civil disobedience, following in the footsteps of Nelson's activist mother, Ruth, and brother, Jonathan.

"We used to call Mary and Kate 'the wild bunch,'" says Marcia Turner, director of external relations for BNL. Turner is also Kate Lane's daughter and a former Sunday school student of Mary Nelson, her current Washington Boulevard neighbor.

Mary Nelson's tenure as president and CEO in leading Bethel New Life, Inc. through many tumultuous years raises the race issue. How did a fair-haired, blue-eyed, and rosy-cheeked white woman successfully lead a minority-based, inner-city organization in a community more than 99 percent black? How did Nelson and the BNL organization deal with racial tension?

"Mary is one of those people in a black community who is not looked at as a white person or a white leader," says Roy Priest, president, National Congress of Community Economic Development (NCCED) in Washington, D.C. Priest first met Nelson more than a decade ago, when he directed the empowerment zone program at the U.S. Department of Housing and Urban Development. He observed how staff and community residents trusted Nelson. He respected Nelson's skill at working with an array of sometimes controversial people to effect change. He also saw how Nelson's close relationship with her church community helped ameliorate backlash. "Faith and religion have a way of neutralizing racial differences."

Wanda Lewis, senior director of senior services for BNL and a longtime staff member, says that the "race card" is sometimes raised by other community organizations that may be jealous of Bethel's success, particularly in raising funds. As far as Lewis is concerned: "The proof is in the pudding. Mary lives right in the heart of West Garfield Park." The word around BNL is that "Mary's heart is here."

In a March 21, 2002, column for the *Austin Weekly News,* a neighborhood newspaper, Frank Lipscomb wrote:

> Mary Nelson of the West Garfield Park Neighborhood was deeply involved in helping black Westsiders fight for civil and human rights—also in obtaining proper housing. She was honest, intelligent, and more 'pro-black' than most Negroes. Mary also suffered the abuses and pains from being in the struggle for freedom in the '60s and '70s. She was raped and beaten and encouraged to leave the movement, but she stayed and fought with us.

While on a driving tour of the community, her Nissan Stanza often lurching between stop signs, Nelson highlights the rebuilt blocks of her neighborhood and the restored Garfield Park Conservatory as evidence of West Garfield Park's comeback.

She also points out where she was brutally attacked years ago. She adjusts her oversized glasses and clears her throat as she heads back to her office. Did the assault intimidate her, cause her to question her conviction? "I was pissed. The police said, 'Lady, you ain't got no business being here.' That got my dander up. It didn't deter me."

Mary Nelson is no quitter, but she is human. She describes many nights during the last five decades when she went home exhausted and frustrated, and cried. She would get through the nights by reading, often a mystery novel (Nelson averages two books of fiction and nonfiction a week), or by calling on her friends. "You have support systems to carry you through the tough times," she says in a clear, resonant voice. She doesn't dwell on personal matters. She has been engaged a couple of times, and now she enjoys "being absolutely freed up. I never was one to worry about any of that. If it didn't work out, it didn't work out."

On the subject of race as with so much in her life, Mary Nelson is a realist: "I'm white. That issue is always there." She admits that she may push her staff a little hard, and that can be misinterpreted as being insensitive or condescending. "At times you have to ask for forgiveness." She counsels white college students who volunteer at BNL from such schools as Princeton, Northwestern, and Loyola: "Your genuineness will speak louder than anything you say."

BNL staffers talk about the Nelson family as "colorblind." The late Reverend David Nelson's widow, Hazel, is a beloved member of the congregation, retired principal of Bethel Christian School, and devoted sister-in-law of Mary Nelson. Mary's brother, Jonathan, heads a multiracial family in Seattle, Washington. Mary Nelson is considered one of the family by those in her church and neighborhood. "She was like my auntie when I was growing up here," says Stanley, an ex-offender and former church youth leader who is rebuilding his life thanks to Nelson and BNL.

As the 1980s drew to a close, Mary Nelson pressed on. "Don't be intimidated. Keep moving forward," she would tell herself and those in her growing organization.

Now armed with a Ph.D. in urban education, she demonstrated her acumen at cobbling together layers of creative financing, joining the resources of government, businesses, private developers, foundations, and charitable organizations in addressing community needs.

The decade ended with two high-profile BNL housing projects: the completion of the Guyon Towers, a $6 million, 114-unit rehabilitation of a former hotel, and the kickoff of the Westside Isaiah Plan, an ambitious inner-city project to build 250 townhouses throughout the West Side of Chicago. The development, under the direction of Bethel New Life, Inc., was sponsored by twenty area churches (each donating $5,000 in construction financing). A decade earlier, Bethel had been forced to go solo when seeking funding for its first housing project. Now it was being supported by a regional network of congregations.

"Instinctively as a community builder you have to find resources and people to work on problems. Mary has long been at the lead end of conceptualizing new approaches to community development," says Jody Kretzmann, a codirector at the Institute for Policy Research at Northwestern University, where Nelson is on the adjunct faculty. She also teaches courses at the University of Illinois, Chicago Circle. Kretzmann had first worked with Nelson when she was principal and he was a tutor at the Christian Action Ministry Academy in West Garfield Park. Years later they would reunite and join John McKnight and other national leaders who were developing progressive approaches to urban problems. These approaches were built on contrarian thinking, such as the novel thought that poor people have resources (assets) that should be identified, developed, and mobilized. Nelson explained in Jim Wallis's 2000 book, *Faith Works:* "The resources poor communities have—time, energy, numbers, relationships, experience, talent, faith, and even some money—when pooled together can become very significant."

At BNL plans begin with an inventory of community assets—what people have, what they know, what they want. By contrast, the traditional, bureaucratic antipoverty program way of dealing with the poor has been to focus on needs and deficiencies. In the case of West Garfield Park these would certainly include a long list of negatives: about one-third of the adult population is unemployed; two-thirds of the high school-age youth are dropouts; about 40 percent of the residents are at or below the federal poverty level; and the neighborhood has the highest crime rate of any Chicago police district. No one at Bethel New Life, Inc. denies these problems exist. They choose to focus on finding solutions: "Well, what are you going to do about it?"

By the dawn of the 1990s, Nelson, McKnight, Kretzmann, and other innovators had further refined the concept of asset-based community development, and it was attracting more true believers, including some of the most powerful leaders in the land.

1990s–PRESENT

"People in power respond to passion."

Photographs of Mary Nelson with four U.S. presidents—Carter, Reagan, Clinton, and George W. Bush—adorn one long wall in Nelson's Beth-Anne Life Center Campus office. The most recent presidential photo is from the January 29, 2001, White House ceremony at which President George W. Bush signed an executive order creating the Office of Faith-Based and Community Initiatives. Mary Nelson stands one person away from the president on his left side. BNL staffers recall how a month before the event, Nelson had slipped on an icy walk and broken her ankle. Surgery required thirteen screws in her ankle. Nelson was insistent on attending the White House meeting without using a wheelchair. She did, thanks to a tripod cane, a wrap-on cast, and her usual dose of gritty determination.

Rick Jascula, former advance man for President Jimmy Carter and current Chicago public relations consultant, says that whenever Mary sets her mind to do something, she does it. He also admits amiably in a recent BNL fund-raising meeting, "I can't say no to you." Jascula, an old friend and well-connected politico, secured an invitation for Nelson to the VIP box at the Democratic Presidential Convention in Chicago in the summer of 1996, where she met such dignitaries as the late John F. Kennedy Jr. "My life is strange," Nelson says. "I'm in the system and out on the streets . . . in the chambers of power."

On Nelson's wide black filing cabinet is a framed signed photo of the late Mayor Harold Washington. A signed photograph of current Chicago mayor Richard M. Daley is also on display. But lately Nelson sounds prickly in her comments about "hizzoner." On his failure to show at the January 31, 2003, dedication ceremony for the new $10 million Beth-Anne Place eighty-five-unit assisted-living wing, a marquee event attended by HUD secretary Mel Martinez, Nelson speculates. Perhaps the mayor didn't appear because of concerns over possible confrontations on the housing set-aside issue currently advocated by BNL and several members of the Chicago city council. Nelson says that a week later Mayor Daley made a brief appearance at the annual Chicago Neighborhood Development Awards program. But there wasn't time to speak with him then.

Over the years Mayor Daley has said some very nice things publicly about Nelson and Bethel New Life, Inc. He was quoted in the August 7, 1994, *Sun-Times* article: "We need more people like her. . . . If we had a Mary Nelson on every block, we wouldn't have a problem." The article discussed how Daley in 1991 had offered Mary Nelson the post of city housing commissioner, which she declined. Photos of Nelson and the mayor have graced the pages of BNL materials, and he is quoted in the 2001 annual report:

> For nearly 20 years Bethel New Life has been a leader in paving the way for re-neighboring, reconnecting, and recreating safe neighborhoods through partnerships with area businesses, public officials, police, and families. . . . Bethel New Life's neighborhood revitalization strategy is a national model for community development helping low- to moderate-income families turn problems into possibilities.

Nelson's response to such acclaim is an observation: "People in power respond to passion." She models that passion in countless interactions while at work and when supposedly off the clock.

"Even in social occasions, she is constantly working the room (schmoozing), trying to build relationships or influence [people] that would benefit Bethel," says Steven McCullough, the "thirtyish" chief operating officer of Bethel New Life, Inc. "She is fearless when it comes to walking up to the commissioner, the mayor, the governor, or even a president, introducing herself and giving two or three salient points or pitches. What's especially powerful is her ability to follow up and 'nag' the same people over long periods of time to get the results that she wants and not take no for an answer."

Mary Nelson's indomitable spirit was the focus of a recent national TV program that touted the success of Bethel New Life, Inc. On February 2, 2003, the PBS program *Religion and Ethics Newsweekly* called Nelson "the catalyst for change" on Chicago's West Side. The show touted BNL's record of developing some one thousand units of new or rehabbed housing and generating more than five thousand jobs and almost $100 million in investment during its twenty-four years of faith-based community development. In typical fashion, Nelson tried to deflect the attention on her: "The myth is that because I'm the one with the big mouth, and I'm out there talking a lot is that people seem to focus in on Mary Nelson. But it is not Mary Nelson. It is this whole host of wonderful people that have really committed themselves, have hung in there through the thick and the thin."

A key case study on the program was the Beth-Anne Life Center Campus: "One of Bethel New Life's most audacious moves was to raise $3.2 million in government funds and private donations (including collateral from the religious order—Ancila Domeni—that had owned the facility) to purchase and renovate a closed hospital."

In late 1989 BNL purchased the closed 9.2-acre, 437-bed former Saint Anne's Hospital campus in the northwest corner of the neighborhood. Over the next decade pieces of an intricate funding puzzle were assembled, with tens of millions of dollars being invested in the revitalization of the health care campus from an array of sources, including the U.S. Departments of Housing and Urban Development (HUD) and Health and Human Services (HHS), the Federal Home Loan Bank, the state of Illinois Supportive Living Program, Chicago's Empowerment Zone, First Bank of Oak Park, LaSalle Bank, the Retirement Research Foundation, Local Initiatives Support Corporation (LISC), and many private donors.

Today the campus is home to 125 units of subsidized senior housing and adult day services, a new 85-unit assisted-living wing, a child development (day-care) center for eighty children, a professional office building, facilities for outpatient mental health services, and office space for community organizations. Mary Nelson points with special pride to the eighteen-thousand-square-foot Cultural and Performing Arts Center, built in the hospital's former chapel, which hosts regular events and encourages creative expression among area youth.

The PBS program closed with an emblematic statement: "Nelson shows no sign of slowing down"—citing her role in BNL's latest project. The Lake and Pulaski Commercial Center is a twenty-three thousand–square-foot, two-story "smart, green" building that will house a day-care center, retail establishments, and offices for BNL's employment services. The energy-efficient structure (featuring photovoltaic cells and other innovations) will be connected to the Chicago Transit Authority's (CTA) Lake Street "El train" platform.

Bethel New Life, Inc.'s introduction to concepts such as energy efficiency, ecological integrity, environmental quality, and sustainable community development dates back to the mid-1990s, when BNL formed a partnership with the Illinois-based Argonne National Laboratory. It was called an experiment in technology transfer and urban restoration. It resulted in such tangible creations as the BNL Recycling and Material Recovery Center, which has returned thousands of dollars and created dozens of jobs in the waste-recovery business. But the relationship with Argonne National Laboratory also elevated BNL's and Mary Nelson's reputation in such fields as environmental justice and smart growth.

Nelson serves on several national boards of organizations such as the National Congress for Community Economic Development, the Christian Community Development Association, Call to Renewal, and the Woodstock Institute. She speaks regularly at national conferences. On February 4, 2003, she flew to Washington, D.C., to address HUD officials from across the country who work with faith-based organizations.

As usual, Nelson's remarks were not scripted. A polished improvisational speaker, Nelson scrawled two pages of notes on a legal pad on the plane, her large cursive handwriting connected with circles and squares around key talking points. Nelson enjoys traveling and meeting with diverse groups and audiences. "One of the joys of this community development stuff," Nelson says, "is you're not segmented. I feel comfortable in the corporate world, in the church world, or on the streets. [I have] . . . the freedom to know no boundaries."

Nelson's reputation as one of the nation's premier community development leaders has been continually buoyed by positive stories in countless publications, such as the June 24, 1992, article by Michael Abramowitz in *The Washington Post,* showcasing the success of community development corporations (such as Bethel New Life, Inc.) as being among the "most effective agents of neighborhood change." But CDCs have not been universally acclaimed.

An article by Rebecca Bauen and Betsy Reed in a publication called *Dollars and Sense* (January–February 1995) cited a controversial *The New York Times Magazine* piece from spring 1994 ("The Myth of Community Development") in which Nicholas Lemann labeled empowerment zones a sham. "Echoing past urban renewal arguments, Lemann held out jobs downtown and migration to the suburbs as the best hope for inner city residents."

A year later (January 1996), Wim Wiewel, an urban planner at the University of Illinois at Chicago, was quoted by Jennifer Halperin in the magazine *Illinois Issues* as questioning the role of community development efforts on Chicago's West Side: "But let's not over blow expectations for this community. . . . I'm not sure this is the best use of scarce resources."

On Thursday, July 12, 2001, the *Austin Weekly News* cited articles in the *Chicago Sun-Times* and *Chicago Tribune,* plus research by Children's Memorial Hospital, that proclaimed West Garfield Park as the worst neighborhood in the city for violence, accidents, abuse, and quality of life for children. The hospital research showed that West Garfield Park ranked first in hospitalizations for preventable injuries and deaths among children seventeen and younger. D. Kevin McNeir quoted Mary Nelson in the article as being concerned about the negative neighborhood description and attitudes it could generate. "Obviously Bethel New Life is committed in its efforts to make this a safe and secure place for children," she said in the weekly newspaper.

Nelson doesn't ignore the harsh realities facing her community, but she refuses to be intimidated by statistics or by city of Chicago officials, such as those staffers in this week's (February 3, 2003) city hall meeting who are mandating that hundreds of thousands of dollars of repairs be made by BNL at the Family Wellness Center before the city will release funding for the rehab of other facilities in West Garfield Park. "You just keep pushing," Nelson says, weaving in and out of bumper-to-bumper traffic en route to yet another meeting.

Nelson gets a needed boost of inspiration on a frigid (5 degrees F.) Friday morning when she meets a group of job-seeking formerly homeless people at the offices of The CARA (which means "friend" in Gaelic) Program, located just east of the Monroe Street Bridge in downtown Chicago. Several residents in BNL's transitional housing program, along with referrals from seventy homeless shelters, are participating in comprehensive life-skills and job-readiness training at The CARA Program's career-transition center. Since CARA's founding in 1991, more than eleven hundred individuals have found employment; the current average hourly salary for participants is almost $10. Almost 70 percent of The CARA Program graduates remain employed longer than nine months, which has helped attract eighty-seven local companies to participate in the job-training and job-placement program.

In a converted bay area of a former fire station, more than thirty men and women in suits and ties and dresses sit in a circle at 8:30 A.M. Tom Owens, head of the Owens Foundation, former IBM executive, and The CARA Program founder, welcomes them. They are greeted and "warmed up" by Eric Weinheimer, president and CEO of The CARA Program. Several in the circle are called out to share a piece of their life story, cite a favorite motivational quote, and lead the group in a feel-good song. These people are looking for a break, a chance to reverse the downward cycle. They will get that break, that chance, that "do-over," through this support-ive program—if they show up on time, work hard, and persevere.

Mary Nelson smiles warmly through much of the thirty-minute motiva-tional program this morning at The CARA Program offices. She applauds with the group when a shy man in a dark suit softly shares the good news that he has a job. He has a job!

Later, Mary Nelson, Steve McCullough, and Kaana Makundi meet with Tom Owens and Eric Weinheimer to explore ways to enhance the relation-ship between Bethel New Life, Inc., and The CARA Program. Nelson presents a preliminary $25,000 proposal for a new program targeting the needs of a rising ex-offender population seeking jobs and a new life. Nelson says that as many as four thousand will return to their neighbor-hood annually for the next three years. This is an introductory meeting for the BNL and The CARA Program execs, and Nelson's proposal will be discussed further at a later date. Differences of opinion are expected. But the "do-gooders" in this room are kindred spirits. They have the same dual mission, the same real goals: to change the way society thinks about the poor, and to change the way the poor think about themselves.

"It's inspirational to see how God moves in people's lives," Nelson says. Now outside facing the bitter breezes of the Chicago "hawk," she makes the block-and-a-half walk to the parking lot in double-time. If you want to keep up with Mary Nelson on foot, you had better not lollygag.

Next stop is a meeting with Ron Gidwitz, the retired CEO of Helene Curtis, whose company had been a major presence in Chicago's West Side community for years. Gidwitz, now a venture capitalist, has long been a loyal supporter of Bethel New Life, Inc. A decade ago his company do-nated $25,000 to BNL's daycare facility, which was patronized by several Helene Curtis employees.

Today Gidwitz is being asked to become a member of the campaign committee, a select group of movers and shakers to lead the Bethel New Life twenty-fifth-anniversary campaign, whose goal is to raise $3 million to ensure long-term financial security for BNL—including $500,000 to "enhance leadership capacity and assure the transition from the founders to the next generation of leaders." Translation: Mary Nelson is retiring in 2005.

"I didn't think that was allowed," Gidwitz says with a smile to the group gathered in his small, windowless meeting room. He sounds savvy as he talks about the potential for gentrification of West Garfield Park—if the schools improve and the gang problem diminishes. He tells Nelson that BNL has to continue to invest in commercial and housing development. Nelson listens, nodding in agreement with much of what Gidwitz says.

Then she again asks Gidwitz, "Ron, will you join us as the fifth member?" After reassuring a somewhat reticent Gidwitz that his time commitment on the committee would be nominal, the deal is done. He agrees to serve.

On the way back to the Beth-Anne Life Center Campus, Nelson celebrates the successful morning meetings with a hasty lunch of an Italian sausage on a roll and a bag of fries from a nondescript drive-through.

When asked about the future of BNL, she responds with a question of her own, "Do we continue to tackle new and risky things, or stay comfortable within and improve our existing framework?" She doesn't answer that question directly. She talks about the organization's $11 million annual budget and its staff of 350 people. She discusses the strengths of the senior management team, including Steven McCullough, the West Side native and MBA-carrying chief operating officer who has expressed interest in succeeding Mary Nelson. A search firm will assist the Bethel New Life board in making the selection. Whoever is chosen will join BNL in 2004 and work alongside Nelson until her retirement in 2005—hence the rationale for funding support from the anniversary campaign. The conversation comes full circle as Nelson states, "I'm going to release the organization to go into new directions."

Late on an afternoon in February 2003, Mary Nelson reflects further about life after Bethel New Life, Inc. She is upbeat about the "many wonderful possibilities and opportunities." She says she will continue to live in West Garfield Park, but she looks forward to travel, to consulting and working with national faith-based organizations, to having more time to spend at the family cabin on that bucolic lake in northern Minnesota, and to mentoring young people who want to make a difference in the community. Nelson, the longtime educator, remains ever the teacher. "This next generation has different tools, and will come at solving problems differently," Nelson says. She sounds encouraged, but there is some concern in her voice as she wonders aloud about up-and-coming activists and their enduring passion for the cause.

A couple hours later, Mary Nelson, today casually dressed in navy slacks, pale blue sweater, and multicolored shawl, joins Kate Lane, who wears a festive black and gold blouse and matching pillbox hat. They sit with some of the other passionate "awesome ladies of the neighborhood" who have stood shoulder to shoulder on the streets of West Garfield Park in twenty-four-hour prayer vigils and forty-day "Take Back the Streets" campaigns. They have stared down gun-wielding drug dealers, offering prayers and white crosses with the names of young men lost to the spiral of violence. Their actions have earned the praise of politicians, newspaper editors, and the grateful residents of their community. Tonight this comely group of heroic women has gathered for an exhibit in the Cultural and Performing Arts Center. They chat about the upcoming Gumbo Gala fund-raiser (featuring Lane's culinary talents) and reminisce, enjoying one another's company on a cold winter night.

"She knows I'm there for her," says Kate Lane about her rock-solid relationship with Mary Nelson. "And I know I can count on her."

Then, when Nelson is across the room greeting some residents, Lane shares a prophetic comment about her friend Mary Nelson, the legendary community builder.

"She's always looking for her keys."

[9]

REVEREND SKIP LONG "WHATEVER IT TAKES"

Photo by Mark H. Massé

At mid-year, Reverend Skip Long had several new developments to report on professional and personal fronts. In May 2003 the National Jobs Partnership (NJP) announced the beginning of its twenty-seventh city in Petersburg, Virginia. By the summer, Atlanta, Georgia, the twenty-eighth NJP city, was scheduled to begin its mentoring and job-training classes. Reverend Long, NJP executive director, announced that more than sixty U.S. communities have expressed interest in joining the National Jobs Partnership network. The organization's track record was winning converts across the country. Closer to home, Skip Long had other exciting news to share. He and his wife, Andrea, were expecting another child in January 2004. Long said life was moving quickly. He, however, was limping along due to a torn anterior cruciate ligament (ACL), suffered in a pickup basketball game. But Reverend Skip Long, weekend athlete and vibrant faith activist, was not about to let a knee injury dampen his spirits.

> Responding to God's call to love Him with all our heart, soul, mind and strength and to love our neighbors as ourselves, we believe that through intentional relationships, we are able to experience a true reflection of the Kingdom of God.
>
> —Mark 12:30–31; Hebrews 10:25

Reverend Skip Long and the antipoverty program he heads have faced many challenges since it began as a local effort seven years ago in his hometown, Raleigh, North Carolina. But neither he nor his organization has ever been so stymied by an act of God—until today. On Sunday, February 15, 2003, officials of the National Jobs Partnership are confronting a near-perfect winter storm that is shutting down Washington, D.C., and threatening to cancel the organization's National Leadership Conference. NJP executive director Long and David Spickard, his director of operations, have been up since before dawn, trying to predict the weather, contacting their board of directors, and making contingency plans that affect more than one hundred people bound for D.C.

"These kinds of events excite me," crisis manager Long says as he works the phones, watches TV news, and checks the Internet. With just a few hours' sleep, he remains upbeat and encouraging to staff and family members gathered in suite 1440 of the Renaissance Hotel on 9th Street N.W. He is wearing the same khaki pants and white turtleneck he wore at dinner last night. The only change in his attire is a dark Mangum Asphalt baseball cap. This morning the stocky, broad-shouldered Long is fueled by Diet Pepsi, handfuls of M&Ms, hearty doses of adrenaline, and the Holy Spirit.

His faith, confidence, and energy have helped grow the National Jobs Partnership from a Raleigh-based program. The Partnership has expanded to twenty-six cities, with eight more U.S. sites pending. In the process the organization, which features a collaboration of local churches and businesses, has become one of the darlings of the contemporary faith-based movement.

The twelve-week, twenty-four-session job training and placement program teaches life and workforce skills using both the Bible and human resources materials. Sample topics: "How I can research work opportunities in a Godly way" and "Communication and spirituality in the workplace." Unemployed (and "underemployed") program participants are sponsored for two years by partner churches, which also provide mentors and necessary support services, such as transportation, childcare, and financial planning. The goals of NJP are secular and spiritual—addressing the needs of job seekers and employers, achieving financial self-sufficiency and economic growth, enhancing race relations, and advancing the Kingdom of God on earth.

"We're trying to change the world one person at a time and in great numbers," says Long. And if you have any sense, you had better listen up, because Skip Long is a very bright, persuasive fellow. The charming forty-two-year-old is also built like an NFL linebacker. One can imagine Long in another time and place, as a knight riding into battle for what he believes is the answer to a host of social ills.

He speaks in a promotional video on the Partnership with a preacher's passion: "Here God has put together a clear plan of how to move forward with those who are in poverty, those who are broken, those who are unemployed. . . . Here is a model that they can embrace and meet the problems they face." He talks convincingly of healing people and transforming lives. But he is more than a talented spokesperson. Skip Long is respected and admired by people across racial lines and from different socioeconomic strata and political affiliations. He has addressed both the 2000 Democratic and Republican conventions, spoken on the floor of Congress, and been invited to the White House by presidents Clinton and George W. Bush.

As one might expect, Long has a healthy ego. But he attracts folks with his wit and ability to laugh at himself and his situation. Several years ago when he was invited to the Clinton White House for a Rose Garden ceremony, related to the passage of new welfare reform legislation, he thought it was a prank call by an old fraternity brother. He told the caller to "fax him something on White House letterhead." A few minutes later, the requested fax arrived.

"You hung up on the White House?" asked an incredulous NJP board member.

"You know I'm just a kid from the 'hood," Skip replied with a hearty laugh.

Or consider this Sunday morning's jovial telephone exchange with one of the managers of the Renaissance Hotel in winter storm–draped Washington, D.C., which now resembles a scene out of a Stephen King novel or an episode of *The Twilight Zone*. "We'll keep dancing," Long says, breaking into a familiar baritone chuckle. "I've worked on all these talks . . . and somebody is going to listen to my vision—even if it's the Marriott staff."

Even that is wishful thinking, because several of the hotel staff are snowbound. There will be no national gathering this week to hear Skip Long's presentations, to meet federal government and private-sector officials, and to read the framed February 3, 2003, letter to NJP from President George W. Bush:

> I send greetings to those gathered for the National Leadership Conference of the National Jobs Partnership (NJP). Every American deserves a chance to learn new skills, reach their full potential, and realize their dreams. Through the important efforts of the NJP, faith-based groups and businesses are working together to provide individuals across our country with the tools they need to build better lives.

I commend the NJP for your dedication to strengthening our communities and for bringing hope, care and comfort to countless Americans. Your efforts to mentor, train and employ those in need are helping to ensure that every person has the opportunity to experience the promise of our great Nation. Laura joins me in sending our best wishes for a successful conference.

—George Bush

By 10 A.M. on Sunday, February 16, 2003, the decision is made to postpone and reschedule the National Leadership Conference, which in contractual terms has been cancelled by an act of God. While Skip Long and David Spickard work their cell phones and David's laptop, sending out a flurry of e-mails, family members in suite 1440 head down to the hotel's concierge lounge for continental breakfast.

Last night in this lounge, Long was approached by a young girl from a suburban Connecticut family. Long was being interviewed by a journalist. The shy girl stepped forward tentatively with pad and pen in hand, as her parents at a nearby table urged her on.

"Are you somebody famous?" she asked softly.

"No, are you somebody famous?" he replied with an impish grin. He made the girl laugh. He told her that many years and pounds ago, he had been an athlete. Actually, Long is an accomplished golfer and tennis player. And the former captain of his college basketball team still plays a mean game of pickup b-ball (though his NJP partner and friend, David Spickard, has more basketball pedigree, having played on the University of North Carolina junior varsity team).

Skip Long says he enjoys meeting people, but it disappoints him when they assume he must be a famous athlete. He recounts traveling with Partnership co-founder Chris Mangum, a handsome silver-haired white businessman. Long notes how often the pair are approached in airports. People talk to Mangum as if he's the sports agent for Long, the black jock. Long wonders aloud why they don't think that he could be a professional other than a pro athlete. If someone happens to make that mistake, Skip Long will likely talk with that person and try to enlighten his or her worldview. It's part of his "ministry of whispering" that he embarked on years ago. It's also a constructive way of channeling his anger, such as in those situations where he may intimidate nervous white store clerks who assume that he could have ulterior motives. In these cases, Long will lower his voice, slow his cadence, and ask the clerks why they thought this black man might be trouble. He will reach out and "engage them at the heart level" to help them see the error of their ways, the bias of their assumptions.

In the days leading up to the NJP National Leadership Conference and for several that follow, Skip Long's life reads like a "lite" version of the Book of Job. Long plays the role of an Old Testament character blessed with the modern-day humor of a folksy comedian like Sinbad or Bill Cosby. Even when he recounts tales of disappointment, loss, frustration, and concern that could drive others to distraction, Long keeps his poise and dignity. These situations range from dealing with the ominous threat of war with Iraq to battles with a computer virus.

Before he, fellow NJP staffers, and his family (wife, Andrea, and son, Matthew) were snowbound in D.C., Reverend Long's laptop went haywire, erasing weeks of conference planning and correspondence, plus all his presentations. At home that week, the family's dryer, dishwasher, and range had decided to break down within days of each other (not to mention that the 1988 Volvo with 158,000 miles was overdue for a tune-up). At the office Long and Spickard were still without a secretary, having had to part ways with a former staff member after Christmas. On a more serious note, at his Raleigh church an ugly racial incident from the previous Easter was still festering, still fragmenting the congregation, and causing associate minister Skip Long sleepless nights.

"My vessel has many holes," Long says, reflecting on a holy host of trials and tribulations. Perhaps this dashing activist could be "morphed" into an African American Indiana Jones, wrestling with various challenges and cliffhangers. He has the leather coat, but instead of a fedora, try a baseball cap. Replace the leather whip with his leather backpack. The relevance of such a fictional comparison may be debated, but as one spends time with Long it becomes increasingly clear that what he is dealing with in the present in February 2003 is a microcosm of the people, events, and issues that have shaped and continue to influence his life.

FAMILY

While in Washington, D.C., Skip Long, with copilot David Spickard, not only has to implement an action plan for rescheduling the conference and improvise two days of orientation strategies for the handful of attendees who made it to the hotel, but also must be a daddy to his precocious eight-year-old son, Matthew, who is wrestling with cabin fever. Long will be the first to admit that Andrea, his gracious and soft-spoken wife, is the behind-the-scenes strength of the family. So far she is keeping Matthew on track with homework and engaged with games and trips around the cavernous hotel, where jackhammers in the lobby have finally grown silent after days of noisy renovation work.

But the slender, doe-eyed boy craves his father's attention. When can we go swimming, Dad? Are you going to take me for a walk, Dad? When are you coming back to the room, Dad? Children, as they say, will try the patience of a saint.

On this Sunday afternoon, Long tidies up the dining/conference room table in suite 1440, tosses out used paper cups and plates, and gathers up Matthew's sneakers. He speaks of parenthood and the behavior he's trying to model for his children (Andrea and Skip also have an adopted eighteen-year-old daughter, Dinesha, now a college student in Florida). He reflects back to his youth and the valuable, but often hard-edged, wisdom imparted by his mother and father.

One of Skip Long's most painful memories is walking as a boy with his father, Matthew Jr., along a Raleigh street when a car of white men drove by and hurled eggs at the father and son.

"My father didn't allow his anger to consume him," Long says, clasping and unclasping his large hands as he shares the tale. His mother, Imogene, a devout Christian, would tell Skip, his two older sisters, and younger brother that these kind of hateful actions were "not the way of the Lord." She told her children that if they were going to change the world, they would have to be smart and act correctly. They would have to be well-spoken and respectful of others. She told her children to remember they were part of a human family: "It is never just about you."

Skip Long tried to do the right thing, but it was hard not to be embittered when he watched his father, a Navy veteran with an engineering degree from the Hampton Institute, having to mop floors in a local ice cream store to earn money when times got hard. "All work honors God," his mother would say. His father, a proud and intimidating man, taught his son to do the best job he could no matter what the task: "A man doesn't quit."

Years later when Long told his father he was dating a white woman (Andrea), his dad disapproved. The son persisted. Just get to know her, he said. Andrea had already won over Skip's mom, who "loved her the first time they met." The elder Long lowered his objections when he got acquainted with Andrea over several days when he installed banks of computers at the Building Together Ministries, where she and Skip worked with poor single moms and their kids in the Halifax Court neighborhood of Raleigh. Two years later Skip and Andrea were engaged.

Not everyone in Skip Long's world was happy. He received negative feedback from members of his Baptist church. Then came the Long family reunion. Long recalls that some members of his extended family took their jokes and sarcastic comments about the engaged couple a little too far. Matthew Long Jr. did not suffer fools gladly. In the middle of the reunion dinner, according to Skip, he announced that his future daughter-in-law, Andrea, was "more like family than the rest of y'all." Then he led his wife, sons and daughters, and daughter-in-law out of the dining room and out to the parking lot. Reverend Long is beaming as he relives the memory: "Dad hit a home run that day."

In 1993 Skip and Andrea married, and his father was there with a joyful and resolute spirit, though his body was weakened from battling cancer. Three years later, when Skip was starting his work with the Jobs Partnership, his father died. "He modeled what it was like to be a man right up to the end," says Long. In 1997, his mother, Imogene, died of a heart attack while undergoing exploratory tests on her liver. To this day, Long believes his mom died of a broken heart after losing her best friend and husband of forty-three years.

The interracial marriage of Skip and Andrea Long was not endorsed by her family. Relations were distant and frosty for years, with brief visits limited to the holidays. But time has healed some if not all wounds. Last year, Andrea's parents gave their son-in-law Skip a beautiful leather back-pack, which he uses in lieu of a briefcase. Recently, Andrea's father built the couple a large wood deck on the rear of their modest ranch-style, fifteen-hundred–square-foot home.

In his talks on the National Jobs Partnership, Skip Long talks about bringing "healing where healing is needed." He is grateful for the improved relations with his in-laws, and he acknowledges how he has called on his faith to get him through difficult times. His compassion for others has continually impressed his peers.

According to John Bender, his friend and the pastor of the Raleigh Mennonite Church that he and Andrea attend: "It is his commitment to Christ that fuels his work and love for those who are hurting and wounded and on the fringes of society. . . . Skip also cares deeply about people and will do anything for them."

Skip and Andrea are proud that they see the same empathy and compassion developing in their young son, Matthew. On a frigid Monday in D.C., Long and his son walked from the hotel to the White House, blocks away. En route they passed a homeless man in a doorway. He was sleeping in cardboard boxes. Matthew couldn't take his eyes off the man. When he looked up at his father, he said, "I almost want to cry, Daddy." He wanted to know what would become of the man. His father couldn't give an answer that would comfort him. Skip Long says that back in Raleigh his son will often give some of his allowance money to homeless people on the street.

RACE

From an early age, Skip Long says, his English teacher mother taught him and his siblings how to live in a multicultural world. "She made sure we were engaged with blacks and whites. As an African American it's part of survival," he says. Long adds that his mother tried to provide him with experiences that would broaden his perspective, such as an eighth-grade class trip to Spain. Years later Long would return to Europe for extended visits after graduating from college.

When it comes to matters of race, Long speaks frankly. He admits that he will talk differently with white CEOs than he will with "brothers on the street." He adjusts his approaches accordingly, depending on the demands of the situation. Long can be confrontational. At dinner during one of the snowbound nights in Washington, D.C., he turns to Joe Crowley, an Irish American professor and member of a contingent (two blacks and one white) of NJP conference attendees from Montgomery, Alabama. With his brow furrowed and eyes focused, Long leans forward and asks Joe if he and his colleague, African American Reverend Aaron McCall, are really friends, or is the black pastor just a "hood ornament"? Professor Joe blushes and stammers briefly as he tries to answer inquisitor Long. He speaks earnestly about having Aaron over to his house on several occasions.

Is there a point to this questioning? What is Skip Long trying to demonstrate? Is he just upset because he ordered the grilled chicken salad instead of the ribs, which he originally said he wanted? He later explains how vital it is to the success of a Jobs Partnership program that matters of race be dealt with directly. "It's going to be rough when you go into your community and try to establish partnerships. Get used to it. You're going to have to deal with the race issue often."

Long also discusses the power dynamics that will occur in Partnership meetings when church folks sit down with business execs. The execs will not be used to relinquishing control, especially to the faith community. But they will have to do just that when black, Hispanic, or other minority pastors take the lead role in launching programs and securing participants. Long wants to make sure that the trio from Montgomery, Alabama, know exactly what they will face.

Skip Long is fond of sharing anecdotes about his journey toward racial understanding. When he was a college student, he took a summer job at YMCA Camp Seagull. Long was the only black on the staff that was serving about fourteen hundred upper-crust white kids. At first he resented his role at the camp. Then a senior counselor named Tracy Howe took rookie counselor Long under his wing. They attended Bible study together. They talked about their faith. Howe encouraged Long to push himself, to challenge preconceptions, and to act as a cultural change agent. In time the black inner-city teen would become a lifeguard, CPR instructor, and sailing instructor. He would learn an important lesson about striving for success in a white-dominated society.

Long also shares a more recent and painful lesson of troubled race relations from within the walls of his own church, where he and Andrea have been members for more than eight years. Last Easter, on what should have been a day of peace, celebration, and reconciliation for the Christian community, an incident occurred at the Raleigh Mennonite Church that continues to haunt Skip Long and others in the congregation.

An African pastor had been invited to lead the service. During his sermon, which focused on racial matters, a white member of the largely white-collar congregation rushed toward the pastor, shouting angrily and flailing his arms. He would later claim to have been inspired by the Holy Spirit. While others were frozen in their seats, Andrea turned to her husband. "You have to do something," she said. Long rushed the man and subdued him. He yelled to the pastor to conclude the service: Do the benediction. Let's go.

In subsequent months, Skip Long refuses to be hardened by the incident. He participates in regular dialogue and sensitivity training with members of the congregation and co-pastors John and Marilyn Bender. Drawing on his reputed gift for consensus building, he pledges to do whatever it takes to help heal the wounds.

"I think Skip has had to put up with a lot of stuff at our church, but he continues to give and stretches us in significant ways beyond our comfort zones," says John Bender, adding that his "significant relationship" with Long, a black man, has broadened and enriched his life. Referring to the Easter 2002 incident, Bender says that because the conflict had racial implications, it was important for Skip Long to be involved and "for all of us to hear his perspective. He was involved from the beginning, and the two of us met with the individual initially. Along the way Skip was a great support to me personally. I know the whole thing got him down, but he continued to help work through it."

Back in Washington, D.C., as the gale winds howl outside suite 1440, NJP director of operations David Spickard leads a training session for the three men from Montgomery, Alabama, and late arrival Jeannie Avery, a slight, gray-haired, English-accented woman from Flemington, New Jersey. Spickard, a trim thirty-three-year-old strawberry blonde–haired, blue-eyed native of Nashville, Tennessee, tells the group how he grew up as a privileged white kid who was disconnected from the poor and isolated from the minority community.

He talks about how he began his career as an MBA-carrying business consultant, but how he ended up dissatisfied and searching for a way to translate his faith into service to others. When he discovered the National Jobs Partnership program in April 1999, he felt he could make a meaningful, lasting contribution to society by working toward the elimination of poverty. But he would have to venture well beyond the borders of his familiar, comfortable white world. He tells how he and Skip have learned from each other about their cultural biases, attitudes, and predispositions. Spickard informs the gathering how he has learned to "get his preach on" by hanging out with Long and other African American pastors during the years he has worked at the Partnership. As Spickard becomes more animated, speaking from the heart about his evolution as a white man being sensitized to the black condition, Skip Long smiles knowingly like a big brother.

MENTORS

In *Collaborating for Employment among the Poor: The Jobs Partnership Model,* a 2001 report by Dr. Amy L. Sherman of the Hudson Institute, Inc., Partnership mentors are described as needing "a strong Christian commitment, a deep love for people, a humble and prayerful spirit, time availability, and emotional maturity in order to be effective." The sixty-seven-page report dedicates more than nine pages to the role of mentors in the job-training and placement program. In his remarks to the Alabama and New Jersey attendees in suite 1440, Skip Long reinforces the importance of mentors to the success of any Jobs Partnership program. The one-on-one relationships between the mentors and the people who are transitioning toward a better life are one of the distinguishing characteristics of the Partnership model versus other welfare-to-work type programs.

Skip Long envisions himself as a mentor not only to those leading Partnership programs in cities across the United States, but also to people he encounters in his day-to-day life. On the way to dinner again tonight in the Renaissance Hotel (because no other D.C. restaurants are open due to the snowstorm), Long runs into the young dark-haired girl who had asked him for an autograph two nights earlier. Long stops and chats with her and her family at their dining room table. It gives him a moment to talk about the work of the Partnership. No, he isn't somebody famous. But he believes he is doing significant work that is more important than being famous. He tells the young girl that he would love to see her engaged in the lives of the poor. Then he exchanges autographs with her. His new friend, Rachel, writes, "To my friend Skip Long."

When Long was about Rachel's age back in Raleigh, he was an angry, overweight boy. He didn't enjoy sports, nor was he fond of school. His mother wouldn't tolerate her first-born son's listlessness. She marched him to a local karate school taught by a five-foot-one, ninety-pound instructor named Vicky Morrow. Miss Morrow was to be the first of many significant mentors in Skip Long's life. She helped him gain confidence and vision in sizing up opponents and opportunities. She taught him how to think strategically and how to channel his anger. She started Long on the road to becoming a successful athlete, who would go on to earn a black belt in karate and a college basketball scholarship.

Sam Lewis, Long's basketball coach at Brevard Junior College, Brevard, North Carolina, selected Skip as starting point guard on the team, telling him: "I want to create a leader." Long continued his solid play on the basketball court and was a member of the golf team when he attended Shorter College, Rome, Georgia. He graduated with a degree in political science and appeared headed for University of California, Berkeley, Law School. But travel to Europe beckoned, and Skip Long went on the road for several months. Upon his return, his strong-willed mother, Imogene, stepped in. She told her son that now it was time to work.

He parlayed his experience at Camp Seagull (and a strong recommendation from mentor Tracy Howe) into a job as a multiple-sport instructor at the Raleigh YMCA. A year later he became assistant general manager of the athletes' dorm, a privately operated building, at University of North Carolina (UNC), Chapel Hill. He was responsible for coordinating room assignments, meals, and logistics for students and summer basketball camp visitors.

In the mid-1980s he returned to the Raleigh YMCA once more, serving as assistant youth director and, later, youth director. He enjoyed working with the kids, and he was grateful for the opportunity to meet Andrea, a fellow YMCA staffer, who five years later would become his wife. In 1988,

Skip Long left the Y and returned to the college campus—this time, North Carolina State University.

He was working for the same firm that he had served under at UNC three years earlier. Assistant general manager Long now managed a high-rise dormitory that was also home to several summer camps. "I was in my element working with the kids," Long says. He was earning good money, living rent-free, and driving a slick Subaru GLX sports coupe. As the cliché goes, he was climbing the corporate ladder. He thought he was on the right path, but his restless spirit told him otherwise. "God began to strip me [of my pride]," Long says. "He was letting me know that I wasn't really in control."

Andrea was now working with Young Life, an inner-city ministry dealing with high school students. Skip began to volunteer with the after-school organization. When he wasn't working on the NC State campus, he took Young Life members on field trips. After one of these trips in 1991, he made up his mind to leave the corporate world and follow his heart to "nurturing the lives of young inner-city children."

He had discovered a new organization with a mission of service to poor families in Raleigh—Building Together Ministries, founded by a white homebuilder, Freddie Johnson, and his wife, Helen. The organization had no money for salaries. If Long wanted to work there, he would have to get sponsors.

He went to his Baptist church congregation, looking for financial support. He was now an ordained minister and youth pastor, and he felt confident that his church family would support his decision. They didn't. They questioned why an up-and-coming black man would leave the corporate world. Skip Long knew the answer. It was right in his Bible, Luke 16:13: "You cannot serve both God and money." Long sought funding elsewhere, from friends and colleagues he had worked with and grown up with in Raleigh.

For the next three years, Skip Long directed youth programs, including after-school enrichment classes. He said he had a gift for finding talented people to work as volunteers in the minority community. He also was attracting the attention of business and community leaders, including Chris Mangum, president of the Mangum Group, a road, bridge, and parking lot paving company.

In 1994 Skip Long reluctantly left Building Together Ministries. He had worked closely with Freddie Johnson, again expanding his multicultural experience. But he clashed with an African American woman executive director, who had a different vision about how the youth programs should be run. Skip Long became a race relations consultant, offering his services to companies in Greater Raleigh. One of his clients became the Mangum Group. A year later, Chris Mangum and Reverend Donald McCoy would start a fledgling organization called the Jobs Partnership. The Partnership began when business executive Mangum befriended inner-city pastor McCoy, and the two men assembled a coalition of a dozen churches and companies to address the local unemployment problem. They were attempting a new approach to solving social problems. These true believers were "casting their vision" to a skeptical world.

During the first six months, the Partnership relied on volunteer staff, including thirty-five-year-old Skip Long. By early 1996, the Raleigh Jobs Partnership incorporated. In June 1996 it qualified for 501(c)(3) non-profit organization status, a crucial step in generating tax-deductible financial contributions and for attracting welfare reform governmental funding. Long now became executive director. "This began my journey with Jobs Partnership," he says. "It's never been my job; it's my ministry."

His mission was now in focus. He would develop the Raleigh program and spread the vision (and the Kingdom) nationwide. Along the way he would benefit from the counsel of Partnership officials, including founders Mangum and McCoy and the current board chairman, James White, a noted Bible teacher and welfare reform consultant.

Seven years later on a Monday evening, February 17, 2003, Skip Long and David Spickard provide the four National Leadership Conference attendees with a short action plan that they will take back with them to Alabama and New Jersey. For this informal presentation, Long wears sharp-creased black dress slacks, a black turtleneck, and polished black loafers. Spickard wears tan, wide-ribbed corduroy pants and a button-down navy sports shirt. The two men intentionally sit at opposite corners of the room.

Spickard takes the lead at the flip chart, noting the four key steps required to launch an NJP program. The first step is forming a steering committee of pastors and businesspeople who could work together in a unique combination of cultures. The second step is praying together as an organization to create a community and to cast a vision. The third step is raising money. For a small community, the minimum NJP fee is several thousand dollars to receive materials and consulting from Long and Spickard. For a larger community, the fee rises to the low five-figure range. But the initial NJP fees are only about one-fourth of the budget suggested to launch a Partnership program.

Skip Long discusses potential funding streams from state and federal government, plus foundations. He speaks on networking and using resources such as the U.S. Chamber of Commerce, which was instrumental in providing the Partnership with a workforce platform to expand its reach to audiences nationwide. Another organization mentioned is the American Institute for Full Employment (AIFE), a novel group dedicated to eliminating poverty (and the welfare system), which was formed by executives of the Jeld-Wen corporation in Klamath Falls, Oregon. Long says he has engaged both Chamber of Commerce and Jeld-Wen execs "at the heart level," and they are ready to help individual Jobs Partnership communities become successful.

The fourth step discussed tonight is vision casting and training. This is where the "ministry of whispering" begins, says Skip Long, "and you speak things into existence." He tells the group that they must convey their passion for serving the poor, and they must challenge members of their communities to support the vision. Long and Spickard try to reassure the three men and one woman studying the flip-chart presentation that they will have support on their mission.

They tell them that many others have been in their situation. They admonish the group to return to their cities and "stick their necks out." But this group is quiet. They seem like nervous disciples about to be sent to the hinterlands.

MINISTRY

Skip Long arrives back in Raleigh on Tuesday, February 18, at dusk on a beautiful midwinter day. He has driven from Washington, D.C., in a rented fifteen-person van, stacked with luggage and boxes of binders, videos, other materials, and equipment intended for the National Leadership Conference. The temperature in Raleigh is about 50 degrees Fahrenheit, without a trace of snow on the ground.

"It's just so unreal, unbelievable," says David Spickard. He and Long discuss what they would be doing about now if the conference had not been cancelled. "Let's see, 5:30 P.M.," says Long. "We'd be wrapping up our table talks and making plans for dinner in Chinatown." Their laughter seems forced and tinny. Their faces look tired.

The unpacking of the van and moving of several elevator loads of boxes, banners, and other conference stuff back to the NJP's aging Six Forks Road headquarters building proceeds smoothly. The men move to and fro quietly, efficiently, in and out of the no-frills offices that are common to

149

local political campaigns and start-up consulting firms—lots of four- and five-drawer file cabinets, small wood bookshelves, secondhand tables, a couple threadbare chairs, and empty computer boxes. Taped to the walls of one office are yellow easel-sized sheets with agendas, calendars, mission statements, and topics that had been planned for the conference that never was: "Work Force Issues," "Strategic Alliances," "Faith-Based Ex-Offenders," "Home Ownership."

There is one piece of good news awaiting Long and Spickard: a letter from the U.S. Department of Housing and Urban Development (HUD). This is the memorandum of understanding (MOU) that the Partnership had been expecting. It formalizes the partnership between HUD and the National Jobs Partnership to "facilitate the planning and implementation of a nationwide series of training initiatives to assist faith-based and community-based organizations' outreach to low and very-low income residents on employment, training and business contracting opportunities through the Section 3 program of the Housing Act of 1968."

The memorandum from HUD is one more example of the Partnership's remarkable rise to prominence in seven short years. Its success has been documented in reports such as the 2001 *Collaborating for Employment among the Poor: The Jobs Partnership Model,* which proclaimed the achievements of the ministry headed by executive director Skip Long. In Raleigh, more than one hundred churches and businesses have worked through the years to train and place more than three hundred people, 92 percent of whom have kept their jobs for at least one year. In Orlando, the Chamber of Commerce has worked actively to mobilize businesses to work with church leaders from the black and Hispanic communities. In Tucson, the mayor's wife, working with clergy and business leaders, became a driving force to establish a Partnership to serve the needs of low-income residents.

A chapter in Jim Wallis's 2000 book, *Faith Works,* touted the proven track record of the Jobs Partnership idea as it spread across the United States. The book praised the networking and community-building of the Partnerships concept as a way to combat poverty. Perhaps most impressive were the words of a female graduate of a Jobs Partnership twelve-week program (about 60 percent of grads are women):

> Dani first heard of the Jobs Partnership through John Bender, pastor of the Raleigh Mennonite Church, and another member of the church, who was coordinating the program. . . . Dani describes the transformation that took place during the Jobs Partnership classes: "I became aware of some forgotten truths in my life. The truth of my own self-worth; the truth of God's love and patience."

When Skip Long hears such testimonials, his faith is bolstered: "We believe this work is a movement that will last beyond our lifetime."

On Wednesday morning, February 19, when Long returns to his office, he has 113 e-mails waiting for him. He also has a call pending to the Renaissance Hotel in Washington, D.C., regarding rescheduling the National Leadership Conference (likely for early April). He chats with Spickard briefly, attends to some paperwork, and then heads to lunch to meet Reverend John Bender to talk about the meeting scheduled at the Raleigh Mennonite Church tomorrow night.

Long greets Bender warmly at a neighborhood pharmacy that has a small soda fountain, featuring tasty hot dogs and other light fare. John Bender is a compact, amiable, plain-clothes minister with thinning dark hair and kind dark eyes. Both he and Skip Long are subdued in their conversation, appearing worried about the Thursday meeting with the congregation.

There will be a motion before the group to ask the offending member from last Easter to take a six-month leave. The man has refused to apologize for his outburst and could not make a commitment not to repeat such actions in the future. Reverend Bender says that the unrelenting stress of the situation has caused him to think seriously about resigning his position. Skip Long says he and Andrea have had serious concerns about their relationship to the congregation in the aftermath of the incident. He will share some of those feelings at the meeting tomorrow. The two men part company after a brief lunch, neither one looking any more at peace than when they met less than an hour ago.

Later, Skip Long pays a courtesy call on Steve Beam, executive director of the Raleigh Housing Authority (RHA) in the Authority's impressive new office building. Long has been on the board of the Housing Commission since 1999. The position has given him the kind of visibility on community issues that has helped build support for the National Jobs Partnership. But Long has done more than just garner publicity; he has worked as an activist in his post. One of his achievements was getting the RHA to cut response time for tenant repair requests from seven days to twenty-four hours or less.

On Wednesday afternoon, Long tours the Halifax Court neighborhood building housing the Building Together Ministries, where Skip and Andrea worked a decade ago. He greets two white retired businessmen who are tutoring a small class of African American boys. One of the men sees Long in the doorway and rushes over to give him a hug and a hearty handshake. The embrace brightens Long's mood, and he smiles for the first time in a couple hours. He points out the multipurpose room in the building, which is the home for the Raleigh Mennonite Church, and the site of the showdown meeting on Thursday night.

Long enjoys a quiet dinner at home with Andrea and Matthew on Wednesday evening, but that night he sleeps fitfully. He awakes at about 2:30 A.M. and can't get back to sleep. He continues to fret about the meeting at the church.

Thursday is rather uneventful. Long waits for three hours for the cable TV guy—who never shows. Then he heads to the museum to catch up with Matthew's class field trip. Afterward he visits the Mangum Group offices, where he chats with Louis Crowder, a graduate of the Raleigh Jobs Partnership's first class in 1996. Today, Crowder is a mentor and assistant class leader in the program.

Not far from the Mangum Group offices is the Char-Grill Takeout Shop, where you can buy the "best burger in Raleigh." For the second day in a row, Long's lunch consists of a couple hot dogs. The gray skies and drizzle reflects Long's mood, and it isn't likely to change until this church meeting gets underway tonight at 7 P.M.

"Have you hugged a black man today?" Skip Long asks Don, one of the elder statesmen of the Raleigh Mennonite Church in the lobby of the building. "Not a good looking one," Don replies, giving Long a hug, a handshake, and a fatherly smile. The two men head to the multipurpose room, where two large banners hang high on the walls: one says, "King of Kings" and is adorned with a star of David, a cross, and a crown of thorns; the other reads, "Through Love Serve One Another." People filter in looking tense and uncomfortable. Most are professionals; some are educators; a few are retired. All but three of the almost forty in the room are white.

Reverend Bender makes a few opening remarks and then turns the meeting over to a facilitator, who discusses the guidelines for the vote that will be conducted tonight. A unanimous vote is required for action to be taken on the motion to ask the offending member to take a six-month leave while the church's pastors, servant leaders, and congregants work through the issues. The church calls it consensus decision making. Its purpose is to "seek the will of God in a particular matter and to build up the faith of the church."

The congregants sit in a large circle about the size of half a basketball court. Neither the member being discussed tonight nor his family is present. But, based on comments, he has supporters in the group. Most in attendance seem anxious about discussing the business at hand. Faces are stony; eyes are cast downward; people shift in their seats; some keep arms crossed; others hold hands to their faces. Skip Long keeps his hands clasped in his lap; his eyes are focused toward the center of the circle; his right knee moves up and down. He wears his gold-rimmed glasses. As the meeting progresses, he opens his Bible and reads briefly.

Andrea arrives about 7:30 P.M. and sits next to Skip. He puts his arm around her, which draws the attention of some people for an extra few seconds. The Longs say they have heard that some in the room are bothered by the show of affection by the interracial couple. Skip's arm remains around his wife. Andrea rests her arm on Skip's leg.

Long doesn't speak to the assembly for about seventy-five minutes into the meeting. When he does, he talks slowly, carefully choosing his words. But he doesn't mince any. "For almost ten months I have humbled myself with an arrogant man." Long explains how he and John Bender and others have worked to find a resolution, to achieve a reconciliation. When others in the group raise objections to the proposed vote, Long raises his voice. "This is what happens when there is not a resurrection." Some turn to him as if to ask what he is referring to. Long replies with a brief on-the-spot sermon about Bible principles. A few nod as Long speaks; others appear unmoved.

After almost two hours, the vote is taken. Skip Long records the vote one by one on a sheet of paper: thirty-three yes, supporting the action, five no, opposing the action. Consensus has not been reached. Now what? More discussion ensues. A proposal surfaces to assemble a subcommittee to talk with the member in question and share with him the results of the vote and the comments expressed on this Thursday night. The subcommittee will meet during the next two weeks and report back to the full congregation. Skip Long is one of five people who have volunteered to be on the subcommittee. The proposal is approved with majority affirmation, but not consensus. (Where are Robert's Rules of Order when you need them?) No one blocks the proposal; time has run out for further discussion tonight. It's well past 9:30 P.M.

John and Marilyn Bender thank the congregation for their time and conscientious actions tonight. As people file out there is relief on many faces. Several shake hands; a few embrace. Some depart without saying a word. Andrea had to leave earlier to take Matthew home. Skip Long hangs around to talk with John and Marilyn Bender. Long says goodnight to Don, the older gentlemen he had greeted earlier this evening.

On the way home, Long sounds weary. He wishes there had been conclusive action taken this evening. But he anticipated the opposition of the five no votes. Still, the issue has progressed one step further. Sometime in the next two weeks, Skip Long will meet once again with the man he had to subdue in the midst of an Easter Sunday outburst. He will try again to get the man to apologize, to see the pain he has caused and the steps he can take to promote healing among the congregation. Long is not optimistic, but he will not give up. As his father often said, "A man doesn't quit."

When Reverend John Bender is asked about his friend and mentor, Reverend Skip Long, Bender says he sees a bright future ahead for the Jobs Partnership program and for its charismatic executive director: "His commitment to Christ will always lead him to ministries of service to others, and to being part of healing the deep wounds in our society."

[10]

RABBI STEVE FOSTER "NEVER IN DOUBT"

After a long, busy winter in Denver, Rabbi Steve Foster enjoyed a spring vacation in a warm desert setting with the full family in tow. He was happy to spend time with his grandkids and unwind on the golf course. Once he returned to Denver, he resumed his full schedule of serving his congregation and his agenda of activism. May 4, 2003, was Mitzvah Day, Temple Emanuel's annual social-action event. Several hundred adults and children went into the Denver community to do volunteer work, including yard cleanup and garden planting, interior house painting, meal preparation, and visits to area hospitals and nursing homes. Temple Emanuel volunteers also continue to participate in Denver-area Habitat for Humanity projects. Rabbi Foster remains outspoken on contemporary social issues, such as the need for a reformed health care system. Building on his reputation as a human rights activist, he is a committed supporter of the Interfaith Alliance, a faith-based group that advocates separation of church and state on behalf of gays, lesbians, and transgendered people. His friend Rabbi Joel Schwartzman says that Foster devotes his time and energy to "causes which affect the quality of life here in the Denver metro area."

> Justice, justice shalt thou follow, that thou mayest live, and inherit the land which the Lord thy God giveth thee.
>
> —Deuteronomy 17:8

The face of social activism in Denver appears grumpier these days as March 2003 draws near and yet another snowstorm hits the mile-high city. The face belongs to Rabbi Steven E. (Steve) Foster, the reputed liberal conscience of this Rocky Mountain community. If Foster is grumpy, there are several possible explanations.

Maybe it's his latest bout with kidney stones, or the fact that he's trying to lose ten pounds. Most likely there is a more substantive explanation why his youngest son, Daniel, says he doesn't have the same sense of humor he had ten or fifteen years ago. His good friend Monsignor Edward Buelt says these days it is understandable why priests, ministers, and rabbis dealing with rising societal problems, including drug use, violence, AIDS, broken families, not to mention war and terrorism, feel stress in trying to serve their congregations.

Rabbi Foster has spent more than thirty years passionately engaged in causes such as civil rights, gay rights, and antiwar and antipoverty work. His advocacy extends to gun control, reproductive choice, more accessible health care, and progressive interfaith dialogue. He wants to build a better world, and if that means taking unpopular stands and rocking people out of their comfort zones—so be it. "My job as a rabbi is to try to bring people together, not tear them apart. But in order to bring people together, sometimes you have to shake them up," he says.

In contemporary matters of faith and social action, Foster considers himself a gatekeeper and sentry; he doesn't like what he sees. He is concerned about the spreading conservative climate in the country and the lack of a coherent, compelling response. He deplores the prejudice, bigotry, and discrimination that continue to shred the fabric of our society. He is disappointed with spoiled youth who expect everything to be given to them, and he is troubled by people who don't put forth an honest effort. Those would include some of his Reform congregants of Temple Emanuel, who are "too busy" to attend synagogue except on High Holy Days (Rosh Hashanah and Yom Kippur). They would also include self-absorbed citizens who are blind to the needs of the poor and underprivileged.

This week in late February, Foster is miffed when some visiting rabbinical students, who are in Denver to receive a week of interfaith outreach training, casually inquire, "Should we call you Steve or Rabbi?" What a question. These "high-maintenance" students are asking their teacher, a senior rabbi, whom they have just met, if it is OK to be on a first-name basis. "Where is the respect, the humility?" fifty-nine-year-old Foster asks hours later as he grabs a quick dinner with his wife, Joyce, an outgoing three-term member of Denver's city council.

"A rabbi is supposed to serve," says Joyce between bites of her T-bone steak as her husband finishes his Cobb salad and turns away a dinner roll. "These students act like they expect to be served." Steve Foster nods wearily, but he doesn't belabor the point. He has a night class ("Introduction to Judaism") to teach, and the roads are starting to get snow covered. But his departure from the casual restaurant is delayed briefly when several friends and members of the congregation stop by to shake hands. The Fosters are a striking, charismatic couple. The media would say they have star quality.

The dapperly dressed Steve Foster, who favors stylish suits, ties, and overcoats, is character-actor handsome, with wavy granite-silver hair and a strong jaw line. His dark eyes can sparkle with warmth, or flash with anger if provoked. A respected orator, the Milwaukee–born and bred Foster speaks in eloquent, sonorous tones. When he laughs, his voice rises, and his compact body revels in the mirth of the moment. But in the heat of battle over a contentious issue such as gay rights, Foster can appear humorless and caustic in word and manner. The way Foster sees it, when you've built your life on principles and staked your career on high-profile controversial causes, you've earned the right to choose your mood, be it gracious or grumpy.

* * *

Remember, I entered a profession of activism.

—RABBI STEVE FOSTER

Irish legend states that St. Patrick used a three-leaf clover to teach pagan converts about the Christian Holy Trinity (God as Father-Son-Holy Spirit). Theologically speaking, Rabbi Foster would beg to differ about the trinity. But he could use a three-leaf clover to explain his tri-part mission as a congregational rabbi: activist for social justice, advocate for interfaith outreach, and pastoral leader to the two thousand member households of the Temple Emanuel community, the oldest Jewish congregation in Colorado and the largest one between the Mississippi River and the West Coast. According to its website: "We are a Reform Congregation in the mainstream of Liberal Judaism. . . . Being a Reform Jew [the other branches being Orthodox, Conservative, and Reconstructionist] means having the responsibility and freedom to seek and to choose the Jewish way of life most comfortable to the individual." Rabbi Foster adds, "Reform Judaism today is a combination of rationalism, intellectualism, religious practice, fervor, and emotion."

Rabbi Foster joined the Denver-based congregation as assistant rabbi in 1970, after receiving his bachelor's degree and master of arts in Hebrew Letters from Hebrew Union College in Cincinnati. The first Temple

Emanuel (means "God is with us") he was affiliated with was located in his hometown of Milwaukee, Wisconsin. The leader of that congregation, Rabbi Herbert Friedman, was a "giant for social justice issues," says Foster, who remembers attending synagogue during the height of the McCarthy era and the emerging civil rights struggle. By the time of his Bar Mitzvah, Foster was convinced he would one day be a rabbi. But in the meantime he would live a typical "Happy Days" teenager's life in Middle America during the 1950s. He was a lifeguard and Eagle Scout, played football and base-ball, and was a diehard fan of the then Milwaukee Braves. Decades later he can still recite the lineup: Spahn, Matthews, Aaron. . . .

Foster was raised in a loving, hard-working family, according to his older sister, Syril Newman. Their father, Milt (Milton), a first-generation Jewish American with Eastern-European roots, owned a small printing company. Their mother, Miriam, one of eight children of German Jewish descent, worked at her husband's print shop while raising Steve and Syril. Money was tight, but there was an abundance of laughter and lively discussion in the Foster household.

Steve Foster attended the University of Wisconsin, where he earned a bachelor's degree in philosophy in 1965. He was a member of SDS (Stu-dents for a Democratic Society) on the Madison campus. During the early 1960s, before protesting the Vietnam War became its raison d'être, SDS was concerned with the civil rights movement. Foster took part in SDS meetings and rallies. He was also active in the Hillel chapter (the Jewish religious/social organization) at the university. In March 1965, as a college senior, he traveled with a contingent of about thirty Hillel students to Alabama to participate in a historic protest march led by Dr. Martin Luther King Jr.

Foster joined thousands of supporters, including civil rights and reli-gious leaders, priests, rabbis, ministers, nuns, students, and "ordinary citizens," who walked the last twelve miles of the fifty-four-mile Freedom March from Selma to the Alabama state capitol in Montgomery. The purpose of the march, according to an article by Roy Reed in the March 22, 1965, *New York Times,* had widened from a campaign to "abolish restric-tions on Negro voting in the Alabama Black Belt . . . to encompass a general protest against racial injustice in the state." Reed wrote that the Alabama march "appears destined for a niche in the annals of the great protest demonstrations."

Two weeks earlier, hundreds of protesters had been clubbed with night-sticks and tear-gassed by state troopers on the Edmund Pettus Bridge over the Alabama River. On this Freedom March hundreds of Army and federalized National Guard troops lined the highway to protect the marchers, who included twenty-one-year-old Steve Foster. His parents, fearing for his safety, had begged him not to go. But he was inspired by the stories of bravery of so many others in the protest movement.

Steve Foster took photographs of Dr. King in the parking lot of St. Jude's Hospital minutes before the march resumed down the unpaved streets of the black neighborhoods. Foster wore a yarmulke (kipah). He was proud to be Jewish. Along the route he routinely heard taunts of whites calling him a "Jew nigger-lover." Although he was aware of the potential for danger, he says he was never frightened in his first major social action protest.

"God, that was a day," he recalls in the quiet of his suburban Denver office, sounding nostalgic as he relives the passion of the Freedom March—the watershed event in his life, when he "stood taller" than he ever had before. In an August 23, 1996, article by Angela Dire in the *Colorado Springs Gazette Telegraph*, Foster described passing through lines of hostile segregationists: "I remember walking down the street and listening to all the intimidation, the anger, the frustration, the hatred in people, and I knew it was the right place to be. For me, it was a God moment, and it wasn't in a synagogue; it was outside with all of those people, doing what I knew to be the right thing. I suppose I became a rabbi for those reasons."

His actions over the two days he was in Alabama would launch Foster's deep, lifelong commitment to social justice and "Tikkun Olam" (Hebrew for the role and responsibility God gives human beings in completing and perfecting the universe). Commenting on his actions in March 1965, Rabbi Foster once said in a sermon, "I felt that there was a religious demand upon me to help my fellow man who needed help."

Foster's unshakable belief in the power of faith to address social problems is one of the driving forces in his life. But his greatest passion is his family, which is centered on his relationship with his wife of almost thirty-eight years. Four months before he marched in Alabama, Foster had met pert, almond-eyed Joyce Cohn, from Benton Harbor, Michigan. Cohn had been sent to relieve Foster as winter weekend director of a Jewish camp in upstate Wisconsin. "She got off the train, and I fell in love with her," he says. "I asked her to marry me the first day I met her."

The attraction was mutual, and Steve and Joyce were soon engaged. They married in December 1965, when Steve was a rabbinical student in Cincinnati.

During the last three of his five years at Hebrew Union College (HUC), Foster had to complete biweekly student rabbi service for about thirty

Jewish families in the Bible Belt community of Union City, Tennessee (some fifty miles north of Memphis). Shortly after Dr. Martin Luther King Jr.'s assassination in April 1968, Foster presided over a Passover Seder. He asked for a moment of silence to honor King's memory. "If looks could have killed," Foster remembers. "They saw me as a rabble-rowser. A few of them could have tarred and feathered me."

Instead of his being intimidated by the rejection of some congregants, Foster's zeal to raise people's social consciousness was forged by the late 1960s. His deep interest in activism became an intellectual as well as vocational pursuit. His June 1970 master's thesis from the HUC's Jewish Institute of Religion was titled "The Development of the Social Action Program of Reform Judaism, 1878–1969."

Foster wrote: "All social action in Reform Judaism is in response to specific social problems within our culture." He noted how at the turn of the century, the Central Conference of American Rabbis (CCAR) took their cue from Gentile clergy in supporting causes such as union organizing, collective bargaining, and advocacy for a minimum wage, health insurance, and the rehabilitation of ex-convicts (now, ex-offenders). By the 1920s, the Reform Jewish leadership had established social justice instead of social service as a national priority. The CCAR issued public statements opposing the racial bias that was "legalized in the immigration act of 1920." The Union of American Hebrew Congregations (UAHC), which had been established in 1873, reported efforts to unite with Catholic and Protestant leaders in making joint social justice announcements on issues of the day such as anti-Semitism.

But support for Jewish activism shifted in 1924 when a special committee of the UAHC recommended that the Union should "concentrate its efforts upon its religious purposes and abandon every other activity which tends to dissipate its energy and depart from the real and essential aims of the UAHC's cultivation of Judaism." Rabbi Foster has experienced that same kind of parochial reaction from members of Temple Emanuel: "Some people say they wish I would stick to religious themes. They don't yet see that those religious themes are played out in everyday life." But he has never been fazed by such a reaction. "That's their problem. It's not my problem."

Foster's conviction is never in doubt. He points to a framed quote behind his desk, written by a noted nineteenth-century cleric, Rabbi Israel Salanter: "A rabbi whose community does not disagree with him is not really a rabbi. And a rabbi who fears his community is not really a man."

Foster refers to the Salanter quote often in conversation, sermons, and writings. It is his moral compass. "I believe that if we're going to create the kind of world God wants us to create, then we have to take a chance and do those things that do not always feel comfortable."

Dru Greenwood, director of the William and Lottie Daniel Department of Outreach with the Union of American Hebrew Congregations in New York, has known Rabbi Foster for almost twenty years. She has worked closely with him on provocative issues such as interfaith outreach, inter-marriage, and religious conversion. Greenwood says Foster is "utterly loyal to the causes he supports. Much of what he accomplishes is done through sheer force of personality and persuasion."

Foster is stubborn—some might say obstinate—in his stances. But he believes many people benefit from his efforts, part of the greater good that results from a rabbi's involvement in the broader societal issues. He fur-ther believes that such efforts ultimately bring a measure of honor to the Jewish community.

That premise, however, wasn't consistently supported by the record of American Jewish social action throughout the twentieth century. The historical research is an intriguing journey of activist ebb and flow. In 1926 the UAHC declared that it was the "duty of the synagogue and its pulpit to speak courageously in defense of human rights as part of its prophetic function."

During the late 1920s and early 1930s, according to Foster, Reform rabbis shifted their focus from dealing with Jewish-specific problems to problems that affected all Americans. In taking such actions, these rabbis would be attempting to honor all three laws of Judaism that direct Jews to maintain reverent, righteous, and responsible relationships—first, with God, second, with their fellow Jews, and third, with their neighbors in the "outside world."

During the height of the Depression, Reform congregations were urged to establish their own committees on social justice, thus decentralizing decision making. But as the decade drew to a close, social justice programs were not being widely supported by local laity. By the mid-1940s race relations were being discussed openly. The CCAR recommended that congregations "invite a Negro to preach from the pulpit."

Foster's research revealed that during the 1950s, "The Jewish commu-nity became very much involved emotionally with the plight of the Negro in the South, and many began to feel that there was some connection between the words of the prophets and social legislation." The pro–social action wing of the CCAR believed that "the worship of God must be transmitted into the work of God." Plans were discussed to establish a National Commission on Social Action in cooperation with Protestant and Catholic groups. But moderate voices in the social action movement made the distinction between "a rabbi's right to speak and a congregation's advisability to take collective action as a Jewish religious organization." Meanwhile, conservative elements in the Jewish community, particularly among many southern congregations, warned of a backlash against Jews if congregations openly supported the cause of civil rights.

In 1961 the UAHC established a Religious Action Center (RAC) in Washington, D.C., to serve as an arm of the Commission on Social Action of Reform Judaism. The goal of the RAC was to "strengthen the ideals of religion in their application to the great moral issues of our time." The UAHC played a visible role in the historic August 1963 March on Washington by Dr. Martin Luther King Jr. But a year later, "the fight over congregational participation in social action projects was still being fought."

Promising developments on the social activism front included the formation of a Mitzvah Corps, a volunteer youth program, launched in 1964 in New York and Chicago. During the mid-1960s, college-age Jewish civil rights workers were a major presence in southern states. As the decade drew to a close, the Religious Action Center expanded its political lobbying role to include education as part of its mission, and a cooperative program with the Harvard Divinity School was established.

Foster's thesis stated that by November 1967, five hundred local social action committees existed in the country. But he noted that "the Jewish community by and large was no longer deeply involved in the great social issues as they once were." A year later, "the whole mood of the Jewish community had shifted to the Right." One bright spot was that the Mitzvah Corps, liberal Jewish youth from Steve Foster's own generation, was still committed to social justice and was now active in several inner cities across America.

At Temple Emanuel in Denver, Mitzvah Day is the congregation's largest annual community service project. On a spring Sunday hundreds of families go into the Denver community and participate in a variety of *mitzvot* ("doing good deeds"). Rabbi Foster believes that such volunteer service activities are important for the young members of the congregation to learn the importance of *tzedakah* ("doing what is right"). Another service program, KVOD (meaning "honor and respect") catering, provides meals for area homeless on a biweekly basis. "I am proud that we do it," says Foster. "I am just ashamed that we don't do it more. I still believe that the synagogue is a place where congregations, not just the clergy, ought to be committed to social justice."

* * *

[A rabbi] must himself have a deep dedication and a pervading
commitment to the ideal of equality and dignity for all men. And he
must be prepared to involve himself in every facet of community and
congregational life that will translate his commitment into the minds
and hearts of those whom he would lead. He must do so with patience
and forbearance and tact—but there must never be the slightest doubt
about what he believes or where he stands.

—RABBI JACOB (JACK) ROTHSCHILD

Rabbi Jacob (Jack) Rothschild, the Atlanta-based protagonist of Melissa
Fay Greene's book *The Temple Bombing,* was a longtime friend of Dr. Martin
Luther King Jr. (According to Greene, he delivered King's eulogy at the
citywide memorial service.) Given Rothschild's courageous stands for civil
rights during the turbulent 1950s and 1960s, he could well have been one of
Rabbi Foster's role models and Foster his protégé. Both men were cut from
the same cloth of conscience and conviction. In Foster's case, his activism
would bridge several decades and embrace many social issues. Arguably,
gay rights would be the cause that defined his career and reputation.

If the Freedom March in 1965 was Foster's first "God moment," his next
divinely inspired awakening came twenty years later in a classroom. He was
completing credits for his doctor of ministries degree at the Iliff School of
Theology, a Methodist institution in Denver. Foster was enrolled in a two-
week summer course on sexuality and the church. A fellow student was
Reverend Charlie Earhart, pastor of the Metropolitan Community Church.
"I didn't know it was the gay church in Denver," says Foster, who admits that
for most of his adult life he had been a homophobe. But in that classroom
he was touched by Earhart's compassion and humanity. "He turned me
around. I saw him as a human being who happened to be gay."

As Foster relates his experience, a beautiful grandfather clock chimes in
his office, which is lined with bookshelves, artwork, family photos, plaques,
and honors—including an "Advocacy Award," presented by the National
Association of Human Rights Workers to Rabbi Steven E. Foster for "Your
dedication and commitment advocating civil and human rights, equality
and justice for all people."

Foster's friendship with Earhart was revelatory. The rabbi who had come
of age on a civil rights march in Alabama was now in the mid-1980s able to
make the connection with gay rights in Colorado. "It changed my life,"
Rabbi Foster says. During the course of the next decade, Foster's classroom
catharsis would have statewide ramifications.

In 1988 Democratic Colorado governor Roy Romer appointed Rabbi
Foster to the Colorado Civil Rights Commission. Foster was a good friend

of the state's political liberals, including then U.S. Rep. Patricia (Pat) Schroeder, D-Colorado. According to Judy Fester, who had served for fourteen years as public information specialist for the Commission, Foster impressed her and his colleagues with his earnest and thorough preparation and review of cases related to civil rights compliance. "He showed good leadership, and argued his positions extremely well," Fester says.

By 1992, in his second term as a commissioner, Foster would prove to be a media-savvy challenger of entrenched Colorado conservatives. The state's right-wingers would attract national attention for their support of Amendment 2, a proposed constitutional ban on gay-rights laws (preventing sexual orientation from being added to other classes of people, categorized by race, religion, age, or gender, who were afforded protection from discrimination). Lifelong left-winger Rabbi Foster now had a new cause to embrace with his deepest conviction—the defeat of Amendment 2.

When Foster informed the board of Temple Emanuel that he was going to accept the position of chair of the statewide Equal Protection Campaign (opposing Amendment 2), members of the board said they would have been surprised if their senior rabbi didn't take on the issue. "I think they saw that as a banner of pride," says Foster. He appreciated the board's support, considering that for five months he would be spending twenty to twenty-five hours a week crisscrossing the state discussing the proposed amendment.

A month before the November 1992 election, Rabbi Foster gave a High Holy Day sermon on the ballot issue: "They have proposed an amendment to the State Constitution that would say that it is OK to discriminate against gays and lesbians. And if this amendment passes, we will be the only state in the United States to legalize discrimination." He told his congregation that he believed that Jews would not be safe "if we begin the process of legalizing discrimination against other minority groups."

Foster's daughter, Deborah, now an elementary school teacher, was a senior in high school during the 1992 Amendment 2 campaign. She was outspoken in her support of her father and his position opposing the ballot issue. She says she was ostracized for her views, but she refused to buckle.

Foster used his bully pulpit as a fiery, flamboyant opponent of Colorado's conservative family-values organizations. "The more the opposition grew, the more adamant Rabbi Foster became in his advocacy for gay rights," says Judy Fester.

His critics accused him of grandstanding and being self-righteous. State Senator Ray Powers, R-Colorado Springs, would later comment in a *Colo-*

rado Spring Gazette Telegraph newspaper story, "If I were accused of something, I'd hate to have Rabbi Foster sitting as judge and jury." But according to David Zaterman, a Republican who succeeded Democrat Steve Foster on the state Civil Rights Commission, there were conservative legislators who disagreed completely with Foster's positions, but still viewed him as a man of principle.

The hyper-competitive Foster lost his major battle in 1992 as the voters of Colorado approved the ban on gay-rights laws. Tired and discouraged, Foster and his eldest son, David, an attorney and a member of the lieutenant governor's staff, arranged a post-election trip to Germany. They invited Holocaust survivors, World War II veterans, religious leaders, and minority community representatives. They called it "A Journey for Justice." The local ABC-TV affiliate covered the weeklong trip, which helped Foster to heal from the rigorous campaign.

In the next few years, he continued to speak out for gay rights and in support of an appeal in the courts to overturn the election results. Four years later, Foster and his supporters were vindicated when the U.S. Supreme Court struck down Amendment 2 as unconstitutional. Politicians have long memories, and in 1996 Republican members of the Colorado Senate came within one vote of blocking Rabbi Foster's reappointment for his third (and final) term to the Colorado Civil Rights Commission.

David Foster watched as his father testified for hours about his positions on gay rights, abortion, and other controversial causes. "People were attacking his values. It almost made me sick to my stomach," David says, recalling the lambasting his father received. But after the grueling renomination process, his father's convictions were unshaken. Rabbi Foster was most concerned with how his family was dealing with the situation.

David Foster says that the older he gets, the prouder he is of his father, though he admits, "I wish he'd be willing to compromise sometimes." The son speaks from firsthand experience. He cites his mother's 1993 Denver city council campaign. David, with a law degree, a master's in public administration, and proven political experience, was in charge of the campaign. But he clashed with his strong-willed father, who "believes he knows how to do things better than anyone." After some sensitive family negotiations, David Foster successfully directed campaign operations, while Rabbi Steve Foster managed an impressive fund-raising effort.

The younger brother, Daniel, also a Denver-based attorney, says he tries to get his father to lighten up. But it isn't easy when he has so much on his mind. Even when father and sons are on the golf course, it isn't very relaxing. Daniel draws comfort from humorous memories of family station wagon vacations from years ago. Back then Steve Foster would tour the Western states with his family, visiting sites such as "the largest reptile in Utah" and conversing with truckers on the CB radio using his "handle," Friar Tuck.

Rabbi Foster, who is still fond of carrying a rubber clown nose in his suit pocket, would insist he hasn't lost his sense of humor. But he admits somberly, "There is no end to this work." He says he has a hard time turning down requests. "The last thing I want to do is to say to someone who has a decent cause, I don't care. Because I do care."

Former Denver mayor Wellington Webb, who calls Foster a "bridge builder," asked the rabbi in fall of 2000 to help broker a peaceful resolution to a growing conflict between Denver's Italian American and Native American communities over plans for a Columbus Day march. Violence was averted, but Rabbi Foster was unable to get the two sides to reach a mutually acceptable agreement.

Previously, the mayor and the rabbi had worked together on the issues of gang violence and school violence in the aftermath of the Columbine High School tragedy. Foster had also lobbied with the mayor's wife, Wilma, for years in trying to get the state of Colorado to officially recognize Martin Luther King Jr. Day as a holiday.

When Rabbi Foster isn't fielding calls from political officials, he is likely to be talking with civic leaders. (A multitasker, Foster will play hearts on his computer while on the phone.) He serves on the boards of several community and religious organizations, including the Rotary Club, the National Conference of Christians and Jews, the Allied Jewish Federation, Planned Parenthood, and United Way. He is particularly interested in his current role as a United Way board member, "pricking the conscience" of his colleagues related to funding decisions about the Boy Scouts, whose national organization voted to not permit gay or lesbian individuals, or those who do not believe in God, from joining as scouts or scout leaders. Foster doesn't believe United Way should fund any organization that practices discrimination.

The issue has special meaning for Foster because he was an Eagle Scout while growing up in Milwaukee. He told his congregation in a 2000 sermon that he was the first Jewish teen in Wisconsin to earn three of the highest awards: Eagle Scout, Explorer Silver, and Ner Tamid (a religious award). He also informed members of the Temple Emanuel community about the letter (excerpted below) he had recently written to the Boy Scouts of America:

It pains me to write and to return in the enclosed envelope those medals that I worked so hard to earn and have prized my entire life. I return them to you now as have others, because I cannot be associated with an organization that has gone out of its way to claim the right to discriminate against other people. The public policy that the Boy Scouts of America has fought for is contrary to all that I hold dear and true.

Predictably, Foster's stance on the Boy Scouts issue garnered media attention, with coverage on local TV and in the *Denver Post* newspaper. But countless other stands that Foster has taken, which never receive publicity, are just as vital to his mission as a social activist. For example, in the late 1990s he recommended to his board of directors that a female associate rabbi be hired at Temple Emanuel. He told them that the candidate had also informed him that she was a lesbian. Rabbi Foster said that if the board chose not to hire her because of her competence, then he would agree with the decision. But if the board didn't offer her the job because of her sexual orientation, then they would have to find another senior rabbi. The job offer was made, but the candidate chose to stay in New York. Years later, Foster says, "I think it would have been wonderful had she been a part of our synagogue."

Fellow Denver-area rabbi Joel Schwartzman opines, "Rabbi Foster is fearless in stating and maintaining his positions."

"I do these things because they're the right things to do," Foster says. He is confident in victory, but he has been humbled by his losses—particularly in those cases where the security of his family was at stake. Some twenty-five years ago, he challenged the presence of a crèche display as part of holiday decorations in front of the Denver City-County Building. He testified in two lawsuits focusing on separation of church and state. He stated that a religious symbol (the Christian Holy Family) shouldn't be displayed on government property. During the court proceedings, Foster received death threats. "I was very concerned about my family's safety," he says, grateful that no incidents ensued.

Two clergy who opposed Rabbi Foster in the church-state cases, a Catholic bishop and a Greek Orthodox priest, testified that in that particular setting, the crèche was a secular symbol. Both of these Christian clerics were interfaith colleagues of Foster's. He describes the late Bishop George Evans as "a dear friend." Six weeks before Evans died, Foster was visiting Bethlehem in the Holy Land. "I brought George back a big wooden cross. . . . In his casket, he was holding the cross."

* * *

Brotherhood-Sisterhood Award Presented to Rabbi Steven E. Foster:
For your distinguished service on behalf of justice, equality and freedom
for all. For your active and innovative promotion of interfaith
understanding. For your strong personal ethic and steadfast belief in the
cultural and religious life of the Jewish community.

—The National Conference of Christians and Jews
(Wednesday, July 11, 1990, Denver, Colorado)

Rabbi Foster is a man of action. But he also appreciates the gift of contemplation. Today he reflects on the painting that hangs at the entrance to his office. His oldest and favorite painting is of Francis of Assisi: Saint Francis of Assisi, a Christian saint. The painting is of a hooded, barefoot monk emerging from the shadows. He is staring at a skull he holds in his cupped hands. The painting, purchased at the Wisconsin State Fair, was a present from Foster's parents when he was graduating from high school. "That painting always spoke to me," says Foster, lost in thought for a moment as his office grandfather clock chimes once more.

Rabbi Foster has steadfastly built a reputation through the decades as a courageous activist for social justice, but in that same period he has led a parallel existence as a pioneer in interfaith dialogue and outreach. This work has ranged from creating coalitions with other religious leaders (he is chair of the Denver Area Interfaith Clergy Conference) to offering innovative strategies to bring unaffiliated families into Jewish life.

In 2000, Foster was integral to establishing the Mile High United Way's "Faith Sabbath, Partners in Compassion" program. The concept was simple: On a designated day of worship, hundreds of thousands of congregants from all faiths throughout the area would be asked to donate one dollar. The funds would be used to provide meals, clothing, shelter, and medical care for needy individuals and families in Greater Denver.

The cooperative, ecumenical fund-raising effort seemed like a natural for this community, which in the late nineteenth century had created the Charity Organization Society of Denver, the prototype for the international United Way movement. The key players in that early community-wide charity drive included a priest, two ministers, and a rabbi named William S. Friedman, from Temple Emanuel.

Rabbi Foster is proud of the trailblazing history of his congregation, and he has continued that tradition recently by participating with the evangelical Christian organization Habitat for Humanity. About eighteen months ago, Habitat officials had asked Foster if he would convene a meeting of area clergy. He helped assemble an initial group of six churches and two Jewish organizations, Temple Emanuel and B'Nai Chavurah. Foster helped raise $50,000 and urged his congregants to volunteer their time in building a house for a local Muslim family. The project had special importance for Rabbi Foster and others who saw it as an act of healing in the wake of 9/11.

Three days after that 2001 tragedy, Foster spoke to his congregation. He told them of his concern for his friend Mohammed, whom he had known for fifteen years. He appealed to his congregants to speak up if they heard others speak ill of Muslims, to have the courage to stand up and say: "Not the Muslims I know. Not the real Muslims. Not the people who really believe that Allah is good and Allah is great." He closed his sermon with a final appeal: "Let each of us find that which is good and transmit it to the next generation, so that these young people will never have to sit again and watch what we watched during this past week."

Concern for the future is one of the vital matters that drives Rabbi Foster, whether he is talking about society in general or the future of "Klal Yisrael," the Jewish people. Foster is fond of using the metaphor of a guardian at the gate to represent his role and responsibility. He says that in an age when an estimated 30 to 50 percent of Jews in the United States are marrying non-Jews, the issue of religious outreach and conversion is one of the most important congregational issues facing the nation's more than six million Jews.

Twenty-six years ago, Rabbi Foster and a handful of other Denver-based Reform, Orthodox, and Conservative rabbis launched a bold experiment to establish a common set of conversion standards and procedures for those individuals interested in becoming "Jews by choice."

"I am one of those who believes that we ought to engage in a more open and accepting policy with regard to those who choose to be part of Jewish life," Rabbi Foster wrote in his doctoral dissertation, "The Rabbi's Role in Counseling Converts to Judaism."

From 1977 until 1983 the Denver Community Rabbinic Conversion Board was a model of cooperation on a very difficult subject—bringing converts into Jewish life with as broad acceptance throughout the community as possible. But after 175 conversions, the experiment ended when participating Orthodox rabbis withdrew their support.

Some say the Conversion Board was a victim of politics. Others point to the Orthodox pullback as a reaction to the decision in 1982 by the Central Conference of American Rabbis to adopt patrilineal descent as valid for Jewish identity (i.e., Reform movement rabbis would now consider children of a Jewish father and non-Jewish mother as Jews if they were raised in the Jewish faith). For centuries Jews had been identified solely on the basis of matrilineal descent.

In a February 1995 article by Diane Solomon in *Moment* magazine, Dru Greenwood, director of the Commission on Reform Jewish Outreach (CRJO) of the UAHC, said, "After pioneering programs in the late '70s for Jews-by-choice, we're now also focusing on interfaith couples, those considering conversion, and those who want to reclaim their Jewish roots." Greenwood, a longtime friend of Rabbi Foster, has praised his advocacy, coalition building, and creative insight in maintaining warm, mutually respectful relationships with "the full spectrum of rabbis in the community," and in establishing Stepping Stones to a Jewish Me, "a ground-breaking and highly effective entry program for interfaith families."

In a recent interview, Greenwood provided details on Rabbi Foster's interfaith innovations that started two decades ago:

> The problem articulated (by) the CRJO was how to invite unaffiliated interfaith families who had not made any decision about their children's religious identify into Jewish life. Rabbi Foster suggested setting up an alternative, time limited, free religious school just for them, an idea that was met with great skepticism. . . .
>
> Steve took it on a dare and created Stepping Stones, for which he built support, participation, and funding across the Denver community. It has been highly successful, with 70 percent of families enrolling their children in mainstream (Jewish) religious education following the two years of Stepping Stones. The program has spread to other cities as well.

In discussing the decisions facing interfaith couples, Foster says, "It's hard. These couples are all vulnerable." He will counsel couples who say they want to raise their children in both religions that it is better to choose a single religious identity; otherwise, the kids will probably choose between mom and dad, or they may become frustrated by the tug-of-war and eventually walk away from any religion altogether.

Foster is a liberal rabbi, but he has rock-solid standards on matters such as intermarriages: He will not officiate in a joint religious ceremony ("The law of Moses does not permit them."). He will also not convert someone who does not believe in God. As he tells visiting rabbinical students, Judaism is a religion; it is not enough to follow traditions or keep a Jewish home.

And don't get him started on "Jews for Jesus." Foster shares an anecdote of calling an Episcopalian bishop, one of his golfing buddies, when the rabbi heard that the "Jews for Jesus" group was meeting in a local Episcopalian church. As Foster explains, he railed on the phone like Vince Lombardi at his friend, "What the hell's going on over there?"

The bishop had already looked into the matter, knowing Foster would call. He apologized, saying that he really couldn't prevent one of his Christian churches from hosting the nontraditional Jewish organization. Foster didn't pursue the matter further, though he groused that the Catholic Church would have had greater control over what went on in their local parishes.

* * *

I became a rabbi because I wanted to bring people nearer to God
through the synagogue.

—Rabbi Steve Foster

Bold acts of social activism and pioneering efforts in interfaith outreach may grab headlines for Rabbi Foster and Temple Emanuel, but the rabbi's pastoral work in serving the spiritual and emotional needs of his congregants has humbler goals: bringing inspiration to the faithful and comfort to the sick, troubled, and grieving. On average, Rabbi Foster spends two to three days a week visiting hospitals and nursing homes and presiding at funeral services. "He makes people feel as if they are the center of the universe," says David Foster about his father's ability to connect with people in need. "He's very compassionate."

As the last week of February winds down, Rabbi Foster has several pastoral calls to make at the Rose Medical Center. En route to the hospital in his late model white and gold-trim Acura, he tries to reach his wife, Joyce, on his ever-present cell phone. "She must be with one of the grandkids."

Once the car is parked, Foster hits the ground at a brisk clip. At fifty-nine and counting, he is in good shape. Six days a week (usually before work) he rides an exercise bike and lifts weights at a local racquet club. Today, in the span of thirty minutes he will stop by six rooms of hospitalized congregants. On one visit he greets three sons and a daughter of an elderly woman who has had back surgery. "You know how Mom is," one son says, shaking the rabbi's hand. "Your grandmother was the same way," Foster replies, leaving laughter in his wake.

On the way back to Temple Emanuel, he catches up with Joyce at his son Daniel's home. (All three of his children reside less than a mile from their parents, who have lived in their comfortable five-bedroom southeast Denver home for more than twenty-five years.) Foster embraces his wife and daughter-in-law Becky and melts at the sight of his sixteen-month-old grandson, Rex Milton, in his high chair. Rabbi Foster clowns for several minutes for the lad, who giggles at his antics. David and Allison Foster's children, Abby and Aiden, are also beloved in bunches by their grandfather, known as "Oppy."

In September 2002 during Yom Kippur, Rabbi Foster's sermon was directed to his grandchildren. It was an ethical will, an ancient Jewish custom where the writer shares something of the values that guide his or her life. He had delivered a similar sermon in 1977 to his three children. In these living legacies he wished for many things for his progeny: to experience God's presence in their lives; to find fulfillment in religious tradition and inspiration in the Torah; to be responsible for their people, their humanity, and themselves; to have a commitment to the land of Israel; and to go forth and try to make the world a better place by their own presence. "Family has always been first, second, and third with my dad," says David Foster. "We all know how much he loves us. That's never in doubt."

"In this day of high mobility, it is remarkable to see the closeness and mutual support of Steve's family," adds Dru Greenwood.

When Rabbi Foster returns to his office, a stack of phone messages awaits, as do sixty e-mails. He works the phones. The e-mails can wait. Later, he will try to prepare his remarks for Friday's "Shabbat Unplugged."

"Shabbat softens the soul," says Rabbi Foster. On this Friday night he looks content as he attends the spirited, moving two-hour service in the impressive, brightly lit nine-hundred-seat sanctuary at Temple Emanuel. The "Unplugged" part of the service refers to the lively music provided by two electric guitars, keyboard, and drums. (This is not your father's Shabbat!)

The week has ended on several good notes: the visiting rabbinical students have returned to New York, Los Angeles, and Cincinnati (most seemed grateful for Rabbi Foster's tutelage and counsel—"Never underestimate the good you can do"); Foster passed two kidney stones with modest discomfort; and he enjoyed Shabbat dinner with his wife, daughter, and sister, plus members of his congregation staff.

At four points during the Friday evening service, Foster leaves his seat, steps to the front of the sanctuary, and addresses the five-hundred-plus congregants. He wears a dark pinstriped suit, white shirt, cream-colored tie, polished tassel loafers. He reads four short sermons, mini-essays intended to bring comfort and inspiration.

In the first two he speaks of surrendering the cares of the world to God, and of appreciating the beauty God has bestowed on the earth. In his third reading, he tearfully remembers the late Israeli astronaut, Ilan Ramon, who perished in the *Columbia* shuttle disaster. Ramon had flown into space, carrying a small Torah scroll, a gift from a Holocaust survivor.

Rabbi Foster's final reading is a mock eulogy: "Our congregation is deeply saddened by the passing of an irreplaceable member—Someone Else. . . . Whenever there was a job to do, a class to teach, or a meeting to attend, everybody turned to Someone Else. . . . He left a wonderful example to follow, but it appears there is nobody willing to fill the shoes of Someone Else."

At the end of the service, Rabbi Foster is smiling. He holds his wife's hand and accepts the greetings of people who have come together tonight to share in worship, in tradition, and in community with their rabbi and one another. Shabbat softens the soul.

[11]

DR. M. BASHEER AHMED "Messenger
OF GOOD NEWS"

Photo courtesy of The Carter Center, Atlanta, Georgia

Dr. M. Basheer Ahmed is an optimist even in troubled times. (The name Basheer means "messenger of good news.") He had several reasons to feel encouraged through 2003. The Muslim Community Center for Human Services (MCCHS), which he founded in 1995, had hired a part-time administrative assistant—a graduate student from The University of Texas at Arlington School of Social Work. The new hire would help relieve Dr. Ahmed of many of his clerical and organizational duties, enabling him to concentrate on more strategic planning, program outreach, and public information efforts. In August 2003 he was chair of a regional conference of the Association of Muslim Social Scientists, sponsored by the MCCHS. The conference, "Extremism: A Threat to Global Peace," featured scholars and speakers from universities such as Harvard, Notre Dame, Clarion, Texas Christian, Southern Methodist, Baylor, The University of Texas, and St. Mary's University, Halifax, Nova Scotia. In previous years, Ahmed had organized regional conferences on domestic violence, the role of religion in promoting world peace, and Muslim contributions to human civilization. For months Dr. Ahmed had been busy coordinating the Interfaith Health Fair, hosted by the Muslim Community Center for Human Services, the Richland Hills United Methodist Church, and the Richland Hills Christian Church. St. John the Apostle Catholic Church was one of several cosponsors. The late September 2003 event marked the first time the annual health fair for low-income Muslim community members and other area poor had received such broad-based support and participation from other religious organizations in the North Texas Metroplex. Based on these positive developments, Dr. Ahmed had every reason to be upbeat about the future of the MCCHS and interfaith relations.

> Whatever you spend with a good heart, give it to parents, relatives,
> orphans, the helpless, and travellers in need. Whatever good you do,
> Allah is aware of it.
>
> —Qur'an 2:[215]

Dr. M. Basheer Ahmed steps lightly but quickly from his office in the compact Al-Shifa Clinic in North Richland Hills, Texas. He tells the other physicians and staff that he is waiting for his final patient of the day, a Muslim woman whose family is caught in the web of domestic violence. She was supposed to be at the clinic an hour ago, but she is lost in the tangled highways and byways of the Dallas–Fort Worth Metroplex. Days earlier she could have blamed a brutal ice storm for her delay, but this spring day is sunny and delightful in North Texas.

Ahmed, a psychiatrist, first spoke with the woman days earlier after she left a message on the twenty-four-hour help line of the Muslim Community Center for Human Services. He recommended she come to the clinic for an intervention. Normally, the clinic closes at 12:30 P.M. on Saturdays, but Dr. Ahmed will keep it open later today, March 8, 2003, until he counsels his client.

This Saturday about fifteen poor and indigent Muslim patients, including elderly, singles, parents, and their children, have visited the medical clinic, housed in one of four 1,200-square-foot suites of a one-story, U-shaped, mission-style brick building. This is the headquarters for the MCCHS, half an hour's drive south of Dallas. Some people have come for their prescriptions for hypertension, others for results of laboratory tests.

A few patients received brief exams for sore throats from Dr. Najam Khan, one of the clinic's rotating pool of seventeen volunteer physicians who donate four hours of Saturday service about every other month. At the Al-Shifa (which means "health" in Arabic) Clinic, patients are not charged for examinations, treatment, or most prescriptions. Once-a-month free diabetes and blood pressure screenings are also conducted on-site. There is a slight charge for off-site diagnostic lab work.

"So many in the Muslim community do not receive medical care because they are poor or intimidated by the health care community," says Dr. Khan, a specialist in internal medicine who has made the fifty-mile drive from Plano this morning. Khan, one of the younger-generation physicians recruited by Dr. Ahmed, says he doesn't mind the drive or the pro bono service. "If I can touch just one life," he says, "I will have succeeded."

Another of Ahmed's recruits is retired surgeon Dr. Siraj Hussain, who supervises the clinic's operation, ensuring that the facilities (two examination rooms, waiting area, dispensary, and offices) are clean, well-equipped, and up to professional standards. The medical equipment, from exam tables to stethoscopes, has been donated by area physicians. Waiting room furniture and clinic bookshelves, file cabinets, and office equipment are also secondhand, but functional. The walls, floors, and mauve carpet are spic-and-span. A faint antiseptic smell hangs in the air.

Dr. Hussain serves on the MCCHS executive/advisory board. Like Dr. Khan, he speaks of the kindness and generosity of Dr. Ahmed, who founded the Muslim Community Center in 1995 and donated a significant portion of the $50,000 down payment toward the purchase of the approximate $250,000 building in 2000. Contributions from several members of the Muslim community in the Metroplex provided the balance of building financing.

The highest praise this afternoon comes from another board member and clinic volunteer Mrs. Asli Abada Parker, a Somalian émigré who has worked often on community health and service projects with Dr. Basheer Ahmed.

"He's a beautiful gift from God," says Parker, who wears a subdued charcoal-gray floor-length garment and a shoulder-length ivory lace headscarf. For many years, Parker wore her nation's military uniform. She was a colonel who flew jets in the Somalian Air Force before coming to America in the 1980s. During the last decade, Parker has worked with thousands of Somalian (Muslim) refugees who settled in the region. As president of the Somalian Community Relief program in nearby Euless, Texas, Parker oversees employment, legal aid, education, and social services. Before the Al-Shifa Clinic was based in its present location, the MCCHS provided its free Saturday medical clinic services in the Somalian Outreach Community Center.

While waiting for his final client of the day (earlier patients were treated for depression and obsessive-compulsive behavior), Dr. Ahmed, dressed in a double-breasted dark gray suit and starched collarless white shirt, chats amiably with Asli Parker. Smiles and laughter punctuate their conversation.

Ahmed speaks in a soft voice that shifts gears from a slow, melodic pace to a near breathless gallop. His dialect reflects his British schooling and South Asian roots (born in India and schooled there, in Pakistan, and in the United Kingdom). Parker's English is spiced with a distinct Mediterranean accent, confirming her many years living in Italy.

Parker, a tall woman with high cheekbones and feline eyes, bears a resemblance to Somalian-born model Iman (Mrs. David Bowie). Dr. Ahmed is of medium height and barrel-chested, with a full face and large, kind brown eyes. If the late Winston Churchill was likened to a bulldog, Basheer Ahmed's visage is more akin to a St. Bernard. At almost sixty-eight, he has a full head of ebony hair.

Dr. Ahmed is a steadfast advocate of progressive change. "My profession, community mental health, is involved in social activism, especially as it pertains to serving indigent clientele." His days and evenings are full, given his responsibilities as chairman of the MCCHS, representative on numerous community, civic, and interfaith boards and organizations, and spokesperson for the regional Muslim community, which is estimated at more than one hundred thousand by the Islamic Association of North Texas. In the last year Ahmed has provided his insights to the U.S. Department of Health and Human Services, and he is participating as a faith-based member of the Arlington, Texas, 2025 comprehensive planning process. Dr. Ahmed continues to work as a consulting psychiatrist an average of two days a week, and he also writes and presents academic papers at national and international conferences.

He says that he enjoys his work, and that helps him maintain his enthusiasm. He adds that he inherited his work ethic from his parents; his father, Qameruddin, was an accountant; his mother, Tahira Begum, was a schoolteacher who later became a physician. When asked about his present workload, which averages fifty hours per week, Ahmed says this is down about twenty-five weekly hours from the late 1990s. Just six years ago he was director of the division of psychiatry at the Plaza Medical Center in Fort Worth, an attending psychiatrist at other area hospitals, and founding director of the MCCHS.

His commitment to establish and nurture the Muslim Community Center, the first Muslim social services organization in Texas and one of a handful in the nation, has drawn the admiration of his peers. He was dubbed a "Lone Ranger" in a local newspaper story for his single-handed efforts to provide the Muslim community with needed social services, advocacy on issues such as domestic violence, and representation in the broader community. But Dr. Ahmed is no glory hound. He is characterized as humble, modest, and a "gentleman from the old school" by his fellow MCCHS board members and area professionals, such as Robert Carter, a Fort Worth attorney who has been friends with Ahmed, his wife, Shakila, their son, Sameer, and their daughter, Araj, since shortly after they came to the Metroplex in 1978. Today, Shakila is a Dallas radiologist, Sameer, a McAllen, Texas, lawyer, and Araj, a law student at American University in Washington, D.C.

Carter says that Dr. Ahmed's goal is to enlighten society about Islam and the Muslim world through his work and interfaith efforts. Ahmed's colleague, board member, and licensed social worker Zeba Salim concurs, noting that Ahmed's faith is expressed through his strong character and charitable service. Salim, who was born in India, was raised in the United Kingdom, and attended The University of Texas at Arlington in the 1980s, says that although Dr. Ahmed's focus has been on the needs of the Muslim population, he is concerned with the community at large.

As chair of a September 2002 regional conference on the "Role of Religion in Promoting World Peace," Dr. Ahmed stated, "The harmony among nations as well as among individuals living in a multi-religious, multi-cultural society can only be achieved through a spirit of tolerance, feelings for other human beings, and sacrifice in the interest of humanity."

Dr. Basheer Ahmed would be the first to remind his friends and admirers of the challenges that lie ahead both for the MCCHS and for interfaith and intercultural relations in America. The Muslim Community Center has achieved nominal success, but it remains a small-scale operation without full-time staff or a base of funding to achieve longer-term goals such as the establishment of a Muslim women's shelter for victims of domestic violence and a facility to treat emotionally disturbed children. In 1998 Dr. Ahmed and Zeba Salim had submitted a grant proposal to the United Way of Metropolitan Tarrant County. They were seeking funding for the MCCHS to create a model of service patterned after other religious-based organizations such as Catholic Charities, Jewish Family Services, and Lutheran Social Services.

The proposal, which targeted a needy, under-served Muslim population, was rejected, according to Ahmed, because it was too parochial. Disappointed but resolute, he has since continued to rely on fund-raising dinners and donations of individual Muslims and other contributors, while still planning to seek "outside" organization funding in the future.

Dr. Ahmed and selected members of his board have achieved recognition for community service, such as their sponsorship of annual health fairs that serve hundreds of Muslim and non-Muslim people (providing free physical, dental, and eye exams, pediatric care, cholesterol and blood pressure testing, and health lectures). But even supporters talk about the need for the MCCHS to secure higher visibility in the community so that the medical and social problems of Muslim Americans will be openly discussed along with those of other minority groups, such as African Americans and citizens of Hispanic descent.

Dr. Ahmed believes that "there is nothing that can't be resolved with patience, commitment, and faith." But he is no stranger to prejudice or to the damage that can be done to noble causes by fear, ignorance, and hatred. "Before 9/11 we were all just Americans. Now we are Muslims first in many peoples' eyes and Americans second."

He has spoken publicly about the threats to destroy the MCCHS and the intimidation felt by members of the Muslim community. But he also cites the many supportive calls he has received from longtime residents of the Dallas–Fort Worth area. Ahmed acknowledges that since the tragedy of 9/11, there has been much more pressure on him for interfaith work and for efforts to dispel misconceptions about his religion and culture in one-on-one conversations and in presentations, such as those launched this year titled "Know Your Muslim Neighbor."

Ahmed was one of the organizers of a January 2003 public forum held in a hall adjacent to a Fort Worth Catholic church. He and other Muslim Americans spoke as part of a series planned by the Interfaith Network for Peace and Justice. Ahmed is a member of the Interfaith Network, which was created by the Tarrant Area Community of Churches after 9/11.

At public events Ahmed tries to debunk myths and reveal truths about the Muslim world. For example, most Muslims come from South Asia and Africa, not the Middle East. During Europe's Dark Ages, Islamic scholars such as Avicenna in the eleventh century advanced the world of medicine. Countless other Muslims contributed mightily to discoveries in math, science, and astronomy. Ahmed also highlights commonalities among the world's three major religions, Christianity, Judaism, and Islam: their joint lineage to Abraham, use of much of the same Scripture, and a Muslim's high regard for religious prophets such as Moses, John the Baptist, and Jesus.

Ahmed is pleased to offer insights into Muslim customs. A devout follower of Islam prays five times a day, with Fridays being the holy day. That is when most Muslims attend a mosque, although it is common for Dr. Ahmed to make brief (fifteen- or twenty-minute) visits to one of three local mosques on other days. His routine begins with him leaving his shoes in an outer hallway before entering the main room of the mosque, a place for reverence and reflection. Inside the quiet, carpeted, white-walled room he both stands and kneels in prone position to offer prayers to Allah. He may be joined by just a small group of other worshippers on these weekly visits. On Fridays hundreds are likely to be in the mosque, with women worshipping separate from the men. Children are expected to be able to read the Arabic text of the Qur'an (Koran) by age eight, and some memorize it entirely by age fourteen (all must memorize key verses by fourteen). While learning the holy book, children sit at the feet of a white-robed imam (prayer leader) in the front of the room near the arch known as the *mahrab* and softly recite their lessons.

Unlike in Christian churches or synagogues, there are no religious statues, symbols, or artifacts in a mosque. The walls are unadorned. In this Arlington mosque where Ahmed prays, a small wooden cart with copies of the Qur'an is near one wall. During the day, light from high windows cascades down on the serene setting.

The majority of Ahmed's audiences have been cordial and appreciative of his lessons, but he recalls one older woman in a recent setting who said, "Oh, why don't all you Muslims just go home." To which the not easily rattled Dr. Ahmed replied: "Ma'am, just like your forefathers didn't want to go home, neither do we. Besides, where would we all go?"

Basheer Ahmed recalls how in 1979 during another Middle East flash point—the Iran hostage crisis—he had been invited to the White House, along with other national Muslim American leaders, by President Jimmy Carter. Ahmed, representing the Islamic Medical Association, met with President Carter and members of his cabinet and advisors. In 2000 he was reunited with the former president and his wife, Rosalynn, at an event at the Carter Center in Atlanta.

The role of problem solver and crisis manager seems to come naturally to Ahmed. According to Dr. Pervaiz Rahman, a senior member of the MCCHS board, "Basheer's reputation was as the trouble-shooter in his family." In 1999 Rahman traveled with Ahmed to his native city of Hyderabad, India, about five hundred miles south of Bombay. He met Ahmed's large extended family, and he was impressed with the tremendous respect they showed him. "He has a God-given ability to encourage people to think, to get involved, and to work toward finding solutions," says Dr. Rahman.

On this Saturday afternoon at the Al-Shifa Clinic, Dr. Ahmed tries to offer hope, if not a solution, to a mother living in an abusive household. Her teenage daughter, who is not with her today, is anxious and depressed, claiming to hear voices. The mother's two adolescent boys wait outside Basheer's office, where Asli Parker engages them in light chatter. At the end of the session, Dr. Ahmed tells the mother he wants to see her and her daughter in a month.

He informed the woman about her options, but he knows he is up against strong cultural, psychological, and social forces. At a February 2001 regional conference on "Domestic Violence—Islamic Perspective," sponsored by the MCCHS, Ahmed and other local and national experts and advocates addressed the issue. In his remarks he said:

> Domestic violence is a universal problem. All ethnic, religious, racial, and age groups are affected. Unfortunately, despite Islamic teachings of compassion, justice, and kindness, many Muslim women in the United States experience these tragedies. . . . If religious leaders, health care professionals, and the community at large are not aware and involved, women will remain in the victims' role for many years.

In spring 2003 Dr. Ahmed adds that given the current climate surrounding post-9/11 and reactionary legislation such as the USA Patriot Act, Muslim women are even more intimidated by the idea of contacting police or any government authorities that could result in their husbands being charged with a crime. They are afraid of the ramifications that could affect the freedom of their entire family, and so they choose to suffer in silence.

In a proactive effort related to domestic violence, the Muslim Community Center in 1998 established an Islamic Institute of Human Relations to offer premarital, marriage, and divorce counseling and educational programs to promote strong family relations. Two local imams, including Dr. Yusuf Kavakci, a professor of Islamic law, are religious advisors. Dr. Ahmed is one of five professional advisors.

"What is important to me," says Dr. (Mrs.) Hind Jarrah, "is his continuous recognition of the role of Muslim women in activism, and his insistence on involving women in the organization of his projects."

After saying goodbye to Asli Parker, Basheer Ahmed leaves the clinic after a five-hour Saturday of service. Now at almost 2 P.M., Drs. Ahmed and Hussain travel to a corner fried chicken establishment. Ahmed orders a small bucket and a glass of ice water. He peels away the outer coating before eating his chicken. He admits that as someone who has high cholesterol, doesn't exercise, and is a little overweight, he needs to watch his diet. He offers a short, silent giggle and returns to his meal. His health is no laughing matter to his family and friends. He suffered a major heart attack in 1988 and underwent quadruple bypass surgery. Dr. Ahmed shrugs off the incident, noting that he was back on his demanding schedule within three weeks. He confirms that most days he spends extended periods of time driving his sleek silver Mercedes Benz 500 SL to his many appointments. His schedule and the nature of his work don't seem to provide him with time to do more walking. Or so the gentle doctor tells himself.

When lunch is over, he begins to share the story of his multilayered journey: how he became a doctor, a psychiatrist, a community mental health specialist, and an American social activist.

* * *

As an immigrant you have to work harder to prove yourself. But America gives you a feeling that you can accomplish so much.

—Dr. M. Basheer Ahmed

Ahmed thanks his parents for helping to shape his character, but he was also very much influenced by his uncle Dr. Manan, a well-known physician in Hyderabad, India, who cared for many patients too poor to pay him. Observing his uncle's work, the sensitive nephew developed a deep sense of empathy, which was to be his constant companion throughout his life. Ahmed was also very religious from an early age.

As a Muslim he believed in "Al-Qadar" (which means "divine predestination"): Whatever God wills to happen will happen. But he was also taught to believe that God had given human beings a free will, the ability to choose right or wrong. Ahmed had a strong conscience from boyhood on. He knew that he was responsible for his choices and that he would ultimately be held accountable for actions in his lifetime.

Ahmed says his interest in psychological matters dates back to high school. "I seemed to be more interested in human issues, problems. My friends and I would talk about family issues. I had a natural inclination to listen. At that time I didn't know there was a specialty named psychiatry."

Ahmed received his B.S. degree from Osmania University in his hometown in 1954. He then attended Dow Medical College at Karachi University in Pakistan. "Once I left home for medical school in Pakistan," he recalls, "my ego strength took over. I saw what I could achieve." He was planning on specializing in internal medicine until one of his professors returned from the United Kingdom with advanced psychiatric training. Up to that point, Ahmed's exposure to the subject had consisted of a few dusty lectures on depression and dementia. Upon graduation from medical school and with the recommendation of his professor-mentor, Ahmed traveled to Glasgow University, Scotland, where he received postgraduate training in psychiatry.

"There was tremendous competition for a foreign-trained doctor to go into a professional unit," Ahmed says. He received the distinction of being assigned to the psychiatric unit of a hospital's acute care ward, when most of his international contemporaries were assigned to work in mental hospitals. In 1964 the Royal College of Physicians and Royal College of Surgeons, London, Edinburgh, and Glasgow, U.K., named him a diplomate in psychiatry. A decade later he would be named a fellow of those institutions as well as the American Psychiatric Association. Dr. Ahmed credits his education in England and Scotland with introducing him to pioneering work in the therapeutic community mental health movement. Back then the United States lagged behind the United Kingdom in innovative approaches to mental health issues. In the early 1960s, during the Kennedy administration, the emphasis was shifting to mass deinstitutionalization of mental patients. For years U.S. communities wrestled with the issue of whom to release, when, and with what support services and safeguards.

In 1968 the St. Louis (Missouri) State Hospital Complex was looking for a progressive clinical director to institute change in mental health patient policies. Dr. Basheer Ahmed was seeking an opportunity to put his ideas into action. "He is representative of what the late President Kennedy called 'a bold new approach' to psychiatry," was how a profile in a state hospital publication described its new director of Unit One in the fall of 1968.

The article explained Dr. Ahmed's philosophy of treatment that featured the patient as a working member of a mental health team. Another innovation implemented by Dr. Ahmed was greater use of group therapy in order to prepare patients for functioning as members of social units (e.g., in a family or home environment, at work, or in day-to-day living) when discharged from the hospital. "The reaction of the staff to these innovations has been extremely cooperative," Dr. Ahmed reported. The publication also mentioned that just before coming to the United States, Dr. Ahmed had married his wife, Shakila. Theirs had been an arranged marriage, according to Indian custom. Shakila was also an M.D., and her sister was a practicing physician in St. Louis when the young couple arrived.

Three years later in March 1971, Basheer Ahmed was featured in a long article by Gerald J. Meyer of the *St. Louis Post-Dispatch*. The story documented how under Ahmed's direction Unit One had reduced its patient population from five hundred to less than one hundred.

More important was how he transformed the unit—from providing essentially custodial care to implementing psychiatry in a therapeutic community setting where patients had a role in decision making. The article also described how Ahmed, "without additional funding from the county or state governments," opened a neighborhood-based mental health clinic in the Kinloch Community Center in north St. Louis County, a largely black urban environment. Dr. Ahmed explained that this preventive psychiatry was designed to serve people in their community rather than removing them for treatment.

When Ahmed confronted racial tension in the community, he couldn't relate to the animosity and polarized attitudes. In his extended family in India, his relatives' skin colors range from fair to bronze to black. As a psychiatrist he was also colorblind. "People's problems are people's problems, regardless of race or ethnicity."

As a pioneer in the mental health community in St. Louis, Dr. Ahmed, according to the 1971 newspaper article, insisted that "psychiatric help must be an accepted part of 'comprehensive community health care,' and that his staff of three doctors, six social workers, two psychologists, one occupational therapist and two vocational rehabilitation specialists operate in cooperation with other agencies." He also created six-month courses on mental health for public health nurses throughout the county. The newspaper article quoted the director of the State Division of Mental Health, Dr. George A. Ulett, who called Ahmed's work with Unit One "in the best tradition of community mental health." At the close of the article, Dr. Ahmed sounded ever the visionary, stating his belief that programs like his would become the wave of the future in psychiatry. Reflecting on his work in St. Louis, Ahmed says he is proud of his contributions, adding ironically, "I wasn't the Muslim doctor then, just the doctor."

Basheer Ahmed continues to be a strategic thinker. He advises members of his board and his fellow community activists that proposed programs should be "doable, achievable, and sustainable." He has applied that formula to his efforts through the years. He has also used that same type of thinking in laying out a career path. Each move, each job was carefully planned to generate specific results.

In mid-1971, at the height of his success in St. Louis, he accepted a position in New York City as director of the Sound View–Throgs Neck Community Mental Health Center, affiliated with the Albert Einstein College of Medicine, where the thirty-six-year-old Ahmed would serve as assistant professor of psychiatry, his first academic appointment. He said it was difficult leaving St. Louis, where his staff gave him a teary-eyed farewell. But in his best paraphrase of Frank Sinatra, Dr. Ahmed says, "If you can work in New York, you can work anywhere."

In New York, Ahmed learned the history of how poor and indigent immigrant groups had struggled for education, employment, health care, and social services throughout the twentieth century. He noted how organizations such as Jewish Family Services and Jewish community centers had developed in response to the needs of religious and cultural minorities who had been subjected to prejudice and discrimination. Years later he would draw on those experiences when creating the concept of the Muslim Community Center for Human Services.

From 1971 until 1976, Dr. Ahmed developed community mental health programs for treatment of acutely ill patients, for comprehensive rehabilitation of non-acute patients, and for decentralized preventive mental health care in the field. He was also teaching psychiatry as a member of the faculty at Albert Einstein College of Medicine, Bronx, New York. ("And I wasn't even Jewish," Ahmed jokes thirty years later.) He and Shakila lived in New Rochelle, about twenty miles north of New York City. The Ahmeds were first-time parents, raising their son, Sameer.

The scenario seemed satisfactory on many fronts. But Basheer Ahmed's career clock was ticking. He realized that to become a full professor at Albert Einstein College, he would have to spend several years conducting basic theoretical research to bolster his credentials. Dr. Ahmed was capable of such research, but it was not his priority. His focus was on applied research. He felt he couldn't afford to spend more years in New York. An entrepreneurial opportunity was calling at a new medical school in Dayton, Ohio. The Ahmeds were on the move again.

In 1976 Dr. Ahmed became a full professor of psychiatry at the Wright State University School of Medicine. He was simultaneously serving as chief of psychiatry at the Dayton, Ohio, Veterans Administration Hospital. The work was rewarding, but he and Shakila felt increasingly lonely and isolated in southwestern Ohio, where there was a small Muslim population, and winters were marked by dreary days and frequent ice storms. Two years later, Ahmed was again scanning the horizon for his next position. The choice would come down to Los Angeles, where he had a pending offer to join the UCLA Medical School, or the Dallas–Fort Worth, Texas, area, with its solid reputation for health care institutions.

In 1978 Dr. Ahmed began a four-year stint as director of the department of psychiatry at the John Peter Smith Hospital in Fort Worth, Texas. During that time he also served as professor of psychiatry, community medicine, and family practice at The University of Texas Health Science Center in Dallas. The Ahmeds found the weather in North Texas more to their liking, and they were comfortable as members of a growing Muslim community.

Over the next two decades, Basheer Ahmed distinguished himself as a medical director, a chief of staff, and chair of continued medical education at institutes, medical centers, and hospitals throughout the region. His reputation as an adult and adolescent psychiatrist grew, with a successful private practice, first in Fort Worth and later in Arlington, where he and his family relocated in 1993. Shakila Ahmed also found success in North Texas as a radiologist at the Dallas Veterans Affairs Hospital and in her own practice. She was profiled in the media as a thoroughly modern woman in dress and liberated spirit. In one account, she told a reporter for the *Dallas Morning News,* "I'm able to do anything as well as a man."

Reflecting on his thirty-five-year career in community mental health, Basheer Ahmed is openly patriotic. He says that this country can give a person what no other country can: opportunity. "There is freedom of achievement, not just freedom of expression, in the U.S."

The Ahmeds live in a stunning home on two-plus acres in a gated estate in Arlington, Texas. The two-story house features glistening Italian marble floors and a sweeping staircase that could rival Scarlett O'Hara's. The home has hosted sit-down dinners for more than two hundred guests. But all who know the Ahmeds praise the couple for their humility and genuine regard for others.

"They go out of their way to make you feel comfortable," says Zeba Salim.

Although Basheer Ahmed wasn't raised with wealth, he typifies the concept of "noblesse oblige," whereby the affluent of society feel a responsibility to aid the poor, whether through making generous gifts to charity or by donating time to worthy causes. "This country had been good to me, and I wanted to pay it back with service to the community," he says. In Ahmed's case, he has spent years responding to the needs of the less fortunate with significant financial contributions, time, and effort to establish the Muslim Community Center.

"My Islamic teachings took root in America," he says, reciting passages from the Qur'an that address one's need to perform acts of charity *(Zakat)* and service to others.

Dr. Ahmed may have been called a "Lone Ranger" in a newspaper story, but he knew it was vital to the success of his plans to have supportive community leadership. In forming the MCCHS he secured the participation of thirty Muslim doctors, educators, professionals, and religious leaders from North Texas to serve on an initial advisory council. A smaller group would later form the executive/advisory board. What had launched the idea for a multipurpose community center was an influx in 1994 of Bosnian, Somalian, and Kurdish Muslim immigrants to the Metroplex. Many were poor and lacking in basic services, notably medical care. Dr. Ahmed and his colleagues spent the next decade implementing a series of community-based responses.

In July 1995 the MCCHS was incorporated; nonprofit tax-exempt status would be secured months later. The first public event was a health fair designed for the Muslim population, but open to the entire community. More than five hundred people attended, and some thirty physicians and nurses from area hospitals donated equipment, supplies, and services. The annual health fair concept would become one of the staples for the Muslim Community Center, and another source for interfaith cooperation with area churches.

In November 1995, two hundred guests attended a fund-raising dinner at a convention center. Those who came to show their support for the MCCHS included the chair of the Texas Republican party, a judge, a county commissioner, and the president of the Jewish Federation of Fort Worth and Tarrant County. Media coverage followed. "His dream to build a Muslim Community Center for Human Services has met all the challenges. . . . He is determined to do it, and he will do it," wrote Aboobaker Ebrahim in the November 23, 1995, edition of the *Asian News*.

In January 1996 the MCCHS launched a twenty-four-hour help line/ telephone counseling service. The Al-Shifa Clinic opened in October 1998. The Islamic Institute of Human Relations (providing marital and divorce counseling) was also formed in 1998.

The North Richland Hills headquarters building for the MCCHS (and the medical clinic) was purchased in 2000. Soon the mainstream Texas media had taken notice of Ahmed and his work with the Muslim Community Center. Patrick McGee of the *Fort Worth Star-Telegram* wrote of Dr. Ahmed's work in providing basic needs for area Muslims in a July 23, 2001, article: "'The problems are the same, but the services are not the same,' Ahmed said," explaining that Muslims need social services delivered in culturally sensitive ways. "That is the driving philosophy behind the Muslim Community Center for Human Services, which was founded by Ahmed and other Muslim professionals six years ago when the Metroplex was receiving Muslim refugees from Bosnia, Somalia and Iraq."

In 2001 and 2002 the Muslim Community Center sponsored regional conferences on domestic violence (in cooperation with The University of

Texas at Arlington School of Social Work), Muslim contributions to human civilization, and the role of religion in promoting world peace, featuring Muslim speakers from across the country.

In 2003 the "Know Your Muslim Neighbor" forums were launched, but a more ambitious community outreach program was underway. On Sunday, March 9, Dr. Ahmed and his executive/advisory board met at the Haveli Pakistani restaurant in Irving, Texas, to discuss their plans for the new program. There would be discussion about interfaith cooperation, sensitivity training, and public information campaigns. But two important questions about the future of the MCCHS could also be answered at that meeting: Would other Muslim community members step forward and take responsibility for programs such as the outreach effort? And could the popular leader Basheer Ahmed loosen his grip on the reins of the organization he had founded more than eight years earlier?

* * *

That's what we do in this country. We put our energies
together to serve humanity.

—Dr. M. Basheer Ahmed

Dr. Ahmed likes to run an efficient meeting. After a pleasant back-room brunch of seasoned, aromatic South Asian food, a "token" platter of scrambled eggs, and pitchers of hot tea sweetened with sugar and cream, Ahmed and his board are ready to work their way through the eleven-point agenda (with attachments), which had been typed and photocopied by Ahmed earlier this morning. The MCCHS has no clerical staff. As Ahmed states, "If I don't work hard, the Muslim Community Center will disappear."

The meeting begins with a recitation from the Qur'an led by Dr. Yusuf Kavakci, a resident scholar imam of the Islamic Association of North Texas and an advisor to the MCCHS. The opening prayer talks of peace, which appears to bring comfort to the gathering, who moments earlier had shared their concerns over the pending Iraq war.

The minutes from the prior month's meeting are approved, and then discussion shifts to building management and maintenance items at the headquarters' site in North Richland Hills. A roof repair estimate of $12,000 has been received. Dr. Ahmed says that more donations may have to be solicited to make the necessary repairs.

Item number six is the outreach program. At the February meeting Dr. Ahmed had said how essential it was for the Muslim Community Center to participate in community-based charitable programs in Tarrant County.

He outlined three program objectives: increasing Muslim representation, participation, and contribution to social services in Arlington; providing services to needy individuals (irrespective of religion, race, or ethnicity) directly or through other institutions; and building coalitions with other social service organizations in the area. He then established a subcommittee to organize the program, asking Mr. Ismail Tahir and Mr. Aftab Siddiqui to co-chair the effort. Now he waits for their report.

Tahir, a certified public accountant, is as reserved as Siddiqui, an operations planner for American Airlines, is animated. One wonders if Ahmed chose the men for the contrasting, and perhaps complementary, styles. Speaking slowly and clearly, Tahir first announces that more than thirty people attended a volunteer meeting on March 1 at the Arlington Central Library. From that group, a six-person committee was formed to identify a list of twenty-two potential projects for the MCCHS outreach program. As the group reads through the list, Siddiqui reminds them in a high-pitched rapid-fire voice of the need to build a continuous presence for the Muslim Community Center in Arlington. Dr. Ahmed and others stress the importance of prioritizing the potential projects list (e.g., food drives, school seminars, library displays of Islam, Earth Day participation, and partnerships with women's and homeless shelters). Tahir nods, and he and Siddiqui inform the group that they will meet with the committee of volunteers and narrow the list to two or three potential projects by the next meeting.

In the past, Dr. Ahmed might well have made the decision on his own because of a lack of time or commitment from other board members. But he has delegated this assignment, and he will let the two men fulfill their responsibilities—though he will certainly monitor their progress.

He will later tell Zeba Salim that he was very pleased with the initiative shown by Tahir and Siddiqui, and with progress to broaden the base of involvement in the MCCHS. By the next board meeting, Ahmed will have learned that the Muslim Community Center's outreach program has become a partner with the Arlington Life Shelter, a public facility for area homeless, and MCCHS volunteers will be scheduled for monthly service activities at the shelter.

The last agenda item at the Sunday, March 9, 2003, executive/advisory board meeting is United Way. Dr. Ahmed, who was the first Muslim in the Metroplex to serve as a committee member of United Way of Metropolitan Tarrant County, announces that he is participating in a review of grant applications. He again discusses the need for a social worker to help the MCCHS write grant proposals for philanthropic organizations, such as

United Way, foundations, and government funding sources. There is brief discussion by the group, but no recommendations on how to proceed. Dr. Ahmed says that until the Muslim Community Center is able to secure grants, it will have to continue to depend on donations and fund-raising dinners.

It has been nearly five years since Ahmed and board member Zeba Salim had first sought United Way funding. When their proposal was unsuccessful, Ahmed confided that he "allowed himself" to be disappointed, to feel sad and hurt for forty-eight hours. But then he "got over it," and it was time to reflect on his best options for the future. He decided that he needed to know more about how United Way operated. He sought out opportunities to get involved, using his community experience and reputation as a psychiatrist in the Metroplex.

About three years ago, he was invited to become a member of the Families Way Impact Council (FWIC) of United Way of Metropolitan Tarrant County, joining twenty-four other representatives from business, education, government, and the religious community. As a member of the FWIC, Ahmed has participated in funding decisions for organizations such as Catholic Charities, Jewish Family Services, and the Salvation Army. This past year, Dr. Ahmed played a lead role in recommending that the FWIC target child abuse and neglect as its priority social issue. In addition to gaining more exposure for the MCCHS, Ahmed's participation with United Way gives him greater confidence for new fund-raising strategies, if and when the Muslim Community Center decides to submit another grant proposal.

When asked about the future of the MCCHS, Dr. Ahmed dismisses any talk of his succession. "Right now my focus is on finding a social worker/coordinator to assist the Muslim Community Center." One intermediate option being considered is the hiring of a part-time administrative assistant. Ahmed does allow himself to speculate on the future of social activism in the Muslim community in North Texas and nationally.

He is encouraged by the potential of the younger generation. He singles out Zeba Salim, the dynamic social worker, who has been a valuable member of the MCCHS board since 1996. Another woman who has impressed Ahmed with her commitment to Muslim causes is Shanaz Arjumand from New York City.

A fifteen-year veteran of the health care industry, Arjumand has been working after-hours and on weekends for two years to conduct research on low-income Muslim populations in New York. She hopes to use her research to launch a citywide community education program to raise people's awareness of available medical and social services. Recently she and Ahmed had dinner when Arjumand was in Dallas on business. Although the focus of their work differed—the MCCHS is a clinic model, and Arjumand considers hers a network model—the two social activists agreed their missions were aligned: to provide the Muslim American community with improved access to resources.

Another bright light on the national scene, according to Ahmed, is a recent Harvard graduate named Zayed Yasin. In his 2002 commencement speech, which was reprinted by the Association of Muslim Social Scientists in the September 28, 2002, program ("Role of Religion in Promoting World Peace"), Yasin explained the correct definition of a *jihad*. He said:

> It is a word that has been corrupted and misinterpreted, both by those who do and do not claim to be Muslims, and we saw last fall, to our great national and personal loss, the results of this corruption. Jihad, in its truest and purest form, the form to which all Muslims aspire, is the determination to do right, to do justice even against your own interests. It is an individual struggle for personal moral behavior.

Basheer Ahmed says that this outstanding Ivy League graduate is forgoing any immediate career decisions to spend two years involved in community service work. Now if only Zayed Yasin wanted to come to Texas. Imagine such a committed young man working for the Muslim Community Center. Dr. Basheer Ahmed appears to file that idea away along with the many he carries with him these very busy days.

[12]

MARK GONNERMAN "DHARMA ACTIVIST"

Photo by Mark H. Massé

During a summer of intensive writing, Mark Gonnerman worked on plans as director of the 2004 Aurora Forum, a returning series of community education programs at Stanford University centered on the theme of American civil liberties in a post-9/11 world. "We want to expand people's horizons and close the gap between rhetoric and reality," he said. In August 2003, Gonnerman also met with Michael Nagler, University of California, Berkeley emeritus professor of classics and cofounder of Berkeley's Peace and Conflict Studies Program. The meeting was one step in the development of the Stanford conference "Cultures of Violence and the Cultivation of Peace," which will likely feature debate and discussion on the role of independent versus corporate media, the economy of violence, and teaching peace (through meditation) to prisoners, among other topics. On October 31, 2003, Mark Gonnerman successfully defended his 560-page dissertation, "On the Path, Off the Trail: Gary Snyder's Religious Education and the Making of American Zen." Afterward, he said he was looking forward to returning to the classroom to teach classes on American religious experience and on Henry David Thoreau. How does all of this relate to Mark Gonnerman's philosophy of activism? The answer is deceptively simple. He believes that education should create socially engaged citizens. "You learn so you can serve the community."

One does not stand still looking for a path.
One walks; and as one walks, a path comes into being.

—Rev. Mas Kodani, Senshin Buddhist Temple, Los Angeles

Breathe deeply, rhythmically, and focus, but don't trip over the curb. No time for *zazen* this afternoon. This is walking meditation as practiced by Mark Gonnerman, Stanford doctoral student, director of special projects, and socially engaged Buddhist.

He is on an unusual quest this pleasant May Saturday in the lotus land known as Palo Alto. He is searching for homeless folks on the streets of this exclusive northern California community, a realm Gonnerman says is dominated by "hungry ghosts," beings with insatiable appetites—the self-absorbed chic.

Gonnerman carries a large covered plastic tray of turkey sandwiches, leftovers from his campus workshop. He moves steadily down the sidewalks in his hiking sandals, jeans, and navy pullover while beautifully tanned, uncovered people stroll with their beautiful dogs by beautiful storefronts. Gonnerman scans the horizon of affluence for any needy, hungry souls. Son of a Lutheran minister, he has the hirsute, intense look of a frontier preacher. Think of a younger, raven-haired Richard Dreyfus in a Robert Altman film.

After several blocks, Gonnerman is about to give up and leave the food on a bench when he spots Karl, an Ahab of a man pushing a shopping cart loaded with his belongings. Gonnerman engages Karl with a quick smile, a sourdough turkey sandwich, and some street-corner conversation. The Urban Ministry Food Closet is closed on weekends; no point in dropping food off there. Best bet is to leave the tray on one of the tables outside the nearest Starbucks.

"They'll find it," Karl assures Gonnerman. While munching on his second sandwich, Karl tells Gonnerman that he recently served four months in jail after being arrested and charged as a "terrorist threat" to the retail establishment. The homeless as terrorists? Gonnerman suspends his disbelief long enough to wish Karl well and accept the man's thanks for his thoughtfulness. The brief encounter appears to have pleased Gonnerman, judging by his spark of laughter. But his emotions are hidden behind his dark clip-on sunglasses. His eyes reveal the real story of this afternoon's mood.

After following Karl's instructions and leaving the tray of sandwiches outside the coffee store, Mark Gonnerman tells his wife, Meri Mitsuyoshi, that he needs some caffeine. But not here. The couple loop the block until they find a quiet shop where Mark orders a large glass mug of orange-colored Thai tea. He removes his clip-ons and begins to debrief about the recently concluded day-long workshop that he hosted on campus. His gray-blue eyes look weary and a little melancholy. His small, well-shaped hands dance anxiously on the tabletop. He wears a brown wooden bracelet (*mala*) on his left wrist, a reminder to try to live in accordance with Buddhist teachings. Gonnerman's voice is clear, betraying his upper Midwest, high school drama club roots. He speaks in the dulcet tones of an NPR program host. "I was hoping we could have spent more time talking about the history of the civil rights movement," he says, moving his trusty olive Timberland backpack by his chair. "We kind of got sidetracked."

Despite Meri's assurances that the workshop went well, Gonnerman remains unsettled. "I'm going to have to process this for a while," he says before finishing his tea.

He will reflect often during the next couple of days on the Stanford continuing studies workshop "You Got to Move: Community, Nonviolence and Social Change." He will analyze how the event that he had spent months preparing for had changed course. He will realize how his good intentions fell short as another workshop leader took control of the discussion. "Mark can be generous to a fault," says grad school friend Gregory Kaplan, now an assistant professor of Jewish Studies at Rice University. "He really is the suffering servant sometimes."

The workshop featured representatives of the Highlander Research and Education Center in New Market, Tennessee, where Dr. Martin Luther King Jr. had visited and Rosa Parks and other civil rights advocates had studied. Gonnerman had intended to use the history of Highlander and the civil rights movement as a case study to help answer the recurring question: How can the average citizen bring about social change in America?

He had envisioned the workshop as a vehicle on empowering ordinary people, demonstrating his belief that social activism is rooted in education and the transmission of knowledge. Instead, the event lost its focus as a series of speakers (including several Bay-area peace activists) presented their own agendas, and the notion of social justice became just one of many topics covered during the five-hour gathering. "That's the difference when you're a facilitator rather than a teacher," he says later. "You can't control everything."

Is this nonchalance or a Zen-like stance? Only a real Bodhisattva—one who works selflessly to awaken and enlighten others—would know for sure. This much may be surmised: Mark Gonnerman won't let this experience slip away without drawing lessons from it.

* * *

He . . . wants to be someone who is an agent of change. He believes in
the power of ideas, of public conversation and of social responsibility.

—ANNETTE SHELBY TODD, associate director of
continuing studies, Stanford University

Mark Gonnerman, forty-five, has spent more than half his life in
academia as student and teacher at distinguished institutions such as
Harvard and Stanford. For almost fifteen years he has been working
toward his Ph.D. Some might offer apologies for so fluid a timetable;
Gonnerman offers insights and reflections.

He says that his longevity on Stanford's campus has strengthened his
interdepartmental, collegial efforts, enabling him to secure fellowships
and sponsors over the years for a range of workshops, courses, and continuing studies programs. His colleagues tend to agree, citing his credibility and efficacy at building bridges between the university and the broader
community. His boss, Dean Charles Junkerman, praises Gonnerman's
staying power, his ongoing enthusiasm, and his unabashed belief in the
values of liberal education: "His influence spreads in concentric circles
from his department (religious studies) and the continuing studies program, where he serves in a staff capacity, through university committees
and collaborative projects to many corners of the institution."

Gonnerman calls himself a lifelong learner, and he notes that such
pursuits can and should make individuals more humane and caring toward others. "A big part of my work is to provide . . . resources that
stimulate learning, the will to learn, and the will to engage with the world
and with other people," he says. "In that sense, I'm an activist inside the
corporate research university."

A May–June 2003 online article from *Sojourners* magazine echoes
Gonnerman's comments about the mission of higher education to inspire
social change. Author Melissa Snarr, a lecturer in religion at Emory College, noted how colleges and universities have "trained and nurtured
numerous social movements and activists that have changed our world."
She referred to this influencing process as "the call to moral learning and
social justice."

Gonnerman has been in and around the "ivory tower" long enough to
warn of attitudes and forces that inhibit liberated thinking and creative ideas
that spark social activism. He says too often the modern academic culture
resists change, and its pervasive socialization dimension muzzles open-
minded exploration. He notes that holding degrees and being educated

are not necessarily the same, especially as degree-granting institutions become more market-driven to offer job training rather than a diversified education. Gonnerman says that "informed optimism" is needed to counter entrenched thinking and thus lead to progressive citizen action on and off campus. "We need to comfort the afflicted and afflict the comfortable," he says, paraphrasing a popular reformers' creed.

Recently Gonnerman has added the term "cognitive activist" to his intellectual arsenal. The concept came from an Alternet article, "Metaphor and War, Again?" by University of California, Berkeley, linguist George Lakoff, who wrote about the importance of "framing" and how changing minds by changing frames for interpretation is good "activist" work. Mark Gonnerman says that a liberal arts education helps cultivate an ability to approach facts and problems from a variety of viewpoints, and this enhances individual lives while helping to develop ethically responsible global citizens.

"Cognitive activist may simply be a fancy word for teacher, but in an age of nonstop media manipulation and the quick fix, the label brings attention to the long-term, ongoing work of cultivating intellectual virtues and exercising them in both private deliberation and public discussion," says Gonnerman, the Stanford religious studies doctoral student, who is finishing his magnum opus this fall, a five-hundred-plus-page dissertation on activist Buddhist poet Gary Snyder.

Gonnerman says Snyder has influenced him as both research subject and mentor. He identifies with Snyder's view on the role of intellect, spirituality, and social action as expressed in these two prose excerpts:

> What the Greeks did do was exteriorize their intellectual life, make it convivial and explicit, define consistency in thinking, and publicly enjoy it. They saw an active and articulate intellectual stance as both modish and practical, sharpening and refining their ability to fulfill the obligations of citizenship in a society where clear and convincing argument counted for much. (Gary Snyder, *The Practice of the Wild*)

> The mercy of the West has been social revolution; the mercy of the East has been individual insight into the basic self/void. We need both. They are both contained in the traditional three aspects of the Dharma path: wisdom (prajna), meditation (dhyana), and morality (sila). (Gary Snyder, "Buddhism and the Coming Revolution," from *Earth House Hold*)

Gonnerman notes that Snyder was one of the founding inspirations for socially engaged Buddhism in the United States. In 1978 the Buddhist Peace Fellowship (BPF) was established. Today there are six thousand

196

members in chapters nationwide who practice contemplation and social action to "help beings liberate themselves—to bring peace where there is conflict, to promote communication and cooperation among sanghas (communities), and to alleviate suffering where we can." BPF-sponsored work includes efforts to promote social justice, prison reform, environmental protection, and other expressions of spiritually based activism.

Mark Gonnerman has been a member of the Buddhist Peace Fellowship for several years, but he hasn't actively participated in BPF programs apart from providing a platform for the Fellowship's speakers at Stanford. Gonnerman's preferred venue for social activism remains community education. "I care about these public programs . . . that are, for the most part, effective, and they generate interest, enthusiasm, and action in the world," he says, citing his work in 2003 as cofounder and director of the Aurora Forum, a series of free monthly conversations at Stanford on current issues and ideas intended to inspire involved citizenship. The Forum was an outgrowth of a number of events in the weeks and months following 9/11. For one of those "healing" sessions, Gonnerman bucked some staff resistance and invited a Muslim scholar for a two-hour dialogue with an interested and anxious audience. Encouraged by the success of such public encounters, Gonnerman worked with Charles Junkerman, dean of continuing studies, and members of the staff, to create an ongoing community dialogue to "articulate and explore American ideals."

Aurora Forum literature quotes U.S. philosopher and educator John Dewey, who said, "Democracy is born in conversation." Gonnerman also recognizes the influence of author Richard Rorty (*Achieving Our Country*), who wrote of the liberal "party of hope, people who believe that the future can be different from and better than the past." The Aurora Forum, whose title pays homage to the goddess of dawn in Roman mythology, invoked two U.S.-based precedents: *The American Aurora*, a leading revolutionary-era newspaper, and *The New York Aurora*, the newspaper Walt Whitman worked for as a young journalist.

Gonnerman wanted the Forum to facilitate a deeper exploration of ideas than other regional public series. He secured the participation of KQED Radio, the National Public Radio affiliate in San Francisco. He also helped line up sixteen "innovative thinkers" to talk about American ideals on six Monday evenings from January through June 2003, among them Angela Davis, human rights advocate and noted 1960s activist; Richard Rodriguez, award-winning PBS television essayist; Joycelyn Elders, former surgeon general of the United States; and Julia Butterfly Hill, writer and

197

environmental activist. The series has been successful, drawing more than five hundred people per event and generating interviews in area media. Gonnerman says he feels privileged to channel university resources into projects and ideas that he cares about.

"Mark's goal is to make the university relevant to the broader community," says Carl Bielefeldt, chair of the Stanford Department of Religious Studies, professor of Buddhist studies, and Gonnerman's advisor. "He's a visionary who is able to bring ideas to fruition."

* * *

> Mark is a tireless advocate of community engagement at the most unpretentious level—starting with conversation.
>
> —DR. CHARLES JUNKERMAN, dean of continuing studies, Stanford University

Mark Gonnerman may have built a reputation at Stanford for creating and directing innovative large-scale events such as the Aurora Forum or the successful year-long, interdepartmental workshop in 1997–98 to discuss Gary Snyder's *Mountains and Rivers without End,* but he is most comfortable in one-on-one conversation. In these small, informal settings Gonnerman engages in "face-to-face activism," striving to offer wisdom–experience, meditation–reflection, and morality–responsible action, befitting one pursuing the dharma path (i.e., the path leading to awakening—the truth and spirit of enlightenment).

Gonnerman says he is guided by the first precept of Buddhism: "Do as little harm as possible." Some could interpret that admonition as a call to passivity, a mere acceptance of karma (consequences of one's actions), or taking things as they are. Inspired by teachers such as Gary Snyder and other Buddhist activists, Mark Gonnerman challenges such preconceived notions of an ethereal Eastern religion.

"There's a deep connection between sitting on the cushion and being in the world," he says. "Meditation keeps your eyes and heart open. It's a continuous process that fosters heightened awareness."

Buddhist monk Thich Nhat Hanh, who was a representative at the peace talks to end the Vietnam War, has explained how the contemplative and active sides of religious behavior are united:

> Overflowing with understanding and compassion, we can appreciate the wonders of life, and, at the same time, act with firm resolve to alleviate the suffering. Too many people distinguish between the inner world of our

mind and the world outside, but these worlds are not separate. They belong to the same reality. (*Interbeing*)

Gonnerman says that his ongoing growth enables him to see that every moment is an opportunity to achieve a fuller humanity and a responsibility to be more sensitive to the suffering of others. He says that simple acts of charity are always possible. "We're all better off if each of us is better off."

By breakfast, Gonnerman is off the cushion. He has lit the incense and placed tiny fresh flowers at the small Buddha altar in the corner of his sparsely decorated living room. He has meditated and chanted. Now it's time to engage with the world of Peet's coffee shop on Lincoln Avenue in the Willow Glen community, west of downtown San Jose.

No need to drive. Peet's is just a ten-minute walk. The 1989 beige Volvo 740 GL with a broken trunk latch, an inoperable taped passenger-side window, and a catchy bumper sticker ("Caribouddhist") sits in the driveway. Gonnerman's 1927 Spanish bungalow on Carolyn Avenue is across from Los Gatos creek. He and Meri, who married in the fall of 2001, have lived in the unassuming two-bedroom house since April 2002.

The home has a minimalist décor that suits the couple's Japanese aesthetic style. An impressive stone fireplace centers the living room, which is framed by a wide bureau, a plush couch, and a dark-wood armoire/entertainment center. The bureau, which contains Meri's extensive CD music collection, is topped by an array of family photos. Several are from their wedding (Meri buoyant in her beautiful heirloom kimono, Mark serious in dark suit and tie). Other photos are of relatives: Mark's from Minnesota and Meri's from the Japantown community in her native San Jose.

In the dining room is Meri's large, colorfully decorated Taiko drum. She played the drum with a professional group for fifteen years. But the drum is dwarfed by the dining room table, decorated in scholarly fashion— books, books, books. Mark and Meri eat their meals in a kitchen breakfast nook on a small table covered with a patterned Tibetan cloth.

The second bedroom/office is lined floor to ceiling with more books, boxes of research, and paperwork. On the worn blue carpet are a dozen stacks of texts on religion, poetry, history, and philosophy (piled at least a dozen high). As if to divert attention from the bibliophile's paradise, several photos catch the eye: a framed eight-by-ten black-and-white of Bob Dylan playing at the 1965 Newport Music Festival, a classic portrait of Malcolm X, and a photo of Christopher, Mark's twelve-year-old son from his first marriage, and Meri.

Mark appreciates Meri's financial contribution as a longtime Silicon Valley engineer, which enabled the couple to afford the house on the tidy corner lot. (It shall be duly noted that Gonnerman makes a "decent salary" in academia and contributes his "fair share to the family coffers.") They love the home's adornment of countless red, white, pink, and peach rose bushes and the apple, plum, and tangerine trees in their backyard. They also appreciate their location—easy access to Highway 280 to Palo Alto and an enjoyable stroll to the heart of Willow Glen.

Today Mark Gonnerman steps lively down sunny tree-lined Lincoln Avenue, past the furniture store whose "going out of business" sign has been up for months, past Barbarella's clothing store (yes, named for the sci-fi Jane Fonda movie), past the Cal-Mex restaurant, yogurt stand, and fruit juice shop.

When he reaches Peet's, Gonnerman carefully removes his clip-on sunglasses and adjusts his eyes for the subdued lighting in the coffee shop. Sitting near the entrance are local sentries Ted and Roy. One is an out-of-work carpenter, the other a self-employed, independently wealthy artist. Both are conversation comrades of Gonnerman. But this afternoon he is on a mission to connect with Josh,* a twenty-three-year-old employee who within days will begin serving a four-month (assault) sentence in the Elmwood Correctional Facility in Milpitas, California. Gonnerman has a book (an autographed copy of *Dharma Punx*) and some kind words for the young man. "I feel a responsibility as a parent to talk to these young people," Gonnerman says, pulling the book from the olive backpack-rucksack that Meri calls his "magic bag," from which books, magazines, and photocopied items just seem to appear.

Josh takes a break from behind the counter, after serving Mark Gonnerman his four-minute brewed tea. He is compact, built like a lightweight wrestler, and clean-cut, with trimmed hair and a tasteful array of tattoos along his arms. He looks surprised at the gift of the book, and warmly thanks Gonnerman, who keeps the dialogue brief. Later, when Josh has finished his shift and ridden off on his bike, Gonnerman fills in some of the blanks. Josh's assault charge was a result of a bar fight. With his sentence due to begin in a matter of days, Josh may appear stoic, but he has spoken of his fear to Gonnerman, who said he would visit him in prison.

"All of us have our struggles, our cares, and our worries. And all of us have responsibilities for our neighbors," says Gonnerman, who admits his

---

*A pseudonym.

first role model was Jesus. He is still very drawn to the "depth of resonance from the Christian texts" he has studied since his youth. "Scripture is nourishing. I can't abandon that."

On a recent visit to the San Francisco Zen Center to hear a lecture on the early history of Buddhist and Christian meditation, "Zen Masters and Desert Fathers," Gonnerman purchased a book, *Jesus: The Teacher Within*, with an introduction by the Dalai Lama. "I like hanging out with literate Buddhists and Christians," Gonnerman says, describing a life journey that sounds as if it belongs in a colloquium on cultural and religious studies.

* * *

Do not be conformed to this world, but be transformed
by the renewing of your minds.

—Romans 12:2

Mark Gonnerman had dreamed of becoming a photographer for *National Geographic* magazine when he was a high school student in the small town of Northfield, Minnesota, about an hour's drive south of Minneapolis. He had won awards for his work, starting in the local 4-H Club, where he first learned the ethic of "selfless service to others." But religion overshadowed creative arts in the serious Gonnerman household.

"There wasn't a lot of humor in our Lutheran Midwestern family," Mark Gonnerman recalls. He talks of a strained, distanced relationship with his father, Frederick, a onetime practicing minister, who had shifted his career to work in public relations at St. Olaf College. But Gonnerman acknowledges that his father shared his love of photography with him and built a "fine darkroom for us in the basement of our Northfield house." His mother, Ruth, was a homemaker while he grew up. Years later, after Mark had graduated with a B.A. from St. Olaf, his mother worked in the school's religious studies department.

Mark, the eldest of four children (two boys, two girls) claims that he tried to not let college interfere with his education. A clever response, but not an entirely accurate one because Gonnerman was enrolled in an innovative Paracollege program during his St. Olaf years. The Paracollege featured an Oxford-Cambridge–type system of tutorials and small-group seminars. In his sophomore year he went on a "global semester" with a tutor to study religious art and architecture overseas.

Gonnerman says his travels to Egypt, Israel, India, and Nepal transformed his small-town worldview. He confronted stark beauty and dire poverty, deciding as a teenager that he would never be driven by money. "I realized my comfortable status was merely an accident of my birth." On his travels, Gonnerman discovered Gandhi and first learned of the power of spirituality-driven activism. Mark Gonnerman, who had taken church seriously as a child and who was a student of the Protestant Reformation, spent a summer and fall at Cambridge University, where he began work on his award-winning bachelor's thesis on Martin Luther's apocalyptic thought.

Though immersed in his college education, Gonnerman also enjoyed diversions such as hiking, swimming, and riding his 360cc Honda motorcycle around the St. Olaf College campus. While in school he met Susan Pennypacker. They were casual acquaintances for two years before starting to date, and they married a few years later.

Gonnerman's first job after graduation was as a counselor at a tertiary care hospital (Rush Presbyterian–St. Luke's) in Chicago. He recalls the work in a hospice environment as pretty sobering for a twenty-two-year-old college graduate. Within a year he was a husband, employed as an English teacher at a YMCA in Fukuyama, Japan, as part of peace education work for the Lutheran Church. He would spend three years (1981–84) in rural Japan, teaching English, studying Japanese, reading, and analyzing the relationship between Eastern and Western religions. By the mid-1980s he was back in academia, enrolled in the master's program at Harvard Divinity School, where he studied Buddhist-Christian dialogue and was a teaching fellow in East Asian Studies. In 1987 he earned his M.Div. from Harvard and a fellowship for Ph.D. work at Stanford.

"Religion at that point in my life was an intellectual pursuit," says Gonnerman, who earned a master of arts degree in religious studies in 1989. He then began work on his dissertation—a study of the philosophy of religion, focusing on William James and nineteenth-century American Transcendentalism. In 1990 his son, Christopher, was born.

For the next several years, Gonnerman embraced the role of doting father, trying to balance time and responsibilities with his son and wife while serving a variety of positions at Stanford: coordinator of teaching assistant training, teaching assistant, research assistant, and teaching fellow.

He and his wife, Susan, were living in graduate student housing. They arranged their schedules so they could share childcare duties. According to Mark Gonnerman, the plan worked well for a while, but eventually something had to give. Focused on raising his son and meeting the demands of his Stanford part-time positions with their "full-time responsibilities," Gonnerman's dissertation began to drift. As time went on, so did his marriage.

Gonnerman is frank and sensitive about the changes that occurred between him and his wife. "At the time, Susan was more and more invested in the world of management consulting and, from that perspective, I wasn't making progress toward many of the things she wanted. I was not the kind of conventional provider that Susan needed. We grew apart and, eventually, were not really there for each other."

By the mid-1990s Gonnerman's work on his dissertation had stalled; he no longer found the subject compelling, and communication with his advisor was breaking down. "I decided that I would either have to leave the academy or reinvent myself," Gonnerman recalls during a discussion over tea at Peet's coffee shop.

In a very real sense, Gonnerman's reinvention was already underway in 1995 when he embraced Buddhism. For a year he "sat daily" in meditation at the Kannon Do Zen Center in Mountain View, California. During that time, he took charge of Kannon Do's involvement with a meal and shelter program for the homeless that was coordinated through various local churches. The onetime devotee of Martin Luther was now a practicing Buddhist. "I was at peace," Gonnerman says. "It felt wonderful, as if I had come home."

But Gonnerman was still searching for answers and seeking direction in his academic career. Then in December 1996 he heard Gary Snyder give a reading from his epic book-length poem, *Mountains and Rivers without End*, at a Bay-area bookstore. From that point on, Mark Gonnerman's life would never be the same.

* * *

Let's become more human and more humane together.

—MARK GONNERMAN

Gary Snyder became a Beat era icon when he inspired the rucksack carrying, Zen-wise character Japhy Ryder in Jack Kerouac's 1958 novel, *Dharma Bums*. The Pacific Northwest native would later win a Pulitzer Prize for his poetry and become one of the founding voices for socially engaged Buddhism in the United States. When he met Mark Gonnerman, he was in his late sixties, on the faculty at University of California, Davis, and a highly visible activist for ecological and environmental causes. Doctoral student Gonnerman's relationship with Snyder began soon after the bookstore reading.

In 1997 Gonnerman received an invitation to apply for Mellon Foundation funds and to arrange a Stanford Humanities Center Research Workshop over three academic quarters—fifteen three-hour presentations on
Snyder's tome, which had been crafted over forty years (1956–96). *Mountains and Rivers without End* encompassed multiple disciplines, including
art history, American literature, Buddhist studies, Japanese drama, and
Chinese poetics, even hydrology. "I saw the poem as a great commons
around which we could gather," Gonnerman says.

According to friend Gregory Kaplan, Gonnerman's vision was "an aston-
ishing success" as hundreds of faculty, students, and community residents
participated in monthly seminars and a five-week course analyzing the
poem and its author, arguably the paradigmatic American Buddhist. Early
in the workshop process, Gonnerman asked the Buddhist poet if he could
research his extensive body of work, with the goal of compiling a bibliography of Snyder's own reading. Gonnerman recalls being overjoyed by the
response: "Snyder was intrigued by my idea and granted me permission to
make use of his library and voluminous journals. The following year
(1988–89) I was awarded the G.J. Lieberman Fellowship by Stanford's
School of Humanities and Sciences in support of the project."

Thanks to the $20,000 fellowship, Gonnerman was able to "reenergize
himself" at Stanford. He had a new dissertation proposal, exploring the
evolution of Snyder's religious vision and spiritual self-formation: "In the
life and work of Gary Snyder, I have encountered a twentieth-century
religious intellectual who has also worried and wondered about what it
means to live humanely in the present age. He has, moreover, articulated
his responses to this question through poetry and prose that offer an
accessible, sophisticated, and helpful vision. . . ."

Gonnerman spent the summer of 1998 with Gary Snyder at his home
(part Japanese farmhouse, part log cabin, and part Indian longhouse) on
the San Juan Ridge. Snyder's influence extended from sage to counsel as
Mark Gonnerman's personal life proceeded into "utter upheaval."

Within a year, he and his wife, Susan, had separated. By 2000 they had
divorced (after eighteen years of marriage) on self-described amicable
terms and without lawyers. Mark and Susan worked out a cordial, sensible
co-parenting plan. Christopher would live mostly with Susan in Palo Alto,
where he would continue to attend local schools. The balancing act between mother, father, and son seems to have proceeded smoothly.

Mark and Christopher talk daily by phone and hold fast to their tradition of taking long regular walks, often going downtown for dinner or to
a favorite spot such as Sausal Pond in Portola Valley. On their frequent

hikes, father and son have a chance to chat about a plethora of topics, from Christopher's little league batting average (about .400) and his drum lessons to world history and pop culture. (They concur: "Ben Stiller is hilarious in *Zoolander*.")

Mark Gonnerman is proud of his relationship with his son, and he speaks of personal growth. "I have strived to be more of a nurturer," he says, referring to his October 2001 wedding to Meri Mitsuyoshi. He admits, however, that his "(over) work ethic" may at times compromise his emotional availability. Gonnerman says he is learning to "really try to be with people when I am with them, especially family members."

When Mark discusses his feelings, Meri's pleasant face warms easily, and the two of them share shy smiles. The pair enjoys hiking ("I was a yak in a former life," says Meri), concerts, and campus events. Mark and Meri also meditate together at home and attend Sunday services at the San Jose Buddhist Church (Temple), one of the oldest Japanese-tradition churches in the United States.

Meri has helped Mark rediscover his love of photography. For a wedding present, she gave him a Leica M-6 camera, which he carries with him regularly in his backpack. She has also tried unsuccessfully to get him back into bicycling. But he has been unable to embrace that former love; the memory of his near-fatal accident two years ago (May 31, 2001) remains too raw, too near.

He reviews the facts as if in a police report (in this case the California Highway Patrol responded). He was on his Bianchi touring bike rounding the curve of a narrow, seventeen-foot-wide road in the Santa Cruz Mountains. He was descending in the middle of the road, making his turn in total control of his bike, when he saw a flash of blue. He would later discover that he had collided with a blue Nissan Maxima heading up the road. He was thrown over the car and landed on the crown of his head. His Bell bike helmet saved his life. Remarkably, the helmet was only scratched, not dented.

Gonnerman was knocked unconscious. He suffered a concussion and a strained neck. He was taken by ambulance to the Stanford Hospital, where doctors told him they couldn't believe he hadn't been more seriously injured. Physically, Mark Gonnerman recovered fairly quickly. But it took him much longer to escape the overwhelming feeling of dread, the post-trauma of the frightening incident.

He says the event changed him. He used to worry often about the future. But now he works on getting the most out of each day. He also tries to free himself from his anxieties. As could be expected, he turns to religious texts for comfort: "Perfect love casts out fear" (1 John 4:18) and "No hindrance, thus no fear" (the *Heart Sutra*).

When Mark Gonnerman says he is grateful to be alive, he is not merely mouthing the words of another Buddhist precept. He shows his devotion in daily chants ("We venerate the Three Treasures . . . Buddha, Dharma, and Sangha . . .") and on Sundays in the spiritual confines of a San Jose Buddhist church, where the chanting of the True Pure Land believers mingles with the musky fragrance of incense, grace, and gratitude.

* * *

If I fail to serve all in need, I will not attain enlightenment.

—San Jose Buddhist Church chant

Sunday, May 18, 2003, is the celebration of the birth of Shinran Shonin, the twelfth-century founder of Jodoshinshu, or the True Pure Land Japanese Buddhist School. Mark, Meri, and Christopher are attending the 10:10 A.M. adult English service on this sun-dappled day in San Jose. The three walk to the Buddhist church in the center of Japantown, where Meri grew up with the sons and daughters of other Santa Clara Valley farmers. Meri, who was raised Methodist, participated in Buddhist Girl Scouts in the community.

Mark wears another of his long-sleeved, button-down Ralph Lauren cotton shirts with the polo player logo on the pocket. Today's shirt is olive. He wears khaki slacks instead of jeans. He still wears his hiking sandals, but has donned gray wool socks. Meri wears a tasteful black dress. Christopher wears jeans and a pale blue pullover shirt. Mark and Meri carry jade-colored prayer beads into the church.

The San Jose Buddhist Church was founded in 1902; the building dates to 1937. The exterior features distinctive Asian architecture, a large garden, and flowing water. But the interior looks very similar to a Christian church. This is no accident. Mark Gonnerman explains: After World War II and the internment of Japanese Americans, religious leaders decided to modify the interior design of the churches to follow Western tradition. In this church are pews, an altar, and a pulpit, as well as beautifully engraved woodwork, two large incense burners at the front of the church, a multitude of candles and lights, and stunning gold decorations on and about the altar.

The service consists of opening remarks followed by sutra chanting. Unlike Zen Buddhism, which emphasizes *zazen* (seated meditation), Jodoshinshu (Jodo = Pure Land; Shinshu = faith tradition) focuses on lay

Buddhist life, including the practices of chanting, devotional study, the cultivation of gratitude, public worship, and appreciative participation in day-to-day community life.

Both Zen and True Pure Land Buddhism have codes of conduct to live by, including responsibility to the *sangha* (community). At today's service, short presentations are made by several organizations. The attending and guest ministers are both dressed in black cleric's garments with colorful sashes. Reverend David Matsumoto presents the dharma message from the pulpit. He is a gifted speaker who talks of the role that everyday citizens can play to improve the world. He tells of overcoming hardship, revealing his own pain of losing a loved one and how it taught him to be more appreciative of the joys of this life.

Mark Gonnerman leaves the service looking like a man refreshed. He and Meri greet fellow churchgoers on the steps and sidewalk. Christopher seems antsy, befitting an energetic adolescent on a warm Sunday morning. On the drive home Mark says he wants to get the church more involved in community outreach activities. He plans to talk with Reverend Sakamoto about this idea. He will also tell him about his dissertation and the relevance of Gary Snyder's work to Jodoshinshu.

Several weeks later, Gonnerman reports that Reverend Sakamoto was very receptive to his suggestions. He has invited Mark to speak to the congregation in the fall about his outreach proposals, which include starting a San Jose Buddhist Peace Fellowship (BPF) chapter at the church. Gonnerman also reveals his plans for the 2004 Aurora Forum programs, dealing with American civil liberties in an age of terrorism. "I want to broaden the dialogue," he says. "It's important that we reach a new generation of activists."

To that end, Mark Gonnerman confirms that he has been thinking for a while for "a way for me to develop something out of that messy May 17, 2003, symposium" that fell short of his expectations. He is laying the groundwork for a two-day institute in the summer of 2004 on "Cultures of Violence and the Cultivation of Peace." He is excited about yet another book: *Is There No Other Way? The Search for a Nonviolent Future* by Michael Nagler, which he says could serve as a blueprint for the institute sessions. Gonnerman seems more confident about his activist life on the dharma path.

EPILOGUE: "LESSONS LEARNED"

> Faith is a quality of human living, which at its best has taken the form of
> serenity and courage and service.
>
> —Wilfred Cantwell Smith, *Belief and History*

As an eight-year-old parochial school student, I was inspired by the words of President John F. Kennedy on inauguration day, January 20, 1961. I recall being struck by the personal tone of that memorable speech: "ask what *you* can do for *your* country." As time passed, like countless other well-intentioned individuals, I filed the line away as I set out to live my life.

The echo of the late president's words stayed with me, perhaps motivating me to be more sensitive to the plight of others, especially the less fortunate. Maybe those words combined with other poignant images from the 1960s influenced me to major in sociology as an undergraduate and later to work in government. But I never truly acted on the heart of the message: "what you can do for your country."

My focus narrowed and became more personalized as I strived to gain a career foothold, to form a family, to care for loved ones. My activism was limited to an occasional walk-a-thon, holiday service at a soup kitchen, donations to charity. Worthy efforts but hardly enough to effect social change.

As a professor at fifty, I recently reread JFK's Inaugural Address of 1961, looking beyond the oft-quoted sound bite. In his words I discovered themes that are central to the mission of social activists, particularly those I have profiled in this book: "If a free society cannot help the many who are poor, it cannot save the few who are rich"; "Let both sides unite to heed in all corners of the earth the commands of Isaiah—to 'undo the heavy burdens . . . and to let the oppressed go free'"; "let us go forth to lead the land we love, asking His blessing and His help, but knowing that on earth God's work must truly be our own."

In writing this book I have been inspired by the actions of people more than mere words. In documenting the lives of faith activists, those who have heeded the call, who have taken risks, who have made God's work truly their own, I serve witness that one person can truly make a difference. One person can make a difference in a neighborhood, a community, a country. As a student of history I knew this as fact. But that fact became reality, a lesson well learned, when I shared in the lives of those I have profiled.

Spending years immersed in the study of social activism has humbled me. I am grateful that there are people of faith who are concerned with "the greater good" in a time of incredible self-centeredness. I value the courage and service of those from different religions who unite in ecumenical efforts to combat social problems and to create progressive change.

Their actions are valued and valuable to a culture where ignorance, intolerance, and self-righteousness too often predominate. Their actions have made me hopeful for a better future. Their actions may lead others to ask what they can do to improve this country and the world in which we all live.

ACKNOWLEDGMENTS

My thanks to Indiana University Press, its editorial director, Robert Sloan, and assistant editor Jane Quinet for the faith shown in this book. I am grateful to my colleagues at Ball State University (BSU) for their support of my research and writing efforts. A special thanks to former dean Scott Olson for his introduction to *Sojourners* magazine. I also appreciate the grant provided by the Freedom Forum Professors Publishing Program in 1997, which helped with writing expenses for some of the early profiles. *Catholic Digest* magazine provided an important vote of confidence when it published my story on Father Gary Smith in June 1998.

I have had several guardian angels throughout the years I worked on this project. Boston University professor Ed Downes has been a consistent friend, a source of encouragement and guidance. He led me to Jerry Berrigan, whom I thank wholeheartedly for his generous assistance. Downes also introduced me to Sister Ann Kendrick. Other referrals came from BSU professor Tom Price, who suggested Reverend Israel Suarez, and from Ron Stodghill II, then Midwest bureau chief for *Time* magazine, who recommended Reverend Richard Tolliver.

University of Pennsylvania professor and former head of the White House Office of Faith-Based and Community Initiatives, John J. DiIulio Jr., was a key source of information. He directed me to Dr. Ron Sider, president of Evangelicals for Social Action, who suggested Doug and Judy Hall, Mary Nelson, and Reverend Skip Long. Father Gary Smith was my introduction to Father Roy Bourgeois. My longtime mentor, University of Oregon professor Lauren Kessler, guided me to Eugene, Oregon, activist Marion Malcolm. Rabbi Joel Schwartzman recommended fellow Denver rabbi Steve Foster. I was introduced to BSU professor Faiz Rahman by Muncie, Indiana, physician Mohammed Bahrami. Professor Rahman suggested I contact Dr. M. Basheer Ahmed. Thanks also to University of Oregon professor Carol Ann Bassett for recommending Buddhist poet Gary Snyder, who referred me to Mark Gonnerman. While citing the influence of academics in my profile selection process, I also want to acknowledge the scholarship of (then student rabbi) Michael Lotker for sharing his dissertation on interfaith relations.

During the course of my research, I have discovered many dedicated individuals, programs, and organizations engaged in social activism. Some of these deserve special mention, although they were not profiled in my book. California-based activist (Ms.) Johnnie Lacy has inspired advocates within the disability rights and independent living movement. (Thanks to Mary Lou Breslin of the Disability Rights Education and Defense Fund and Susan Sygall of Mobility International USA for the referral.)

In Salt Lake City, Utah, the Church of Jesus Christ of Latter-day Saints (LDS) has long been a significant financial and volunteer supporter of The Road Home (formerly Travelers Aid Society), a social services agency for area homeless. Two notable LDS volunteers are Deanna and Bruce Hammond, who have served the agency for several years.

Man of faith, Vietnam War hero, prisoner of conscience. Those words just begin the story of former Catholic priest and Congressional Medal of Honor recipient Charlie Liteky, who has spent decades as an antiwar and human rights activist. Reverend Rodney Hart is executive director of the New England headquarters of Teen Challenge International, a global Christian-based drug treatment and rehabilitation program. He also shares a remarkable, inspirational tale of self-actualization. Eric Weinheimer, president and CEO of the Chicago-based CARA Program, and David Phillips, cofounder of Cincinnati Works, are enabling scores of people annually to make the transition from welfare to productive new lives. As I traveled across America, I encountered the good faith and good works of countless individuals serving the antipoverty housing program Habitat for Humanity.

In closing, I greatly appreciate the time and contributions of all who helped shape this book with information, insight, and counsel. A hearty thank you to family and friends who lent a helping hand. A special blessing on my wife, Mykie, for her steadfast love. My last acknowledgment is a prayer of thanks to God for guiding, inspiring, and empowering me.

September 2003

INTRODUCTION

1: *"Father Gary Smith: Street Angel"*: Mark H. Massé, "Convert, Priest, Activist, Servant," *Catholic Digest,* June 1998, 117–121.

2: *"I think there might be"*: Roger Gathman, "How the Novel Imagines Us," *Poets & Writers,* January–February 1999, 43–46.

2: *"there was evidence"*: Harold Quinley, *The Prophetic Clergy* (New York: John Wiley and Sons, 1974), 2; Robert Wuthnow, *The Restructuring of American Religion* (Princeton, N.J.: Princeton University Press, 1988), 147–149; interview with Rabbi Steven E. Foster, 24 February 2003.

2: *"Charitable Choice"*: Ronald J. Sider, *Just Generosity* (Grand Rapids, Mich.: Baker Books, 1999), 86.

2: *"Call to Renewal"*: Ibid., 94.

2: *"White House Office of Faith-Based and Community Initiatives"*: Transcript of President George W. Bush's announcement, 29 January 2001, eMedia Mill Works, © 2001 *The Washington Post Company.* URL: www.washingtonpost.com/wp-srv/onpolitics/elections/bushtext012901.htm (accessed 25 February 2002).

3: *"presidential executive order in 2002"*: Wire Services (Muncie, Ind.) *The Star Press,* 2 February 2002, 3A.

3: *"passage of the CARE Act in 2003"*: Jim Wallis, "The Things That Make for Peace," *Sojourners,* July–August 2003, 8.

3: *"political rhetoric had far exceeded reality"*: Ibid.

3: *"Finding Common Ground"*: Working Group on Human Needs and Faith-Based and Community Initiatives, *Finding Common Ground,* January 2002, 13, 18.

3: *"Research shows that"*: Winifred Gallagher, *Working on God* (New York: Random House, 1999), 25.

3: *"faith's secular definition"*: David B. Guralnik, editor-in-chief, *Webster's New World Dictionary, Second College Edition* (New York: Prentice Hall, 1986), 503.

4: *"And hope is the single"*: Jim Wallis, *Faith Works* (New York: Random House, 2000), xxv.

1. FATHER GARY SMITH

7: *"The Catholic Sentinel"*: Deb Shannon, "Religious Communities Focus New Ministries on Poor," *The Catholic Sentinel,* 16 September 1994, 9.

7: *"Radical Compassion"*: Gary Smith, *Radical Compassion* (Chicago: Jesuit Way, 2002).

7: *"Redeem"*: David B. Guralnik, editor-in-chief, *Webster's New World Dictionary, Second College Edition* (New York: Prentice Hall, 1986), 1189.

9: *"We are called to be bearers"*: Father Gary Smith, S.J., *Outreach Update* (newsletter of Outreach Ministry in Burnside, Portland, Ore.), Winter 1997.

2. THE REVEREND DR. ISRAEL SUAREZ

12: *"In Spanish"*: Roger Williams, "Reverend Asks Public to Donate Turkeys, Food" (Fort Myers, Fla.) *News-Press*, 10 March 1997, B1.

13: *"annual report"*: Nations Association annual report, December 1997.

15: *"upwards of half a million acres"*: "Even If People Get Hot, Florida Needs More Fire," *Palm Beach Post* (Florida), 19 July 1998, Opinion 2E.

18: *"If all the churches"*: Ann Rodgers, "United They Stand," *News-Press*, 23 October 1983, D1.

3. SISTER ANN KENDRICK

22: *"she was profiled"*: Carrie St. Michel, "A nun among migrant farmworkers," *Good Housekeeping*, September 2003, 118.

22: *"In November 2002, Amnesty International"*: Sandra Mathers, "Nuns Give Lift to Lives Weighed Down by Poverty," *Orlando Sentinel*, 20 November 2002, B1.

22: *"first public disclosure"*: Kate Santich, "Sister Ann," *Orlando Sentinel*, 6 Dec. 2001, E3.

23: *"We have a great people"*: Mother Teresa, *Words to Love By* (Notre Dame, Ind.: Ave Maria, 1983), 67.

23: *"St. John's Water Management District"*: The Associated Press, "Farms' Last Day Signals Start of Lake Restoration," *St. Petersburg Times*, 1 July 1998, 5B.

24: *"She's trouble for us"*: Billy Bruce, "Nun Finds Mission in Migrant Workers" (Daytona Beach) *News-Journal*, 28 February 1993, A11.

25: *"The town of Apopka"*: 2000 United States Census, Apopka City, Orange County, Fla. (pop. 26,642). URL: www.factfinder.census.gov (accessed 26 Sept. 2003).

26: *"The Farmworker Association of Florida"*: Association literature.

27: *"I don't understand"*: Billy Bruce, "Nun Finds Mission in Migrant Workers" (Daytona Beach) *News-Journal*, 28 February 1993, A11.

27: *"We take this Christian deal"*: Sharon McBreen, "Four Minister to Farmworkers," *Orlando Sentinel*, 23 December 1989, D1.

28: *"Sisters of Notre Dame de Namur"*: Base communities brochure citing the "Constitution and Directory: 1984."

28: *"Then came the call"*: Diane Divoky, "Turning the Tide," *Green Class Journal* (alumni publication of Trinity College, Washington, D.C.), Summer 1998, 9–10.

30: *"The revered image"*: The Associated Press, "Our Lady of Guadalupe," *The Star Press*, 16 January 1999, 1D.

31: *"In 1978 Kendrick and the other SND sisters"*: Mark Pankowski, "20th Anniversary Adds Fuel to Nuns' Fire to Help," *Orlando Sentinel*, 26 December 1991, SE2, 11.

32: *"have written an essay":* Teresa McElwee, Gail Grimes, Cathy Gorman, and Ann Kendrick, "Collaboration in Ministry Challenges the Apopka Four," 1998, 2–3.

33: *"The volunteers serve":* "Apopka Americorps Mission," *La Vida en la Papa Grande,* Winter–Spring 1998, 5.

35: *"An old newspaper photo":* Rhonda Abrams, "Nuns Show Social, Personal Concern for Migrants," *Orlando Sentinel,* 3 August 1972, 2.

4. THE REVEREND DR. RICHARD L. TOLLIVER

36: *"SERC will have developed":* St. Edmund's Meadows, Chicago, Ill., fact sheet from The Rev. Dr. Richard L. Tolliver, 6 June 2003.

36: *"Front-page coverage":* Joshua S. Howes, "Church to Make CHA Sites Home Again," *Chicago Tribune,* 12 August 2003, 1–2.

37: *"sermon":* The Rev. Dr. Richard L. Tolliver, "Moral Leadership for the 21st Century," 23 February 2003.

37: *"In a feature on urban rehab":* Ron Stodghill II, "Bringing Hope Back to the Hood," *Business Week,* 19 August 1996, 70–73.

38: *"before the population plummeted":* Nile Harper, *Urban Churches, Vital Signs* (Grand Rapids, Mich.: Wm. B. Eerdmans, 1999), 158.

39: *"progress, not pipedreams":* St. Edmund's Redevelopment Corporation Projects fact sheets, 11 May 1999.

39: *"In some of our urban neighborhoods":* Nile Harper, *Urban Churches, Vital Signs* (Grand Rapids, Mich.: Wm. B. Eerdmans, 1999), 165.

39: *"the Low Income Housing Tax Credit":* Introduction, *Celebrating Ten Years of Investing in Affordable Housing for America,* 1997 report of the National Equity Fund, Inc., Chicago, Ill.

39: *"The Local Initiatives Support Corp":* Ibid.

39: *"Entrepreneurial ability":* Nile Harper, *Urban Churches, Vital Signs* (Grand Rapids, Mich.: Wm. B. Eerdmans, 1999), 166–167.

44: *"Turner":* Edith Turner, *It Happened in Springfield* (Springfield, Ohio: Springfield Tribune Printing Co., 1958).

46: *"The day you decide":* Zondra Hughes, "South Side Holy Man Restores Community Spirit," *N'Digo,* 3 December 1998, 7.

47: *"The so-called Negro church":* Dr. Martin Luther King Jr. quote cited in a sermon by The Rev. Dr. Richard L. Tolliver, "Jesus, Are You the One?" 13 December 1998.

48: *"Cone's book":* James H. Cone, *Black Theology and Black Power* (New York: Seabury, 1969).

48: *"even if it kills you"* and *"Yes, that's what I want to be remembered for":* Zondra Hughes, "South Side Holy Man Restores Community Spirit," *N'Digo,* 3 December 1998, 7.

52: *"current books":* Laurence Otis Graham, *Our Kind of People: Inside America's Black Upper Class* (New York: HarperCollins, 1999); Derek Dingle, *Titans of the Black Enterprise 100* (New York: J. Wiley, 1999).

56: *"The 1927 building"*: Information compiled by The Rev. Dr. Richard L. Tolliver, received May 1999.

56: *"St. Edmund's Church"*: Laurence T. Young Sr., ed., *History of the Church of St. Edmund* (Chicago: Bankers Print, 1966).

56: *"God didn't just reserve"*: Andrew Herrmann, "Black Episcopalians Rich in Tradition," *Chicago Sun-Times,* 20 May 1996, 4.

57: *"I wish more ministers"*: CAPA Presse TV, France, September 1996.

57: *"I have built a new sense of hope"*: Ibid.

57: *"The heroes of community development"*: "Developer Sparks Revival of South Washington Park," *Chicago Defender,* 25 July 1992, 39.

57: *"Reverend Tolliver and his church"*: James Rosenthal, "Pastoral Visit. USA Is Alive and Well," *Anglican World,* Michaelmas (Fall) 1996, 26–29.

5. DOUG AND JUDY HALL

61: *"reasons to celebrate"*: Steve Daman, ed., *Inside EGC,* April–May 2003, 1.

64: *"The Reverend Dr. Michael Haynes"*: Steve Daman, ed., *Urban Update,* Fall 1995, 2.

66: *"We came to the city"*: Ibid., 1.

66: *"In his 1995 testimonial"*: Ibid.

68: *"In what the Center's research"*: Rudy Mitchell (director of research and library services, EGC), "An Overview of Boston Church Trends," publication of Emmanuel Gospel Center (EGC), Boston, Mass.

68: *"The Coalition"*: *Investing in the Vitality of Urban Churches and Communities* (EGC Capital Campaign publication, 2002), 5.

69: *"The BEC's mission"*: "Boston Education Collaborative (BEC)," fact sheet of Emmanuel Gospel Center, January 2002.

72: *"In his writing"*: Peter Senge, *The Fifth Discipline* (New York: Doubleday Currency, 1990).

73: *"As Doug Hall explains"*: Doug Hall, "A Model for Faith-Based Initiatives," 3.

75: *"The Hall plan"*: Ibid.

76: *"He summed it up"*: Steve Daman, ed., *Urban Update,* Summer 1999, 1.

6. FATHER ROY BOURGEOIS

77: *"We must learn"*: James William Fulbright, speech in the U.S. Senate (March 27, 1964); Emily Morison Beck, ed., *Bartlett's Familiar Quotations* (Boston: Little, Brown and Co., 1980), 862–863.

79: *"From the website"*: "What Is SOA Watch?" URL: www.soaw.org/new/faq.php (accessed 7 September 2002).

79: *"Other remarks"*: Jeff Ament, Jackson Browne, Graham Nash, Bonnie Raitt, and Harvey Wasserman, "Statement of Support for School of the Americas Watch Rally and Protest," Fort Benning, Ga., 15–17 November 2002.

79: *"Massachusetts Congressman"*: James P. McGovern, U.S. Representative, "Statement for the Annual Protest Gathering at the Western Hemisphere Institute for Security Cooperation (School of the Americas)," 15 November 2002.

82: *"Truth never"*: Mohandas K. Gandhi (1869–1948), *The Star Press,* 27 May 2003, 8C.

82: *"Investigations into the killings"*: Amnesty International USA Publications, *Unmatched Power, Unmet Principles* (New York: Amnesty International USA, 2002), 4–5.

82: *"During its almost sixty-year history"*: Douglas Waller, "Running a School for Dictators," *Newsweek,* 9 August 1993, 34, 37; Peter Carlson, "The Priest Who Waged a War," *The Washington Post,* 29 November 1998, F1, F4.

82: *"In addition to"*: Amnesty International USA Publications, *Unmatched Power, Unmet Principles* (New York: Amnesty International USA, 2002), 43.

83: *"In a National Public Radio broadcast"*: Robert White, National Public Radio, 24 March 2000. URL: www.ciponline.org/colombia/032401.htm (accessed 23 August 2002).

83: *"In January 2001"*: Amnesty International USA Publications, *Unmatched Power, Unmet Principles* (New York: Amnesty International USA, 2002), 45.

83: *"Bourgeois was unimpressed"*: Jonah House Community, eds., *Year One,* Winter 2002, 6.

83: *"In a 2002 publication"*: Amnesty International USA Publications, *Unmatched Power, Unmet Principles* (New York: Amnesty International USA, 2002), 44, 67–69.

83: *"Note: In September 1996"*: Dana Priest, "U.S. Instructed Latins on Executions, Torture," *The Washington Post,* 21 September 1996, A1.

84: *"Newsweek magazine"*: Douglas Waller, "Running a School for Dictators," *Newsweek,* 9 August 1993, 34, 37.

85: *"The Washington Post"*: Dana Priest, "U.S. Instructed Latins on Executions, Torture," *The Washington Post,* 21 September 1996, A1; Peter Carlson, "The Priest Who Waged a War," *The Washington Post,* 29 November 1998, F1, F4.

85: *"The New York Times"*: Editorials, "School of the Dictators," *The New York Times,* 28 September 1996.

85: *"A Chicago Tribune"*: "Lights Out at the School of the Americas," *Chicago Tribune,* 16 April 1999, Sec. 1, 22.

85: *"The Los Angeles Times"*: Editorials, "Bury This Relic," *Los Angeles Times,* 21 May 1999.

86: *"In a 1998 video"*: Linda Panetta, producer, "School of the Americas: An Insider Speaks Out!" *Maryknoll World Productions,* 1998.

86: *"In a 2002 publication"*: Margaret Knapke, ed., *From Warriors to Resisters* (Washington, D.C.: SOA Watch, 2002), 5.

87: *"He had learned of"*: Paulo Freire, *Pedagogy of the Oppressed* (New York: Herder and Herder, 1970).

87: *"Growing up"*: Margaret Knapke, ed., *From Warriors to Resisters* (Washington, D.C.: SOA Watch, 2002), 4.

89: *"Then, as recounted"*: Peter Carlson, "The Priest Who Waged a War," *The Washington Post,* 29 November 1998, F4.

90: *"In the name of God"*: Mike Wilson, *The Warrior Priest* (Evanston, Ill.: John Gordon Burke, 2002), 19.

90: *"The Salvadoran soldiers":* Ibid., 26.

91: *"The case was":* "Worst," *The American Lawyer,* July–August 1983, 115.

93: *"Among those sent":* Mike Wilson, *The Warrior Priest* (Evanston, Ill.: John Gordon Burke, 2002), 75–76.

93: *"In his fourth prison sentence":* Ibid., 80–81.

94: *"In every country":* "In Praise of Dissent," *Columbus Ledger-Enquirer,* 17 November 2002, F1.

94: *"According to the November 7 issue":* S. Thorne Harper, "Both Sides; Downie, Bourgeois Share Stage in Public for First Time after Several Private Meetings," *Columbus Ledger-Enquirer,* 7 November 2002. URL: www.soaw.org/new/newswire_detail.php?id=143 (accessed 3 December 2002).

96: *"Someone browsing":* The Associated Press, "Colombian Army Troops Rescue Catholic Clergy," *Columbus Ledger-Enquirer,* 16 November 2002, A16.

97: *"By then they had started":* Bob Koenig, "Influenced by the Vietnam War and Catholic Worker Movement," *Year One,* Jonah House Community, eds., Winter 2002, 4.

97: *"By then they had started":* Tess Koenig, "What Bob and I Do Now: Our Work for Peace!" *Year One,* Jonah House Community, eds., Winter 2002, 5.

98: *"Our greatest enemy":* Margaret Knapke, ed., *From Warriors to Resisters* (Washington, D.C.: SOA Watch, 2002), 8.

101: *"Nowhere can man":* Marcus Aurelius, quoted in *Columbus Ledger-Enquirer,* 16 November 2002, A18.

7. MARION MALCOLM

102: *"Social progress never":* James Melvin Washington, ed., *A Testament of Hope: The Essential Writings of Martin Luther King Jr.* (San Francisco: Harper and Row, 1986), 213.

109: *"For Central American Christians":* Marion Malcolm, "How I Have Changed," speech to Central Presbyterian Church, Eugene, Ore., 6 December 1992.

110: *"In Central America":* Marion Malcolm, "Ways We Understand and Experience Jesus," speech to Trinity United Methodist Church, 7 March 1989.

110: *"CALC's Mission":* Marion Malcolm, ed., *CALC* (Community Alliance of Lane County) Newsletter, Autumn 2002, 2.

110: *"Working in solidarity":* Marion Malcolm, "On Being an Ally," Erev Shabbat talk at Temple Beth Israel, 28 June 2002.

110: *"Malcolm's co-workers":* Paul Neville, "Activist Community Losing Legend," *The Register Guard,* 20 December 1999, 1A, 11A.

115: *"In one of her talks":* Marion Malcolm, "About Being an Ally," Churchill Human Rights Workshop Panel, 16 January 2002.

8. MARY NELSON

117: *"Mary Nelson's message"*: *New Life News,* Newsletter of Bethel New Life, Inc., Chicago, Ill., Summer 2003, 2.

117: *"Bethel New Life, Inc. Mission"*: *Good News Bible,* Today's English Version (New York: American Bible Society, 1976), Isaiah 58:9–12.

119: *"Bethel New Life, Inc. is organized"*: "Built on a Rock," *Bethel New Life, Inc. Annual Report Fiscal Year 2002,* 2–6.

119: *"She was born in"*: Tom Seibel, "Building on Faith," *Chicago Sun-Times,* 7 August 1994, 6A.

121: *"She explained the source"*: "Bethel New Life, Inc.," video produced by The Annie E. Casey Foundation, 2002.

121: *"The first of several riots"*: Karl Plath, "Mary Nelson's Own West Side Story," *Chicago Tribune,* 7 January 1990, Sec. 16, 1; Tom Seibel, "Building on Faith," *Chicago Sun-Times,* 7 August 1994, 1A, 6A.

122: *"In late 1965"*: Tom Seibel, "Building on Faith," *Chicago Sun-Times,* 7 August 1994, 6A.

122: *"In the twenty-year period"*: Diane A. Meyer, ed., *On the Ground with Comprehensive Community Initiatives,* The Enterprise Foundation, March 2000, 46.

123: *"Mary Nelson explained"*: Tom Seibel, "Building on Faith," *Chicago Sun-Times,* 7 August 1994, 6A.

123: *"Reverend Nelson appealed"*: Patrick Barry, *Rebuilding the Walls* (Chicago: Bethel New Life, 1989), 49.

123: *"This community was redlined"*: Tom Seibel, "Building on Faith," *Chicago Sun-Times,* 7 August 1994, 6A.

124: *"By mid-1981"*: Patrick Barry, *Rebuilding the Walls* (Chicago: Bethel New Life, 1989), 52–57.

124: *"By mid-1981"*: Hank DeZutter, "Self-Help in Slum Buildings: Can Community-Based Management Work?" (Chicago) *Reader,* 13 August 1982, 3.

124: *"A year later, Bethel received"*: "A Bethel Project Creates Low-Income Housing Without Federal Money," *Forum* (a newspaper for the philanthropic community), Fall 1983.

124: *"Later that year"*: Cheryl Devall, "'Miracle' Puts a Roof Overhead," *Chicago Tribune* (city/suburbs), 15 September 1986.

125: *"But . . . the banks"*: Patrick Barry, *Rebuilding the Walls* (Chicago: Bethel New Life, 1989), 62.

126: *"In a March 21, 2002, column"*: Frank Lipscomb, "Women's History Month: A Good Time to Highlight Urban Divas," *Austin Weekly News,* 21 March 2002, 3.

127: *"The decade ended"*: Karl Plath, "Mary Nelson's Own West Side Story," *Chicago Tribune,* 7 January 1990, Sec. 16, 1.

128: *"Nelson explained"*: Jim Wallis, *Faith Works* (New York: Random House, 2000), 104.

128: *"In the case of West Garfield Park"*: D. Kevin McNeir, "West Garfield Park among City's Worst?" *Austin Weekly News,* 12 July 2001, 1, with supporting documentation from Bethel New Life, Inc., Local Initiative Support Corporation ("Building Community"), National Neighborhood Coalition ("Transit-Oriented and Focused Area Development").

129: *"We need more people":* Tom Seibel, "Building on Faith," *Chicago Sun-Times,* 7 August 1994, 1A.

129: *"For nearly 20 years":* "Connecting for Community Sustainability," *Bethel New Life, Inc. Annual Report Fiscal Year 2001,* 3.

130: *"On February 2, 2003":* Judy Valente, reporter, "Religion and Ethics Newsweekly," PBS-TV, 2 February 2003.

130: *"In late 1989":* "Built on a Rock," *Bethel New Life, Inc. Annual Report Fiscal Year 2002,* 2–6.

131: *"The Lake and Pulaski Commercial Center":* New Life News, A Newsletter of Bethel New Life, Inc., May 2003, 1.

131: *"Bethel New Life, Inc.'s introduction":* Restoring Our Urban Communities: A Model for an Empowered America, a report by the Argonne National Laboratory, Argonne, Ill., n.d.

131: *"Nelson's reputation":* Michael Abramowitz, "Stepchildren of Urban Policy Are Agents of Inner-City Change," *The Washington Post,* 24 June 1992, A17.

132: *"An article by":* Rebecca Bauen and Betsy Reed, "Our Cities, Ourselves," *Dollars and Sense,* January–February 1995, 15.

132: *"A year later":* Jennifer Halperin, "Here Comes the Neighborhood," *Illinois Issues,* January 1996, 13.

132: *"On Thursday, July 12, 2001":* D. Kevin McNeir, "West Garfield Park among City's Worst?" *Austin Weekly News,* 12 July 2001, 1.

132: *"Since CARA's founding":* CARA, A Newsletter from The CARA Program, Fall 2002.

135: *"They sit with some":* Editorials, "Neighbors Take Back Their Streets," *Chicago Tribune,* 18 September 1994, Sec. 4, 2.

9. REVEREND SKIP LONG

136: *"Responding to God's call":* Amy L. Sherman, *Collaborating for Employment Among the Poor: The Jobs Partnership Model* (Indianapolis: Hudson Institute, 2001), 19.

137: *"The twelve-week, twenty-four session":* Jobs Partnership brochure, National Jobs Partnership, Raleigh, N.C., 2001.

138: *"He speaks in a promotional video":* The Jobs Partnership Video, 1999.

138: *"I send greetings":* Letter from President George W. Bush, 3 February 2003.

145: *"In Collaborating":* Amy L. Sherman, *Collaborating for Employment Among the Poor: The Jobs Partnership Model* (Indianapolis: Hudson Institute, 2001), 27.

148: *"The Partnership began":* Ibid., 20.

150: *"Its success has been documented":* Ibid., 7, 21.

150: *"A chapter in Jim Wallis's 2000 book,"* Jim Wallis, *Faith Works* (New York: Random House, 2000), 180–181.

10. RABBI STEVE FOSTER

157: *"the Temple Emanuel community"*: "History of Congregation Emanuel." URL: www.congregationemanuel.com/aboutus.htm (accessed 14 January 2003).

157: *"According to its website"*: "An Introduction to Congregation Emanuel." URL: www.congregationemanuel.com/aboutus.htm (accessed 14 January 2003).

158: *"The purpose of the march"*: Roy Reed, "The Big Parade: On the Road to Montgomery," *The New York Times,* 22 March 1965. URL: www.nytimes.com/learning/general/onthisday/big/0321.htm/#article (accessed 22 March 2003).

159: *"In an August 23, 1996, article"*: Angela Dire, "Gay Rights Are Merely Civil Rights to Crusading Colorado Rabbi," *Colorado Springs Gazette Telegraph,* 23 August 1996, 5E.

159: *"Commenting on his actions"*: Rabbi Steven E. Foster, sermon, "An Ethical Will to My Children," Kol Nidre, 1977, 5.

160: *"Foster wrote"*: Rabbi Steven E. Foster, master's thesis, "The Development of the Social Action Program of Reform Judaism, 1878–1969," June 1970.

160: *"But support"*: Ibid.

161: *"That premise, however"*: Ibid.

161: *"During the late 1920s"; "During the height"; "Foster's research"*: Ibid.

162: *"In 1961"; "Promising developments"; "Foster's thesis"*: Ibid.

162: *"At Temple Emanuel"*: "Social Justice." URL: www.congregationemanuel.com/aboutus.htm (accessed 14 January 2003).

163: *"[A rabbi] must"*: Melissa Fay Greene, *The Temple Bombing* (Reading, Mass.: Addison-Wesley, 1996), 428–429.

163: *"Rabbi Jacob"*: Ibid., 429.

164: *"A month before"*: Rabbi Steven E. Foster, sermon, Kol Nidre, 6 October 1992, 3.

164: *"State Senator Ray Powers"*: Angela Dire, "Gay Rights Are Merely Civil Rights to Crusading Colorado Rabbi," *Colorado Springs Gazette Telegraph,* 23 August 1996, 5E.

164: *"He told his congregation"*: Rabbi Steven E. Foster, sermon, Kol Nidre, 2000, 3.

168: *"The cooperative, ecumenical"*: "United Way Faith Sabbath Partners in Compassion," brochure, 2000.

169: *"Three days after that"*: Rabbi Steven E. Foster, sermon, 14 September 2001, 3.

169: *". . . 30 to 50 percent"*: Steven E. Foster, "The Rabbi's Role in Counseling Converts to Judaism," dissertation, March 1985, 10.

169: *"one of the most important"*: U.S. Census Bureau, Statistical Abstract of the United States: 2000, #74 Religious Bodies (self-reported membership of religious bodies: 1998 Jewish population = 6,041,000), URL: www.census.gov/prod/www/religion.htm (accessed 23 July 2003); Glenmary Research Center, Religious Congregations and Membership: 2000 (Jewish, with 6 million adherents in 3,727 congregations), URL: www.glenmary.org/grc/RCMS_2000/findings.htm (accessed 23 July 2003).

169: *"I am one of those"*: Steven E. Foster, "The Rabbi's Role in Counseling Converts to Judaism," dissertation, March 1985, 11.

169: *"From 1977 until 1983":* Steven E. Foster, "The Community Rabbinic Conversion Board—The Denver Model," *Journal of Reform Judaism,* Summer 1984, 25–32.

170: *"In a February 1995 article":* Diane Solomon, "Outreach, In Reach and Over Reach," *Moment,* February 1995, 54.

172: *"In September 2002":* Rabbi Steven E. Foster, sermon, Kol Nidre, 15 September 2002; "An Ethical Will to My Children," sermon, Kol Nidre, 1977.

11. DR. M. BASHEER AHMED

177: *"His days and evenings":* Jeffrey Weiss and Lori Price, "When Home Is Violent," *Dallas Morning News,* 10 February 2001, 1G.

178: *"As chair of a September 2002":* M. Basheer Ahmed, M.D., "Religion, Peace, and Justice," *Role of Religion in Promoting World Peace,* Association of Muslim Social Scientists, 28 September 2002, 9.

181: *"In his remarks":* M. Basheer Ahmed, M.D., "Domestic Violence—Causes and Consequences," *First Regional Conference on Domestic Violence, Islamic Perspective,* Muslim Community Center for Human Services, 10 February 2001, 9.

183: *"He is representative":* Bess Dutson and Modeena Nolan, eds., *Outlook,* Fall 1968.

183: *"Three years later":* Gerald J. Meyer, "Shrinking One Mental Hospital," *St. Louis Post-Dispatch,* 28 March 1971, Sec. 14G, 1.

184: *"As a pioneer":* Ibid.

187: *"His dream to build":* Aboobaker Ebrahim, "Muslim Community Center for Human Services Holding a Fundraiser," *Asian News,* 23 November 1995.

187: *"Patrick McGee":* Patrick McGee, "Custom Aid," *Fort Worth Star-Telegram,* 23 July 2001, 10.

191: *"In his 2002 commencement speech":* Zayed Yasin, "My American Jihad," *Islamic Horizons,* September–October 2002, 44.

12. MARK GONNERMAN

192: *"One does not":* Rev. Mas Kodani, Senshin Buddhist Temple, Los Angeles, Calif. (quote courtesy of Mark Gonnerman).

194: *"Only a real Bodhisattva":* Diana Winston, "You Too Can Be a Bodhisattva," *Turning Wheel,* Spring 2002, 35–37.

195: *"A May–June 2003 online article":* Melissa Snarr, "The University of Social Justice," *Sojourners,* May–June 2003. URL: www.sojo.net/index.cfm?action=magazine.article&issue=soj0305&article=030520 (accessed 15 May 2003).

196: *"The concept came":* George Lakoff, "Metaphor and War, Again?" URL: www.alternet.org/story.html?StoryID=15414.

196: *"What the Greeks":* Gary Snyder, *The Practice of the Wild* (San Francisco: North Point Press, 1990), 57.

196: *"The mercy of the West":* Gary Snyder, "Buddhism and the Coming Revolution," *Earth House Hold* (New York: New Directions, 1969), 90–93.

196: *"In 1978":* Buddhist Peace Fellowship website. URL: www.bpf.org/html (accessed 4 August 2003).

197: *"Gonnerman also recognizes":* Richard Rorty, *Achieving Our Country* (Cambridge, Mass.: Harvard University Press, 1998).

198: *"Mark Gonnerman may have":* Gary Snyder, *Mountains and Rivers without End* (Washington, D.C.: Counterpoint, 1996).

198: *"Buddhist monk":* Thich Nhat Hanh, *Interbeing* (Berkeley, Calif.: Parallax, 1993). Source: BPF History, www.bpf.org.

200: *"Gonnerman has a book":* Noah Levine, *Dharma punx* (New York: HarperSanFrancisco, 2003).

201: *"Gonnerman purchased a book":* Laurence Freeman, *Jesus, the Teacher Within* (New York: Continuum, 2000).

201: *"Do not be":* Jim Wallis, *Faith Works* (New York: Random House, 2000), 183.

203: *"Gary Snyder became":* Jack Kerouac, *Dharma Bums* (New York: Penguin Books, 1958).

204: *"In the life and work":* Mark Gonnerman, dissertation proposal ("On the Path, Off the Trail"), OTP Preface, May 2002, 5.

206: *"Sunday, May 18, 2003":* Charles S. Prebish, "Buddhism," *Encyclopedia of the American Religious Experience,* Charles H. Lippy and Peter W. Williams, eds. (New York: Charles Scribner's and Sons, 1988), 678.

207: *"He is excited about":* Michael Nagler, *Is There No Other Way?* (Berkeley: Berkeley Hills Books, 2001).

EPILOGUE

208: *"Faith":* Wilfred Cantwell Smith, *Belief and History* (Charlottesville: University Press of Virginia, 1977), 93.

208: *"the words of President John F. Kennedy":* *Inaugural Addresses of the Presidents of the United States.* Washington, D.C.: U.S. G.P.O: for sale by the Supt. of Docs., U.S. G.P.O., 1989; Bartleby.com, 2001. URL: www.bartleby.com/124/ (accessed 1 October 2003).

208: *"I never truly acted":* Ibid.

208: *"If a free society . . .":* Ibid.

Alinsky, Saul D. 1972. *Rules for Radicals.* New York: Vintage Books.

Amnesty International USA Publications. 2002. *Unmatched Power, Unmet Principles.* New York: Amnesty International USA.

Coles, Robert. 1993. *The Call to Service: A Witness to Idealism.* Boston: Houghton Mifflin Co.

———. 2000. *Lives of Moral Leadership.* New York: Random House.

Cone, James H. 1969. *Black Theology and Black Power.* New York: Seabury.

Corbett, Michael, and Julia Mitchell Corbett. 1999. *Politics and Religion in the United States.* New York: Garland.

DeBenedetti, Charles. 1986. *Peace Heroes in Twentieth-Century America.* Bloomington: Indiana University Press.

DeLeon, David. 1994. *Leaders from the 1960s.* Westport, Conn.: Greenwood.

Dingle, Derek. 1999. *Titans of the Black Enterprise 100.* New York: J. Wiley.

Elie, Paul. 2003. *The Life You Save May Be Your Own: An American Pilgrimage.* New York: Farrar, Strauss and Giroux.

Freedman, Samuel. 2000. *Jew vs. Jew.* New York: Simon and Schuster.

Freeman, Laurence. 2000. *Jesus, the Teacher Within.* New York: Continuum.

Freire, Paulo. 1970. *Pedagogy of the Oppressed.* New York: Herder and Herder, 1970.

Gallagher, Winifred. 1999. *Working on God.* New York: Random House.

———. 2001. *Spiritual Genius.* New York: Random House.

Graham, Lawrence Otis. 1999. *Our Kind of People.* New York: HarperCollins.

Green, John C., James L. Guth, Corwin E. Smidt, and Lyman A. Kellstedt. 1996. *Religion and the Culture Wars: Dispatches from the Front.* New York: Rowman and Littlefield.

Greene, Melissa Fay. 1996. *The Temple Bombing.* Reading, Mass.: Addison-Wesley.

Harper, Nile. 1999. *Urban Churches, Vital Signs.* Grand Rapids, Mich.: William B. Eerdmans.

Holsworth, Robert D. 1989. *Let Your Life Speak: A Study of Politics, Religion, and Antinuclear Weapons Activism.* Madison: University of Wisconsin Press.

Kerouac, Jack. 1958. *Dharma Bums.* New York: Penguin Books.

Kessler, Lauren. 1990. *After All These Years.* New York: Thunder's Mouth.

Knapke, Margaret, ed. 2002. *From Warriors to Resisters.* Washington, D.C.: SOA Watch.

Levine, Noah. 2003. *Dharma Punx: A Memoir.* New York: HarperSanFrancisco.

Lippy, Charles H., and Peter W. Williams, eds. 1988. *Encyclopedia of the American Religious Experience.* New York: Charles Scribner's and Sons.

Lotz, David W., ed. 1989. *Altered Landscapes: Christianity in America, 1935–85.* Grand Rapids, Mich.: William B. Eerdmans.

McGinniss, Joe. 1976. *Heroes.* New York: Viking.

McNeal, Patricia. 1992. *Harder than War: Catholic Peacemaking in 20th Century America.* New Brunswick, N.J.: Rutgers University Press.

Meissner, W. W. 1992. *Ignatius of Loyola.* New Haven, Conn.: Yale University Press.

Nagler, Michael N. 2001. *Is There No Other Way?* Berkeley, Calif.: Berkeley Hills Books.

Nhat Hanh, Thich. 1997. *Interbeing.* Berkeley, Calif.: Parallax.

O'Malley, John W. 1993. *The First Jesuits.* Cambridge, Mass.: Harvard University Press.

Polner, Murray, and Jim O'Grady. 1997. *Disarmed and Dangerous: The Radical Lives and Times of Daniel and Philip Berrigan.* New York: Basic Books.

Quinley, Harold E. 1974. *The Prophetic Clergy: Social Activism among Protestant Ministers.* New York: John Wiley and Sons.

Rorty, Richard. 1998. *Achieving Our Country.* Cambridge, Mass.: Harvard University Press.

Senge, Peter. 1990. *The Fifth Discipline.* New York: Doubleday Currency.

Sider, Ronald J. 1990. *Rich Christians in an Age of Hunger.* Dallas: Word.

———. 1999. *Just Generosity.* Grand Rapids, Mich.: Baker Books.

Smith, Christian, ed. 1996. *Disruptive Religion: The Force of Faith in Social-Movement Activism.* New York: Routledge.

Smith, Gary. 1994. *Street Journal: Finding God in the Homeless.* Kansas City, Mo.: Sheed and Ward.

———. 2002. *Radical Compassion.* Chicago: Jesuit Way (Loyola Press).

Smith, Wilfred C. 1977. *Belief and History.* Charlottesville: University Press of Virginia.

Snyder, Gary. 1969. *Earth House Hold.* New York: New Directions.

———. 1990. *The Practice of the Wild.* San Francisco: North Point.

———. 1996. *Mountains and Rivers without End.* Washington, D.C.: Counterpoint.

Teresa, Mother. 1983. *Words to Love By.* Notre Dame, Ind.: Ave Maria.

Turner, Edith. 1958. *It Happened in Springfield.* Springfield, Ohio: Springfield Tribune Printing Co.

Wald, Kenneth D. 1997. *Religion and Politics in the U.S.* Washington, D.C.: CQ.

Wallis, Jim. 2000. *Faith Works.* New York: Random House.

Washington, James M., ed. 1986. *A Testament of Hope.* San Francisco: Harper and Row.

Wilson, Mike. 2002. *The Warrior Priest.* Evanston, Ill.: John Gordon Burke.

Wuthnow, Robert. 1988. *The Restructuring of American Religion.* Princeton, N.J.: Princeton University Press.

Abraham, 179

Activism, 1–6 passim, 9, 28–29, 37, 46, 48–49, 73–74, 76–77, 87, 90–91, 102–116 passim, 118, 155–173 passim, 177, 181, 190, 192, 194–195, 197–198, 202, 208–209, 211

Ahmed, Basheer, 174–191 passim, 210, 221nn178,181; activist philosophy, 175, 177–179; community mental health advocacy of, 183–186; description of, 176, 181; education and training of, 182; family relationships of, 177–178, 181–182, 185–186; influences on, 182; interfaith advocacy of, 178–180; introduction to, 1, 5; Muslim Community Center leadership by, 177, 181, 187–191; praise for, 176–178, 180–181; psychiatric work by, 175, 183

Albert Einstein College, 184–185

Alinsky, Saul, 69, 88

Al-Shifa Clinic, 175–176, 180

The American Lawyer, 91

AmeriCorps, 3, 24, 30, 33–34, 214n33

Amnesty International, 22, 83–84, 213n22, 216nn82–83; *Unmatched Power, Unmet Principles,* 83, 216nn82–83

Anglican, 48, 56

Anglican World, 57, 215n57

Aurelius, Marcus, 101, 217n101

Aurora Forum, 192, 197–198, 207

Austin Weekly News, 126, 128, 132, 218n126, 219n132

Bahrami, Mohammed, 210

Bassett, Carol Ann, 210

Bender, John, 142–154 passim

Berrigan, Daniel, 1, 88–89, 93

Berrigan, Jerry, 210

Berrigan, Philip, 1, 89

Bethel Lutheran Church, 118, 121, 123

Bethel New Life: 117–135 passim, 218n117, 219nn128–131; awards, 124; community support, 133; founders, 118; future, 134; leadership, 125, 127, 129,

135; organization, 119; philosophy, 128, 132; programs, 125, 127, 130–132; publicity, 130

Black Theology and Black Power, 48, 214n48

Blair, Joseph, 86

Bourgeois, Father Roy, 77–101 passim, 210, 216n83, 217n94; activist spirit of, 101; acts of civil disobedience, 90–92, 94; description of, 78–79; early activism of, 89; family relationships of, 77, 87, 94, 98–99, 216n87; founding of SOAW by, 82; introduction to, 5; lessons learned in Latin America by, 86–87; ordination of, 88; prison sentences of, 84, 91–93; SOAW leadership by, 85–86, 95–101; speeches by, 80–81, 100; upbringing of, 87–88; Vietnam experience of, 88

Boy Scouts of America, 166–167

Breslin, Mary Lou, 211

Brown v. Board of Education, 44

Buddha, 5, 199, 206

Buddhism, 198, 203, 221n196, 222n206; Jodoshinshu Buddhism, 206–207; socially engaged Buddhism, 196, 203; True Pure Land Buddhism, 206–207; Zen Buddhism, 206–207

Buddhist Peace Fellowship, 196–197, 207, 222n196

Building Together Ministries, 141, 147, 151

Bush, President George, 29

Bush, President George W., 128, 138–139, 219n138

Business Week, 37, 214n37

Call to Renewal, 2–3, 131, 212n2

CARA Program, 132–133, 211, 219n132

Carter, President Jimmy, 59, 124, 128–129, 180

Carter, Robert, 177–178

Casey Foundation, Annie E., 121, 218n121

Catholic Charities, 178, 190

Catholic Digest, 1, 212n1

Catholic Sentinel, 7, 212n7

Catholic Worker, 1, 27, 89, 91, 97, 217n97. *See also* Day, Dorothy
Catholicism, 11, 30
Central American University, 82
Central Conference of American Rabbis, 160, 169
Charitable Choice, 2, 212n2
Chavez, Cesar, 1, 25, 30, 80, 111
Chicago Defender, 55, 57, 215n57
Chicago Sun-Times, 36, 56, 123, 129, 132, 215n56, 218nn119,121–123, 219n129
Chicago Tribune, 36, 55, 85, 132, 214n36, 216n85, 218n121
Christ, Jesus, 5, 10, 18, 34, 47–48, 56, 63, 66–67, 88, 90, 109, 170, 179, 201, 222n201
Christian Action Ministry, 122–123, 127
Christian Science Monitor, 36
Christianity, 51, 66, 109, 179
Church of Jesus Christ of Latter-day Saints, 211
Cincinnati Works, 211
Civil rights movement, 1, 47–48, 156, 194
Clergy and Laity Concerned, 107
Clinton, President Bill, 59, 128, 138
Colorado Civil Rights Commission, 163–165
Colorado Springs Gazette Telegraph, 159, 164–165, 220n159
Columbine High School, 166
Columbus Ledger-Enquirer, 94, 96, 217nn94,96,101
Commission on Reform Jewish Outreach, 170
Community Alliance of Lane County, 108, 110–115, 217n110
Community Development Corporation, 36, 118, 131
Community Reinvestment Act, 125
Cone, Dr. James, 48, 214n48
Cornell University, 104–105, 115

Daley, Mayor Richard M., 41, 129
Day, Dorothy, 1, 27, 80, 91
Daytona Beach *News Journal,* 24, 27, 213nn24,27
Denver City Council, 165
Denver Post, 167
Dewey, John, 197
Dharma Bums, 203, 222n203
Dharma Punx, 200, 222n200
DiIulio, John J., Jr., 210
Dingle, Derek, 52, 214n52. *See also Titans of the Black Enterprise 100*

Disability Rights Education and Defense Fund, 211
Downes, Ed, 210
Downie, Colonel Richard, 94–95

El Salvador, 81–83, 89, 92, 97, 101, 108
Elliott, J. Robert, 91–92
Emmanuel Gospel Center, 61–76 passim, 215nn68,69; fund raising, 63; goals, 75; history, 62, 67; operations, 64, 68–69; urban ministerial education, 71–76
Enterprise Foundation, 124
Episcopalian community, 56, 215n56
Evangelical, 2, 4–5, 61, 64, 66, 122, 168
Evangelicals for Social Action, 210

Faith Works, 4, 128, 150, 212n4, 218n128, 219n150, 222n201. *See also* Wallis, Jim
Faith-Based, 2–3, 39, 65, 68, 73, 130–131, 134, 137–138, 150, 155, 177
Farmworker Association of Florida, 22, 26–27, 34, 213n26
Fester, Judy, 164
Fort Benning, 77–101 passim, 109, 215n79
Fort Myers *News Press,* 18, 213nn12,18
Fort Worth Star-Telegram, 187, 221n187
Foster, Rabbi Steve, 155–173 passim, 210, 212n2, 220nn159–162,164,169, 221n172; activist philosophy of, 156, 159–162, 167; civil rights experiences of, 158–159; conversion and intermarriage outreach by, 169–171; description of, 155–157, 172–173; ecumenical work by, 168; family relationships of, 155–159, 164–166, 168, 171–173, 220n159, 221n172; gay rights experiences of, 163–166; introduction to, 4; pastoral work by, 171–173; upbringing of, 158
Freedom Forum, 210
Freedom March, 158–159, 163
Freire, Paulo, 87, 216n87. *See also Pedagogy of the Oppressed*
From Warriors to Resisters, 86–87, 216nn86,87, 217n98. *See also* Knapke, Margaret
Fulbright, James William, 77, 215n77

Gallagher, Winifred, 3, 212n3. *See also Working on God*
Gandhi, Mohandas (Mahatma), 20, 80, 82, 202, 216n82
Gathman, Roger, 2, 212n2. *See also Poets & Writers* magazine

Gidwitz, Ron, 133–134
Godbold, Jim, 103
Gonnerman, Mark, 192–207 passim, 210, 221n192, 222nn197–198,200–201,204; activist philosophy of, 193, 195–196, 200–201, 207; Aurora Forum leadership by, 197; Buddhist influences on, 198, 203–207; description of, 193–194; family relationships of, 193–194, 199–207; graduate education of, 202; home of, 199–200; introduction to, 5; upbringing of, 201
Good Housekeeping, 22, 213n22
Gordon-Conwell Theological Seminary, 64, 70–71
Gorman, Cathy, 25, 28, 32, 214n32
Graham, Lawrence Otis, 52, 214n52. *See also Our Kind of People*
Greene, Melissa Fay, 163, 220n163. *See also The Temple Bombing*
Greenwood, Dru, 161, 170, 172
Grimes, Gail, 25, 28, 32, 214n32
Gustavus Adolphus College, 120
Gutteriez, Gustavo, 87

Habitat for Humanity, 29, 124, 155, 168, 211
Hall, Doug and Judy, 61–76 passim, 210, 215nn73,75; activist history of, 65–70; activist philosophy of, 65; description of, 62–64; family relationships of, 63, 65–66, 74–75; introduction to, 4; legacy of, 75–76; residence of, 62–63; urban ministry education by, 70–74
Hammond, Bruce and Deanna, 211
Hart, Rev. Rodney, 73, 211. *See also* Teen Challenge International
Harvard University, 47–49, 162, 174, 191, 195, 202, 222n197
Haynes, Rev. Dr. Michael, 64, 66, 215n64
Hebrew Union College, 157, 159
High Holy Days, 156
Highlander Research and Education Center, 194
Howard University, 49–51
Hudson Institute, Inc., 145, 219nn136,145

Iliff School of Theology, 163
Imam, 180–181, 188
Iraq, 79, 103, 113, 140, 187–188
Isaiah, 45, 118, 127, 208
Islam, 51, 178–179, 189
Islamic, 112, 174–191 passim, 221n191 ·

Islamic Association of North Texas, 177, 188
It Happened in Springfield, 44

James, William, 202
Jefferson, Thomas, 94
Jeld-Wen, 149
Jesuit (Society of Jesus), 1, 5, 9, 11, 81–82, 88, 92, 96, 98
Jesuit Refugee Service, 7
Jesuit Way, 7, 212n7
Jewish Family Services, 178, 185, 190
Jihad, 191, 221n191
Jonah House, 89
Judaism, 155–173 passim, 220nn160–161, 221n169; Conservative, 157, 169; Orthodox, 157, 169; Reconstructionist, 157; Reform, 157, 160–162, 169–170
Junkerman, Dr. Charles, 195, 197–198

Kaplan, Gregory, 194, 204
Kendrick, Sister Ann, 22–35 passim, 210; activist history of, 25, 28, 30–31; activist philosophy of, 27, 32, 34; community action of, 29, 33; crises of, 32, 33; description of, 24; education of, 28; family relationships of, 27, 32; introduction to, 4; migrant worker advocacy by, 23, 24; praise for, 26; Sisters of Notre Dame relationship with, 32, 34, 35; upbringing of, 27
Kennedy, Bobby, 47
Kennedy, President John F., 83, 208, 222n208
Kennedy, John F., Jr., 129
Kennedy, Joseph P., II, 85
Kerouac, Jack, 203, 222n203
Kessler, Lauren, 210
King, Dr. Martin Luther, Jr., 1, 4, 18, 47, 56, 80, 102–103, 122, 158–160, 162–163, 166, 194, 214n47, 217n102
Knapke, Margaret, 216nn86,87
Kodani, Rev. Mas, 192, 221n192
Koenig, Bob and Tess, 97, 101, 217n97
Kretzmann, Jody, 127–128

Lacy, Johnnie, 211
Lama, Dalai, 201
Lane, Kate, 118, 125, 135
Liberation Theology, 1, 48, 87, 89, 109
Liteky, Charlie, 85–86, 92, 211
Local Initiatives Support Corp., 39, 130, 214n39, 218n128

Long, Rev. Skip, 136–154 passim, 210;
activist philosophy of, 137–138, 142–
143; description of, 137, 140; family
relationships of, 136, 140–143, 154;
introduction to, 4; Jobs Partnership
leadership of, 145, 148–151; ministry of,
139, 147–148, 151–154; racial
experiences of, 141–144; upbringing
of, 146
Los Angeles Times, 85, 216n85
Lotker, Michael, 210
Luther, Martin, 202–203
Lutheran Social Services, 178

Makundi, Kaaneli, 120–121, 133
Malcolm, Marion, 102–116 passim, 210;
activist influence on, 105; anti-war
activism of, 106–107; description of,
103; family relationships of, 102, 104–
106, 108, 113, 115–116; interfaith
advocacy by, 112–113; introduction to,
4; mentoring by, 104, 115; migrant
worker advocacy by, 110–111; sanctuary
movement work by, 109
Mangum, Chris, 139, 147–148
Maryknoll Order, 5, 78–79, 86–90, 92
Maryknoll World Productions, 90, 97,
216n86
McElwee, Teresa, 25, 28, 32, 214n32
Mellon Foundation, 204
Merton, Thomas, 10, 91
Miami University, 46, 59, 230
Mitzvah Corps, 162
Mitzvah Day, 155, 162
Mobility International USA, 211
Moment magazine, 170
Moreno, Blanca and Tirso, 26
Moses, 5, 37, 170, 179
Mountains and Rivers without End, 198, 203–
204, 222n198. See also Snyder, Gary
Muhammad (Mohammed), 5
Muhammad, Elijah, 49
Muslim, 5, 49, 51, 79, 112, 169, 174–191
passim, 197, 221n178
Muslim Community Center for Human
Services, 174–191 passim,
221nn181,187; conferences, 181; future,
178, 188–189; mission, 186–187, 190–
191; organization, 176–177, 180, 188–
189; services, 175, 177; support, 187

National Conference of Christians and
Jews, 166, 168

National Jobs Partnership, 136–154
passim, 219nn136–138,145; goals, 137;
history, 148, 150; leadership, 137;
Leadership Conference, 139–140;
mentoring, 145, 152; organization, 138,
140, 148; support, 138, 149
Nations Association (Charities), 12–21
passim, 213n13; donors, 13; offices, 14,
17; volunteers, 15
Nelson, Rev. David, 119–123, 127
Nelson, Mary, 117–135 passim, 210,
218nn117,121,127; community
leadership of, 123–129; description of,
118; early Chicago years of, 121–122;
family relationships of 119–121, 123,
125, 127, 134; future challenges for,
133–135; introduction to, 4; national
media coverage of, 130–131; racial
attitudes of, 127; sacrifices of, 126
New York Times, 60, 85, 158, 216n85,
220n158
Newsweek, 84, 216n84
Nhat Hanh, Thich, 198, 222n198
Northwestern University, 127

Office for Farmworker Ministry, 24–26, 29;
advocacy, 31; award, 29; mission, 34;
offices, 29; services, 25; volunteers, 24
Olivier, Father Lucien, 88
Olson, Scott, 210
Orlando Sentinel, 22, 35, 214n35
Our Kind of People, 52, 214n52
Our Lady of Guadalupe, 30, 213n30
Outreach Ministry, 9–10, 213n9

Parker, Asli, 176–177
Parks, Rosa, 56, 59
Peace Corps, 50
Pedagogy of the Oppressed, 87, 216n87
Pentecostal, 5, 13, 68
Phillips, David, 211
Poets & Writers magazine, 2, 212n2
Prebish, Charles S., 206, 222n206
Price, Tom, 210
Protestant Reformation, 202
Public Broadcasting System (PBS), 130–
131, 197

Qur'an (Koran), 175, 180, 186, 188

Radical Compassion, 7, 212n7
Rahman, Faiz, 210
Raleigh Mennonite Church, 142, 144,
150–152

Reagan, President Ronald, 128
Register-Guard, 103, 110, 217n110
Religious Action Center, 162
The Road Home, 211
Romero, Archbishop Oscar, 82–83, 89–90, 101, 108
Rorty, Richard, 197
Rothschild, Rabbi Jacob, 163, 220n163

SAFER (Springfield Alliance for Equality and Respect), 113–115
Salim, Zeba, 178, 186, 189–190
Salvadoran, 82, 89–90, 217n90
Salvation Army, 20, 190
San Francisco Zen Center, 201
San Jose Buddhist Church, 205–206
San Jose State University, 10
Santa Clara University, 11
School of the Americas, 77–101 passim, 215n79, 216nn85–86
School of the Americas Watch (SOAW), 77–81, 84–86, 90, 92–96, 98–101, 215n79, 216n86, 217n98
Schwartzman, Rabbi Joel, 155, 167, 210
Senge, Peter, 72, 215n72
September 11, 2001 (9/11), 169, 179, 181, 192, 197
Shabbat, 113, 172–173
Sheen, Martin, 81, 93, 96
Sider, Dr. Ron, 210, 212n2
Sisters of Notre Dame de Namur, 24–26, 28, 31–34, 213nn28,31
Smith, Father Gary, 7–11 passim, 210, 212nn1,7, 213n9; college years of, 8, 10; conversion of, 10–11; description of, 8; family relationships of, 10; introduction to, 1, 5; Outreach Ministry work by, 9–10; social activism of, 9–11; walking tour by, 8; working-class upbringing, 10
Smith, Wilfred Cantwell, 208, 222n208
Snyder, Gary, 192–207, 210, 221n196, 222nn198,203
Social Gospel, 1, 48, 57, 67, 90, 109
Sojourners magazine, 3, 195, 210, 212n3
Somalia(n), 5, 176–177, 187
Spickard, David, 137, 139–140, 145, 148–149
St. Anne's Hospital, 118
St. Edmund's Academy, 39, 51, 54–55, 57–58
St. Edmund's Church, 36–60 passim, 215n56
St. Edmund's Meadows, 36, 43

St. Edmund's Redevelopment Corp. (SERC), 36–60 passim, 214nn36,39; goals, 51; projects, 39; staff, 43
St. Edmund's Towers, 38, 40
St. Edmund's Village, 41–42, 54
St. Francis of Assisi, 168
St. Ignatius, 11
St. Louis Post-Dispatch, 183, 221n183
St. Olaf College, 201–202
Stanford University, 192–198, 202, 204–205; (Department of) Religious Studies, 195–196, 198; (Division of) Continuing Studies, 194–195, 198
Stodghill, Ron, II, 37, 210, 214n37
Straight Ahead Ministries, 71–72
Suarez, Rev. Dr. Israel, 12–21 passim, 210; Buen Samartino church of, 19, 21; description of, 12, 15, 19–20; devotion to social causes by, 13; evolving social activism by, 16; family relationships of, 13, 16–18, 21; fund raising by, 14; introduction to, 4; journey to Fort Myers by, 13, 15; Nations Association leadership by, 13–14; religious philosophy of, 15, 19; tour of transitional shelter by, 20; youth of, 17
Sygall, Susan, 211

Teen Challenge International, 73, 211
The Temple Bombing, 163, 220n163
Temple Emanuel, 155–173 passim, 220nn157,162
Teresa, Mother, 23, 213n23
Thoreau, Henry David, 192
Time magazine, 37, 210
Titans of the Black Enterprise 100, 52, 214n52
Tolliver, Rev. Dr. Richard, 36–60 passim, 210, 214nn36–37, 215nn56–57; childhood of, 44–46; community involvement of, 59–60; description of, 37–38, 54; family relationships of, 44–46, 50–51; introduction to, 4; pastoral work of, 40–41, 43–44; Peace Corps experiences of, 50; professional development of, 53–55; redevelopment corporation leadership of, 41–43, 57; religious influences of, 46–48; residence of, 52–53; social activist evolution of, 48–50; St. Edmund's rectorship of, 51, 55–56, 58–59; visionary nature of, 37–39; Washington Park tour by, 38, 40
Trappist, 11, 91–92
Trinity College, 28, 33, 213n28

Union of American Hebrew
Congregations, 160–161
United Way, 166, 168, 178, 189–190
University of California–Berkeley, 105,
146, 192, 196
University of Oregon, 102–103, 106,
111, 230
University of Texas, Arlington, 174, 188
University of Wisconsin, 158
Urban Churches, Vital Signs, 39, 214n39
U.S. Chamber of Commerce,
149–150
U.S. Department of Defense, 83
U.S. Department of Health and Human
Services, 177
U.S. Department of Housing and
Urban Development, 42, 123, 126,
130, 150
USA Patriot Act, 181

Veterans for Peace, 86, 100
Vietnam, 5, 9, 78, 85–89, 92, 98, 106–109,
113, 198
Villafane, Dr. Eldin, 64, 68, 70, 73
VISTA, 3

Waite, Gerry, 98
Wall, Pastor Bruce, 62, 68, 73
Wallis, Jim, 3–4, 128, 150, 212nn3,4,
218n128, 219n150, 222n201
The Warrior Priest, 90, 93, 216n90,
217nn90,93. *See also* Wilson, Mike
Washington, Mayor Harold, 125, 129
Washington Park, 36, 38–40, 56–57
Washington Post, 85, 89, 131, 216nn85,89,
219n131
Webb, Wellington, 166
Weinheimer, Eric, 133, 211
West Garfield Park, 117–135 passim,
218n128, 219n132
Western Hemisphere Institute for Security
Cooperation, 83, 94, 215n79
Weston, Rev. M. Moran, 49
White, Robert, 83, 216n83
White House Office of Faith-Based and
Community Initiatives, 2–3, 128, 210,
212n2
Wilson, Mike, 90, 216n90, 217nn90,93
Working on God, 3, 212n3

Zazen, 193, 206

MARK H. MASSÉ

is Associate Professor of Journalism at Ball State University.
As a freelance writer for more than twenty-five years, he has authored
articles, essays, and stories in international, national, and regional
publications. A New York native, he has degrees from the University of
Oregon and Miami University, Oxford, Ohio.